Management in the 21st Century

About the book...

Business environment has become highly competitive in the wake of liberalisation and privatisation wave sweeping across the world. After the establishment of WTO and enforcement of its regulations, the world has moved fast towards free trade. Business firms are gearing up to face intense competition in the 21st century. It is going to be the survival of the fittest. The new scenario offers both opportunities and challenges for present and prospective entrepreneurs in industry and trade. It obviously calls for an integrated knowledge of management techniques like communicative skills, leadership qualities, organisational behaviour, human resourcing and decision-making.

In the context of 21st century challenges, the present work is intended for business executives, government officials, legislators and teachers and students of business management and public administration.

About the author...

Mr. Jetli is currently associated with Jaquar & Co. Ltd. as General Manager (HRD & Administration). The contents of this publication also include a series of lectures delivered by him during training programmes of the company.

A post-graduate in English Literature and a university topper in journalism, K. Narindar Jetli's first published work was a collection of 50 poems, Buds & Blossoms. He has written articles, plays and stories in Urdu and English in several publications including the Milap, Poona Herald, Poona Daily News, and Mid-Day (Mumbai). In 1963, he joined the Indian Oil Corporation (after a stint with the Indian Railways) and worked in the marketing, sales, operations, public relations and aviation departments. In 1965, he became the first Indian to translate the American play, Death of a Salesman by Arthur Miller, that ran four full-houses. E. Alkazi, the then Director of National School of Drama designed the sets and composed the music. In 1997, his second book of poems, Witherings, was published.

Management in the 21st Century

K. Narindar Jetli

NEW CENTURY
NC
NEW CENTURY PUBLICATIONS
DELHI INDIA

NEW CENTURY PUBLICATIONS
34, Gujranwala Town, Part-2,
Delhi - 110 033 INDIA
Tel.: 7247805, 7138192
Fax: +91-11-7464774
E-mail: indiatax@del2.vsnl.net.in

First Published 2002

ISBN: 81-7708-016-4

Published by New Century Publications and printed at Print Line, New Delhi-110 002

PRINTED IN INDIA

Acknowledgements

I am grateful to Mr. N.L. Mehra, Chairman, Jaquar & Co. Ltd. who invited me to share some of the responsibilities of the company thereby affording me an opportunity to bring out this volume. I also express my thanks to Mr. Rajesh Mehra, Director (Marketing) of Jaquar & Co. Ltd. whose untiring schedule, hardwork, dedication, commitment, all-round knowledge and love for his staff, inspired me to write this book.

I am thankful to Mr. Vijai Kumar, my Executive Secretary, who took special pains to contribute extra hours to type the pages of the work on time. Special thanks are due to Mr. V.K. Garg (CEO, Foreign Trade), Mr. Anand Sharma, Mr. Sanjay Dutta (EDP), Mr. Vijay Pal Singh (EDP), and my team members at Jaquar who helped in their own way to make this work see the light of the day. I am also thankful to all the Managers, Officers and Staff who gave patient hearing to my lectures, which gave me inspiration to compile this book

Preface

This is not a text book. This is a real life experience in print.

My long experience of working at several places in various capacities in so many organisations like government offices, public undertakings, private enterprises and NGOs, inspired me to share my experiences with others.

Having worked for a long time since 1948, and necessitated by family compunctions after moving down to India in 1947, I learnt my first real lessons when I walked three days and three nights to cross the border at Fazilka. With no jobs, homes or contacts in free India, we had to survive.

No management principles or textbooks or formal training could provide that knowledge and survival techniques that we imbibed by fighting out the odds.

I completed my entire education while working for more than six years in Indian Railways. After obtaining my post graduation in English literature from the University of Delhi, I joined Indian Oil Corporation. While at IOC, I had the opportunity to study Journalism and topped the Pune University. During the final years of my service, I headed the Aviation Stations at Santacruz and Sahar. Being the location in-charge, I was actively associated with the Training Department which organised training courses at Sahar International Aviation Fuelling Station.

After retirement, I joined an ISO-9002 Plastic Moulding Company as a General Manager and established and handled the training of the employees. At Jaquar, I have been fully involved in the training of all its employees at Delhi for over forty months.

This book will prove handy for all those persons who could not attend the training lectures delivered by me in person. All the lectures on all subjects dealt with therein have been serialised and arranged in this book. Most of the chapters included in this volume are based on personal experience, real-life incidents, real problems and provide implementable solutions, which would not be easily available in most text-books. This book would remind the working managers about their knowledge on management. It would revise their educational study in management.

The 21st century demands a new set of managers, a new set of traditions, new procedures, new techniques and absolutely fresh methods of managing people. This century is a great era of change. Those who would accept this change and imbibe it would succeed.

I am fortunate to be a part of the vision of Mr. Rajesh Mehra of Jaquar who is keenly involved in the development of staff, dealers and everyone associated with our company.

Delhi
January 1, 2002

K. Narindar Jetli

Contents

1

Communication: The Best Virtue

God has blessed mankind with several virtues. The best of all is the art of speaking. When this art is converted into communication it adds all the wealth in a person which cannot be fathomed. Fortunate are those who are gifted with the art of communication. It is said that the function of Art is to give pleasure and good communication gives much pleasure. It adds vitality, warmth and wealth to an individual.

Communication takes place in several forms, such as, written, verbal, visual, body language, paralinguistic, eye-to-eye and listening.

All living creatures communicate. Each species has its own method of communicating. Start from the ants: when they are moving in a line they meet each other stop and move on, thus conveying something. Even when a calf is born of a cow their body language tells intense communication, particularly, when the cow licks the calf. Similarly, the birds feed their offsprings, touch each other and communicate. An infant immediately after birth moves his limbs seeking and by this telling something: is involved in communication. His ooh!, aah!! makes him a Khussar-Phussar which is audible to his mother and as these "Khussar-Phussars" grow they chisel the art of conveying messages and receiving signals and with each passing day they improve learning this art, blow-by-blow. If you analyse the verbal sounds of infants periodically you can draw an upper moving graph of their new techniques of learning.

From the origin of birth to the age of maturity and with the help of education, society, friends, media, this art is enhanced to such heights that the original khussar-phussars become versatile speakers in public fora.

Shakespeare in his last play, 'The Tempest', puts words in the mouth of Miranda when she uttered on seeing the man for the first time, "*How beautiful this mankind is!*"

Really how beautiful this mankind is when he pours out his heart and communicates either verbally or in writing or through any part of the body when he transfers his thoughts and emotions into beautiful words.

Communication is a very vast subject to deal with, but here we would deal with only when this art is used in the modern management in our day to day working.

Management apart, communication is necessary at each and every level of activity in life. I recall my experience where the good communication solved *three of my serious problems in a day*. It was the year 1975 when I had gone on holidaying in the South. The Indian Airlines had gone on strike and all the flights were inoperative. I was stranded in Bangalore. I had to rush to the Railway Station for my return journey by train. No first-class accommodation was available on any train. I used all my talents of expressing smiles, using polite words and convincing tactics to impress the booking clerk - all failed. Finally I sneaked into his enclosure and told him that he must be considerate to his own colleagues. I reminded him of my past in the Indian Railways. I told him that I was the best scout in the Railways. To this he yielded to some extent that he could give me one seat for my wife in the lady's coupe and I had to vacate the coupe if any other single lady boarded the train en route. I had no alternative, but had to agree to it. At the time of payment of tickets I ran short of cash because he did not accept the travellers cheques. It was 9 in the morning and the banks had yet to be opened. I requested the booking clerk to keep the cash with him and the balance would be paid as soon as I encashed the travellers cheques when the banks opened. We rushed to the nearest State Bank of India Branch.

The bank had not yet opened and the sweepers were cleaning the premises while I waited. A middle aged man entered the bank who looked to be a petty official and I told him the embarrassing story of the morning and requested him to help in getting the travellers cheques encashed as early as the bank opened. More and more employees of the bank trickled in. That gentleman collected cash from his colleagues and encashed my travellers cheques sufficed to pay the railways and cleared me even before the banks opened. My wife was surprised the way I had communicated. We rushed to the Railway Station again, paid the cash, got the first-class tickets for the evening train and as we were walking on the road there was a huge rush since the Raj Kapoor magnum opus, "Mera Nam Joker", was to be released at 10.30 a.m. show. My wife challenged that if I could show her the movie only then she would be convinced about my art of communication.

At that point of time when she had completed the sentence, we had reached the main gate of the cinema hall which was closed and a very smart guard wearing smart uniform was keeping the crowd away. A sentence flowed out of my mouth, "Has the sahib come?" He got up, saluted and said, "Yes", and then opened the gate for us. We both entered and he closed the gate behind and in no time we reached an office where the so-called 'Sahib' sat in the company of 7 or 8 important people.

As soon as we entered the room, I introduced myself and instantly asked the **sahib** whether he was married. He smiled and said, "Yes". I responded immediately, "In that case you must have escaped several embarrassing moments by fulfilling the whims of your better-half". He smiled more and offered us seats. I told him that we had been to South for the last 25 days and everything went very well till the booking of the seats and encashing travellers cheques before the banks opened. A new threat has loomed large that if I don't show my wife this film, the entire tour would go waste. I convinced him that we were the transient passengers leaving by train in the night and we were not the residents of the city, so please help the poor husband. He rang the bell and ordered two Coca Colas and asked which show we would like to see the movie. I replied, "Any show would do before our departure". He asked the peon to bring two balcony tickets for the first show. We enjoyed the coke, more than the tickets. The wife was convinced and satisfied. After the show, we went to him again to thank him but could not get him.

From the above episode you would see that there was no magic, no jugglery of words and no tricks applied anywhere, when simple methods of communication which brought the results at the railway station, at the bank and at the theatre with ease.

Verbal Communication

Verbal communication is used by human-beings most of the time. Man by nature and necessity is a social animal. Even if he is not educated, he is tamed to be a civilised being. He likes to be talked softly and affectionately.

Always be soft while speaking whether face to face or on telephone or any other means of communication. If an elder person speaks softly to you and to young ones, the response is equally soft and respectful. A good manager always speaks softly with his staff, particularly, to the uneducated workers who give very positive response.

Choose the simple words which are audible, understood and meaningful. This would make the communication clear. If you use difficult words and speak fast, and in anger or in a hurry, the receiver of the message would not understand. By using the appropriate words three things are very important, i.e. the level of understanding, the level of age, and the lever of position. If the teacher talks to another teacher the level would be the same. If a teacher talks to a student, the level of understanding, education and age would differ and if the same teacher talks to any other uneducated person, he would have to bring his level down to the level of a child or the uneducated person. While making an effective communication, these levels have to be maintained. If you are soft in speech, use the appropriate words clearly, you would sound helpful, considerate and often affectionate.

I have been in Maharashtra for over 26 years, but I learnt one line in Marathi, which was very meaningful, "*SHABD HAY SHASTRA AHE ZAPUN VAPRA*". This means that the words are like weapons, these should be used sparingly and carefully.

Smile is the Best Dress

Smile is the most precious ornament, it not only adds to the beauty of face, but it makes you very attractive. Smiling face is liked by every one. A simple smile on your face makes you more communicative because it attracts attention, it establishes a friendly bond. Smile is a powerful adhesive to the bond of communication. This weapon is used very effectively in the art of marketing and winning friends.

Brief and to the Point

Any person who talks big and loose he cannot establish and maintain control on the language and he loses the target. But if you are attentive, brief and to the point you become very effective communicator.

In the year 1970 I had led the students of journalism of the Pune University to visit Delhi on a study tour during which we met several prominent personalities like Smt. Indira Gandhi, the then Prime Minister of India, Shri Yashwant Rao Chavan, Shri Mohan Dharia, Shri Kuldeep Nayyar, Shri Frank Moares and several others. During the course of our discussion with Frank Moares, who was the Editor-in-Chief of The Indian Express at that time, he discussed with the group about the importance of the Republic Day Parade, which was to be held during those days. During that period of 40-45 minutes, he must have received 100 telephone calls in our presence and to each call he used only one or two words like yes, no, later, ok. Very seldom he used three words or in one or two cases - four words. This was a glaring example of getting brief and to the point and attending so many calls in such a short time and that too while discussing with the group.

By being brief it not only saves energy and time, but it makes the communication very pointed and very meaningful. By being brief doesn't mean that you must talk telegraphically. The information shared must be correct and complete. In case of doubt the point must be clarified with details, statistics, truth and if necessary by exchanging notes. If the information is correct and complete the message becomes clear and the communication effective. In 'Army' whenever oral instruction is given it is always stamped with two words, "Koi shaque?", that is "Any Doubt?" That seals the stuff, that the information is not only complete, correct, but understood as well.

Tongue: A Deadly Weapon

Tongue is a Deadly Weapon in the armoury of communication. Tongue-twisters are seldom liked. Several slips of tongue distort communication. Forked tongues injures the listener, but the sweet tongue cements the friendship. It is said that the tongue can win friends and make enemies.

Oily tongue is often used in the offices while greasing the technique of flattery. A good communication not only wins friends, but it wins enemies as well.

Listening

Listening is also a very effective part of verbal communication. Without listening the communication is incomplete. There is difference between the hearing and the listening. You can hear several voices, but you listen only to one of them. Listening means hearing specifically. Listen attentively to give importance to others. It also helps to grasp the message or communication. You must have noticed that when you talk to an elderly or wisely person and when he gives a patience hearing you feel very important. Similarly, when you listen to others it enhances your respect in their eyes. If you use all these principles of verbal communication you would find a thrill in the conversation and that thrill is converted into another sweet and strange language, which is called the body language. It adds to the beauty of communication. The best example of body language is displayed when the dancers, artists perform on the stage. You can see those bhavs/mudras, expressions of people by their acts and actions. The dialogue on the stage becomes more meaningful when the artist delivers the dialogue with action. Body language is spoken by even without speaking a word. The silence is another golden rule of communication.

Over the ages the art of communication has rapidly changed because of the scientific advancement. About fifty years back the telegrams and telephones were very rarely used. I remember when I was a primary student, if anybody received a telegram the household people used to start crying as if some one had died and whosoever gathered from the neighbourhood would also start crying without knowing the contents of the telegram. Even in those days the use of telephone was also very rare and now look around you have fax messages, where you can send a document and the same is received at any corner of the globe, i.e. a duplicate of the original document. You have e-mail which can be transmitted through the satellites all over the globe in matter of seconds. You have mobiles, you have car radios which can send messages across the continents. You can have tele-conferences by talking to each other while sitting in different countries. In this scenario the verbal communication apart, the written communication also plays a major role in sending across messages. Thus the written communication includes composing, punctuation and displaying an error-free document. These documents are often passed around in various departments as memos, inter office memos, notes, letters, statements, statistics involving necessary and need-based paper work turning into records. Even this scenario is changing faster. These records which were hitherto kept in files are now stored in the computers or hard-disks. These documents stored in any way become a part and parcel of the official communication. The effective communication is the blood stream of any organisation.

Essentials of a Good Document

A written communication is done in a specific language and any language must have a grammar, use of words, construction of sentences, observing the rules of grammar, spellings, punctuation, a strict control on common errors, contents of the draft, layout, graphics, good printing on a well designed letterhead made out of quality paper. Everything must have quality and style. Quite often documents also carry enclosures, etc., to make the communication complete.

Grammatically the official communications have salutations, topping and tailing with complimentary close, which make a document complete in itself.

I attended an international seminar held in Delhi, which was largely attended by most countries. The chief guest was a minister in the central cabinet, who had graphically displayed the written documents sent by various top companies in respect of goods exported from India. He emphasised while our products matched with the international standards, the communications, particularly, the documents let the products down. The letterheads used by the companies were of very inferior quality, the printing used to be horrible, the design of the letterheads sloppy and the contents of the letter were often funny, the condition of the envelopes wayward and the hand-written address on the envelopes could kill any communication. While the audience went into peals of laughter the way he described the communications the message went home that the Indian firms should take care of these vital cosmetics of communication.

Quite often it is commendable that our postal staff could decipher the addresses written on the envelopes when mail is distributed. With the advancement of science there is lesser scope in written documents or even typed documents and with the help of computers and electronic printing the written communications have certainly improved. It is said that if anything that goes out of your office or house, does a PR job.

In written communication one should avoid criticism or complaining. In its place, the consideration and courtesy should dominate. You may discuss but avoid argumentation. You have the time to pick and choose your words carefully. Proper use of words makes the document a diamond studded jewellery. The composition of written communication must invite, compel, motivate the reader to go through the document. The modern manager is an educated individual who is very professional and knowledgeable while making a written document, but the traditionalist don't compromise and adhere to the archaic style. Please go through this example of old official communication.

While working for railways for over six years I noticed that some of the senior head-clerks used to sit late after office hours. Getting delayed, missing their shuttles carrying them home and even while going home they would carry the files for completing the jobs at night. This aroused my curiosity to find out as to what they did sitting late. I hid myself from their view and observed them in action. One of them was Ram Lal and the other was Kundan Lal. Ram Lal read one sentence in the draft and said, "We must put a comma here". Kundan Lal didn't agree and said, "The comma is not required". To which Ram Lal argued that comma was put when a similar draft was sent last week. Kundan Lal said he used the same draft which was signed by the other officer without putting the comma. Ram Lal could not digest this, he opened another bundle of files and took out a couple of folders and read them to Kundan Lal. In reply Kundan Lal also opened a bundle of files and showed some drafts to Ram Lal showing that similar sentences didn't carry a 'comma' and it was approved by their boss. Both of them argued and argued and none of them could change the construction of the sentence and concentrated all their efforts on the "use of comma or not to use the comma". They sat and discussed for three hours and finally carried about a dozen files home to complete the job and the next morning Ram Lal was jubilant that his comma added draft was approved by the boss. This is a story of 1955-58. Can anybody afford this luxury now, the answer is 'No'.

From the above examples you would find the difference between the old style and the modern style of writing. However, there is a sea-change for writing the business letters. We conclude the following observations, which must be kept in mind while communicating in writing:

- The most important factor is the central idea of the topic. The topic should never be digressed nor incomplete. The skill of the writer is to keep it concise and to the point.
- Use simple words, in short sentences giving the complete message.
- In case of a lengthy note or long letters, please split the body of the letter into small paragraphs and if necessary give headings or sub-headings and each paragraph must be synchronised that the matter should run in serial order without breaking the direction and thought.
- The writing must have a cordial tone. Tone of the communication is very important to have the total impact which would give a positive result.
- When responding to a letter start to refresh the subject matter so that the receiver may link up the previous communication.
- Always begin from the beginning. The start of the letter must indicate as to what is to be followed.
- Don't complain or argue, but give full information so that no confusion is created. If there is any confusion created by the sender it should be clarified.
- Always accept mistakes if committed and be bold to apologise.
- Edit the copy so that all mistakes, specially, the spellings of the names are properly corrected if required. It is very embarrassing for the receiver to have his name written incorrectly.
- The written communication must be drafted in such a way as if you are speaking to some one, i.e. a language which is well

spoken, well heard and nicely understood.

Communication by Word of Mouth

- Oral communication is mostly used by all of us, small, big, poor, rich, young, old, literate, illiterate, men, women, in various languages all over the world. We exchange words at each level depending upon the mood, place, purpose, but we forget the basic essentials of communication by word of mouth, some of which are given below:
- As a civilised person it is necessary that one must be soft, clear, helpful and affectionate. Soft-spoken words evoke better response.
- Whenever you meet any person always greet with a smile. One smile would get several smiles in return. Each smile would enrich you with the wealth of happiness.
- In any oral communication you have to be attentive and polite. This would make the other persons important and he would equally treat you important.
- Wisemen speak less. Therefore, please be brief and to the point. Bragging is not welcomed.
- Listening is an important part of communication. Those who learn and practice to listen become good communicators.
- Information exchanged should be correct, complete and concise in itself.
- Good mouth can win friends and big mouth always make enemies. The people with big mouth in offices are generally ignored.
- Pleasant communication can win even enemies.
- Always learn to enjoy the thrill of verbal communication.

Communication on Telephone

The modern manager uses this gadget in a big way, whether he uses office telephone, personal mobile or car phones and so on. Telephone puts you in contact with people all over the world at the touch of few buttons. Most people in most offices don't use this facility properly. They forget that communication on telephone costs money. Saving money in commercial organisations adds to profit. We had given the example of brevity of telephone communication during our visit to the newspaper editor mentioned earlier. We must use the following skills while speaking on telephone:

- Disclose your identity before speaking on telephone. It has been observed that a lengthy communication is exchanged without identifying the caller as well as speaker.
- Be clear, pleasant, polite and helpful.
- Answer the call promptly. Telephone must be picked up within three rings. If it takes longer, keep the caller informed in between that you are already attending him.
- If there is longer delay for one reason or the other, please apologise for the delay. If required, you can give reason/s.
- Always keep a notebook or a pad or a diary handy to note down the names, addresses and the identity of the caller.
- Be brief, attentive and sweet.
- Always remember that telephone is one of the wonderful invention of science, it must be and should not be misused for making nuisance to others.
- Always remember words are weapons, use them carefully.

1.1 Public Speaking Brings Confidence

In modern management culture; speaking is very important USP. Day in and day out, every manager is to address a gathering small or big, whether it is staff meeting, a seminar, a sales conference, meeting of the HRD and on the occasions of welcoming a person to the organisation or bidding farewell.

Public speaking is an art. The function of the art is to give pleasure. Therefore, public speaking must give pleasure to the speaker as well as to the audience. In public speaking all elements of communication, such as, language, style, smile, sense of humour, body language, information and knowledge, all play a prominent part. In other words the public speaking is the accumulated communication.

Speaking Projects Competence: Your speech and manner describes your competence in terms of knowledge and information. It brings confidence and sincerity. Any speaker having the mastery of the subject matter reflects confidence and sincerity. In absence of this, the speaker fumbles, forgets, frowns, gets fear and ultimately fails. Competent managers and knowledgeable speakers enhance their position and prestige.

Be Relaxed: While addressing the audience you must stand erect and relaxed without any tension. If the limbs of body, particularly, the ankles and below knees are stiff that shows that your body is tense. In this situation, the stream of consciousness and the flow of words don't run smoothly.

We were the first in India to stage the famous American play, "The Death of a Salesman", by Arthur Miller. We had hired a Director from the National School of Drama. For the first time in India we had shown the flashback on the stage, did not use microphone and each scene was sketched. The Director invariably would feel the muscles of the artists to ensure that they were not stiff and until they were relaxed he would not allow any artist to deliver the dialogue. When he did the same exercise on me I was embarrassed in the beginning, but later it became very comfortable to deliver the dialogue.

Even if you address a small number of people, stand erect, be relaxed and let your body language be normal. The results would be fantastic.

Know Your Audience: Long time ago, I used to be invited to perform on the stage as a singer as well as an actor. My first consideration used to be, "What is the audience?". The selection of the item to be performed depended on the type of audience. You cannot talk something serious and philosophical to the children and you cannot give tit-bits to the educated gathering. For artists these things can be planned well in advance if you know the audience as well as schedule, but for managers you are often asked to make a public speaking without any notice. There you have to decide promptly and on the spot as to what is the audience you are supposed to address. Could it be a union meeting, a staff meeting, HOD meeting, annual function or a festival gathering. If you know it and are aware of this, then deliver the speech suitably.

Body Language: Body language is a means of communication where no word is spoken, but the movement of the limbs of the body can convey more meanings than the words. All our classical dances are based on body language. A new born child conveys many things by body language only. For instance he lifts his body into a bow indicating to be lifted up, the anger of mother, boss and wife can be found out the way they look at you. All the limbs of the body move and with the words those are spoken and the feelings those are expressed.

In a public speaking, generally the gestures are made by hands or the shoulders or the movement of the head, but most important is the eye-to-eye contact. If the speaker maintains eye-to-eye contact with the audience, the communication becomes purposeful. The smiles, the laughters and other facial expressions provoke the audience into the intended responses. A synchronised body language enhances the beauty of the speech.

Eye-to-Eye Contact: While eye-to-eye contact is a positive sign of a confident speech, the facial expression also tell the knowledge, the confidence and the command over the language. The face should reflect bubbling cheerfulness. The happiness should dance on the face.

Maintain Continuity: Whenever a story is told its continuity has to be maintained and it should flow like a running stream. Water gushing forth in a regular rhythmic manner. In literature it is called stream of consciousness. In the sub-conscious mind, the ideas and the words are arranged in a serial order so that when it flows, it flows like a stream. Generally, a speech is classified into three parts, viz. Beginning (the face), body (the content) and the end (the bottom). These parts are not the isolated ones, but integrated as one part called the speech. The speech can be further split into smaller paragraphs or portions each related to the other. Just as a music each instrument is synchronised with the other in such a way that it becomes pleasant and lilting. If the instruments are not co-ordinated properly into a tune, this would become noise and not music. To maintain this continuity it is advisable to jot down the main points of the speech and then arrange in such an order so that each event is told and related to the previous one in order to achieve the continuity.

Proper Tone and Pitch: The tone and pitch are important ingredients of a speech. You come across several politicians, who deliver the speech at the top of their voice raising the pitch, some time they shriek, but that is just to keep the audience alert and attract to create a dramatic effect. Some people are fond of very low pitch and their tone is also lowered. The synchronising of pitch and tone should be smooth, regular and continuous. It must appear to be silky touch. A gentle pour of rain right into the brain, very smooth and refreshing. The amalgamation of tone and pitch creates balmy sensation.

Projection of Words: The use of words in a speech should be chosen carefully and spoken artfully. There should not be gurgling of words. Each word should be projected properly so that it is audible to the last man sitting in the audience. At the time of staging the "Death of a Salesman by Arthur Miller, we were directed to project vowels with a thrust so that the sound is pushed for a longer distance in order to reach the last man. This helped all the artists a lot because we had not used the microphones and the play was well received by the audience. This must be practised repeatedly and preferably tape recorded and heard to ensure that each word spoken is heard and chiselled like a diamond.

Oral Punctuation: In literature the grammar safeguards the punctuation as to where you have to put a comma, a colon, and a full stop, etc. In a speech the oral punctuation is done by a pause, sudden change of tone, sudden raising and lowering the pitch of the voice, gestures by hand or head making and maintaining eye-to-eye contact by circling the dramatic glance of the audience. In theatre, we give a break or a hold to give a dramatic effect to the audience. This pause is also given in orchestra to achieve musical hold. A good pause in a speech not only maintains the interest, but it acts like an ornament.

Avoid Abrupt Ending: Out of three important constituents of the speech, the conclusion of this exercise must reach its climax because the entire speech terminates into an effective end the climax. It must warm the hearts of the audience. This should not give a jolt. The speech should not be finished abruptly. It must encourage and motivate the listeners to long for the speech again. The music of the speech must ring bells in the ears of the audience, if not, a standing ovation. The speech must end in a thunderous applause.

1.2 How to Prepare a Speech?

Special skills are required to prepare a speech. By all means it is not difficult. I still remember the speeches which I have attended personally of Netaji Subhas Chandra Bose, Mohammed Ali Jinnah in Lahore, Mahatma Gandhi, Jawaharlal Nehru, Indira Gandhi, Rajiv Gandhi, Jaiprakash Narayan, T.A. Pai, Shyama Prasad Mookerji, A.K. Gopalan, Madhu Limaye, Krishna Menon, Atal Behari Vajpayee and several other leaders. One feels proud to have such remarkable orators in our country. While getting ready to prepare a speech one must keep a role model in mind. Cicero was a great orator, Mark Anthony in Julius Caesar is a classic example. While identifying a role model, you may work out the mannerism, the style of speaking, vocabulary, body language, style of addressing, the grace of their handling difficult subjects - all these factors imbibe in you an image which you would like to portray if you select a role model for your self. Our Krishna Menon created a world record for continuously speaking for more than eighteen hours in the United Nations on Kashmir issue. This reminds me of an instance which occurred when I was doing my M.A. in literature from Delhi University.

In the University elections, we had put up candidates to contest. I personally did not contest the elections, but I supported and campaigned for my friends. Coincidentally, all of them were elected. The elected body organised a function thereafter where Krishna Menon was the Chief Guest. Besides several artists from the institute, we had invited the prominent radio singers of that time including Asa Singh Mastana, Ramta, to quote a few, the group of students who had lost the election did not want the function to be successful. They hooted out all the items one by one. The radio artists including Asa Singh Mastana, Ramta and others were also not allowed to perform. The Principal of the Institute, looked embarrassed. At that moment I came on the stage and addressed the gathering in a challenging way, saying that I was one of them, the difference being I was on the stage and they were in the audience. I asked them if they would listen any song of their choice, I accepted to perform. If I fail to do so they could hoot me out and if I satisfy them they would help the function to succeed. There were several voices from the audience giving me a list of songs to be performed. I accepted three of them - a lullaby from Do Bigha Zamin sung by Lata Mangeshkar, a duet of Hemant Kumar and Lata Mangeshkar from Patita and Kishore Kumar's voice Nakhrewali from New Delhi. The audience clapped in jubilation. The songs went very well which were heard peacefully and attentively. The programme proceeded thereafter and all the artists were invited again to perform one by one. At the end of the programme the Principal of the institute and Krishna Menon personally complimented me not only for the songs, but for handling the situation which had become explosive. The shouting brigade became close friends thereafter.

If you observe minutely the way the noted speakers perform, this would help you a lot in making your speech. Try to deliver a speech before a mirror and tape it. You listen the tape again and again and make corrections wherever necessary. The mirror would give you the live commentary on your lip movements, facial expressions, how you look when you speak and over all body language. Try this exercise wearing different kinds of clothes and you will feel the difference yourself.

Remember TV Personalities: Electronic media has played an important part to influence the style of man in the 21st century. Even the children born in this age are producing an improved specimen of man. Please remember the famous TV personalities who used to broadcast on radio, earlier or joined the electronic media and transformed the very styles of speaking. Observe the response of the listeners and try to build up your image while delivering speeches.

Style and Modulation: Every man has his own style, but the modulation of the voice is an artful skill which increases the dimension of the talent. Remember the style of Raj Kapoor and voice modulation of Amitabh Bachchan and the dialogue of Sohrab Modi and Raj Kumar, visualise the style of Dilip Kumar, pinpoint their qualities and improve your style and voice modulation. When the country won freedom, the famous speech of Pt Jawaharlal Nehru, "At the strike of midnight when the nation sleeps, India becomes free ...." All these have become history.

Highlight the Traits: If you visualise your role models try to highlight their energy, the enthusiasm, conviction, clarity, expression, confidence, animation, sense of humour and ease with which they perform.

Compare Yourself With Role Models: Always compare yourself with your role models in terms of your voice speaking before the mirror, tape recording your voice and hearing it, but it is recommended not to copy anybody's style, individual style is recommended. Always maintain individuality.

Take Inventory Of Good Points, Bad Points: While listening your taped voice, please identify your sound whether it is nasal or wobbling, use of negative words or irritative phrases or repetitive words. Too much repetitive words look irritating. Avoid speech ticks like oh!, mum, well, ok, etc.

Check Speed: Speech must be completed within a stipulated time. During the electronic age when the speeches are made with slides, projections and presentations, the time allotted is very restrictive. Please span your speech in the allotted time. In doing so, please ensure that you do not speak fast in order to complete the speech in time and it should not be slow so that it does not look abrupt ending, but everybody likes brief speeches. You may remember the story of a minister who was blamed for delivering long speeches. He was asked by his boss to make the speeches short. The minister asked his secretary to draft brief speeches in future to which he obliged. The minister was reprimanded again for delivering a lengthy speech. In return he reprimanded his secretary. The secretary responded that the speech was drafted very brief, but he made five copies and the minister had read all of them.

But the fact remains that most politicians play to the gallery and make speeches their audiences want. They know their audiences well.

1.3 Speech Habits Need Careful Studies

Every man has his own style of speaking, but there are several common habits which are observed by the audience without the knowledge of the speaker. These habits should be identified and eliminated after close scrutiny.

Elimination of Annoying Habits: Most of the speakers are in the habit of repeating some familiar words repeatedly like, 'I mean to say', 'nevertheless', 'make no mistake', 'you see', etc. etc. They would also scratch their foreheads, nose, ears or buttons, etc. Such habits may look natural to speakers, but they look odd to the audience. The best way to eliminate these habits record your voice and listen to it again and again.

Problem Words: Most often some difficult words cannot be pronounced easily. You must have seen on TV that the names of foreigners are not pronounced properly. To make it easier for the announcer the media journalists split such words into small pieces and then rehearse to pronounce. Other than the names, the problem words can be displayed around so that you don't miss them but practised repeatedly. Alternatively, you can read such words allowed in a closed room, preferably in front of a mirror.

Avoid Long Pauses: If the passage of the script is long, you may give suitable pauses and break the long paragraphs into shorter and in order to make the speed uniform, the passages should be read again and again so that they should not look uneven when read.

Be Comfortable: The best speech is that which is delivered in comfortable posture. To achieve this please start reading or speaking the words few and fewer in the beginning till you are comfortable with the language. If you speak few words each time the pronunciation will become clearer.

Ensure Audibility: It is the sole response of the speaker to ensure that his words are audible to the audience. This can be measured by making eye to eye contact. Those who cannot hear you would be disinterested in your speech, would look restless and start gossiping, laughing, sleeping and even leaving. Therefore, please maintain the tone and the pitch of the speech uniform so that they are heard by them.

Avoid Strain to Listeners: If your voice is quiet or low in tone or a whisper, this may cause of strain to listeners. It is very difficult and painful to address the strained listeners.

Sense of Humour: Don't ever look like a dull speaker. You should display your sense of humour in such a way that the speech should reflect bubbling enthusiasm for every one.

Use of Anecdotes: Every one has read a life of tragedy and comedy. People give a cold ear to your tragedies, but they warmly receive your stories containing humour. Keep a good stock of tit bits, anecdotes for every type of occasion, humorous speaker is always liked and welcomed.

Importance of Posture: The speaker has to project his voice in such a way that the speech is clear as well as audible. The posture of the speaker whether sitting or standing is important to voice projection. The posture of the body becomes different and more emphatic when the speaker intends to lay emphasis on the voice projection. A well projected voice beautifies the meaningfulness of the speech.

Eye-to-Eye Connection: While delivering a speech, the eye to eye connection with the audience is very essential. It has been observed that eyes should be in action constantly and not the tongue.

Step by Step Method: If you have to deliver a successful speech, step by step method for speech making has to be understood.

Earlier we have discussed in theory the art of preparation of speech. We would now discuss the technical aspect or let us say literary aspect for the preparation of speech.

Step No. 1: Depending upon the identity of the audience the first step is to decide as to how long the speech should be. No audience prefers to sit for a long speech. The speech should be to the point covering all aspects, should be juicy, informative, entertaining and delivering a message. It should be along enough to cover the vitals and should be short enough to bare the essentials. The drafting of the speech must be done keeping in view of the standard of the audience.

Be Punctual: One must be punctual to deliver the speech on time. If you cover the professional seminars or management meetings where you make a speech, you should not report late because the time allotted to you is always in minutes. A few minutes delay here and there cuts your own time span. Similarly, please don't exceed the time limit set for you. It not only annoys the following speakers, but it angers the audience as well and it angers the organisers more if the speech is lengthy and dull.

Begin from the Beginning: Your very appearance on the podium should be presentable and the very first word or the sentence should be a warm invitation to the listeners to listen to you. Some speakers even go to the extent of starting the speech with a joke. It goes well with the youngsters, but not with the board members who have very short time at their disposal for such occasions.

Build Bridges: As soon as you attract the attention of the audience you start building bridges to the listeners' interest. A good speaker knows fully well the purpose of the function and the core issue of the audience. Start addressing the core issues immediately as soon as the audience accept your invitation to listen to you, the mention of the core issue steps to build the bridge and the audience would be attracted at once to venture to cross the bridge. The immediate response from the listeners would be reflecting the warmth as well as the cheer and jubilation.

Tie the Interests: As soon as you establish the audience link, audience would expect how their interests are taken care of right from the opening of the speech. Therefore, the listeners must be given ample proof in the beginning itself as to how you tie with their interest. You should speak to them in the manner as if you are one of them, but you have more in-depth knowledge than them.

Use Support Material: The verbal speech gives an audio impact on the listeners whereas the support material gives the visual impact on the audience. The visual impact is longer lasting. In the modern methods of teaching, the visual methods are more used in the institutions. While developing the speech used examples, anecdotes, charts, slides, diagrams in support of your views during the speech. The support material acts as evidence to convince the audience.

Information Based on Knowledge: The audience must be convinced and satisfied that your information is based on knowledge not only the theoretical knowledge, but the practical knowledge from which the benefits have been achieved by the speaker. It is only then the audience would be convinced. By citing personalised examples, the speaker can also enhance his credibility.

Action-Oriented: Before the conclusion of the speech, the intelligent speaker demands, requests and motivates and cajoles some specific action from the audience, e.g. to join, to vote, to support, to buy, to invest to learn or to practice. In all, the speech should be crisp, entertaining and informatory so that it should have lasting effect on the audience.

Types of Speeches

Impromptu Speech: Impromptu speech is given by a speaker suddenly on any occasion. In this speech the success depends on the ability to organise and phrase your thoughts quickly at the spur of the moment. It is not difficult for any intelligent executive to make such a speech. This type of speech is very short and your opening remarks should be carefully chosen taking cue from what some one else has already said, e.g. the organisers say, "Now I request Shri .... to say a few words on the implementation of the new scheme in respect of incentive scheme for punctuality." The speaker will take the cue in his opening remarks with very few words on punctuality as well as the incentive scheme.

Though the speech is for a very short duration, the speaker must marshal his thoughts in a logical sequence and he should focus on the points of any controversy or doubt and make an attempt to clarify them without raising any controversial doubt. While doing so, you can correlate with your ideas to the experience of the listeners. It is quite possible the audience may react promptly either positively as a sign of approval or negatively as a sign of dissent. The speaker must respond suitably without raising any further, and the best way is you must stop as soon as you have said what you wanted to say.

The impromptu speech is never expected to cover all aspects of the topic. Try as far as possible to be simple and direct, and you need not be apologetic for not being prepared as every one in the audience would know that you have been asked at the spur of the moment to speak. The success of this speech would be the simplicity of words, brevity of thought and the concise logical sequence and a bit of humour, if possible, for the comfort of the audience.

Speech of Introduction: Invariably, we have to introduce a new entrant into the organisation, a new member to your club and to introduce a guest speaker who is to make a speech or he is to inaugurate a function.

Since you have to introduce a new personality, it is necessary to know about him, try to either obtain his bio-data, alternatively gather as much information as possible to know him. Doubly check that the information about him is correct and the pronunciation of his name is properly announced. His name should not be announced in any incorrect fashion. Avoid clichés and ornamental phrases. The guest speaker should not feel embarrassed for either exaggerated or under-rated achievements. However, please inform the audience the purpose of the occasion and what is the subject to be spoken of and what was the necessity for bringing this guest speaker and what is the name and background of the speaker. These points should never be missed and they should be very carefully told to the audience in the short introduction of your guest because it will create harmony between all the elements like the subject, the audience, occasion and the choice of the speaker. Introduction speech should work like a tonic to the audience and it must raise their expectations. The time taken for those introduction speech should not exceed two minutes in any way. The longer introduction spreads boredom.

This reminds me of an interesting situation when I was the secretary of Indian Oil Club and the then Chairman of Indian Oil, Shri P.A. Gopala krishnan, the last of cadre of ICS in India was the Chief Guest. In my introductory speech I said, "Now the variety programme is over, I request the Chairman to kindly say a few words on this occasion." The Chairman quietly and gracefully got up, looked at me with piercing eyes and said, "As the Secretary has announced, my item seems to be outside the programme and hence not relevant." The audience exploded in laughter. The Chairman made a point.

After the function was over, the Chairman took me aside and advised me saying, "Very well done, please include the Chief Guest item in the programme itself." I remembered his advice till date.

Speech of Thanks: Speech of thanks is given at the end of a function/programme wherein the speaker is asked to thank the main speaker without any notice. Therefore, it is very essential that he knows about his understanding of his speech. In doing so the speaker must pinpoint and highlight the most significant point made by him in the speech. The speaker should also single out something special which he has liked and the audience has also appreciated the same. You may conclude by thanking him personally and at that moment, please do not miss to glance at him and must stop as soon as the audience starts applauding. This speech should also be less than two minutes or the 100 seconds, the maximum.

The speech of thanks is also given at a formal function attended by a huge gathering where you have to thank all the participants and all the major contributors to the success of the function, so much so that you don't forget to miss the names of caterers and the microphone suppliers, furniture suppliers, etc. etc.

Speech of Welcome: Speech of welcome can be compared with the speech of introduction, but it's a longer version and it needs elaboration. This speech is given to welcome new entrants in the organisation, some of the persons at very senior and professional level and they have to be introduced to the organisation. Similarly, besides introducing the chief guest or to the function of the organisation they have to be welcomed to such functions in a formal way. Therefore, while doing so, start your speech as early, in the proceeding, as possible. Be objective, sincere and avoid jokes while welcoming, particularly the honoured guest, but to the newcomers to the organisation you must be warm and friendly because your purpose of welcoming is to make the new entrants feel a part of the organisation. By welcoming the new members introduce them by name, designation and their background, both academic as well as professional, by recalling your own feelings when you joined the organisation. Similarly, you introduce the organisation as well explaining in brief the goals of the organisation, culture of the organisation and little bit of history of the organisation to the new entrants so that new members may also get inspiration to contribute their talents to the organisation.

In case of welcoming the guests, you must describe the goal of the organisation and how the chief guest or the special guest would contribute his experience, talent and participation in respect of achieving such goals. While welcoming the guest, please describe his name, his career, his achievements and the reason for selecting such a guest to the function. The speech of welcome should not be more than three minutes in any case and it should inspire confidence and sense of achievement to the new entrants.

Farewell Speech: Quite often the members of the staff or the employees have to leave the organisation either on resignation due to switch over to the new company or due to the retirement. The speech on these occasions is generally of sentimental values. On such occasions a function is usually arranged and some time a gift is presented. In this short speech the contribution of the leaving employee is mentioned, his achievements are revealed, his relationship with the colleagues is remembered without giving a full story of his life history.

On such occasions most of the gathering is gently standing, therefore get over the speech as early as possible. However, it should look like the speech of the audience, i.e. the majority of the staff rather than the organiser and it should be addressed as, "We" instead of "I" so that the leaving person must feel the gratitude of saying good bye from all of them. The purpose of this speech is to make the leaving person feel that his association was valued and his absence will be missed. You must thank thc audience who have chosen you to make such a speech. If you are given enough notice in advance, please ensure that your farewell speech should evoke emotions and sentiments. You can do so by appreciating his valuable contribution relating some of the instances and express affectionate recourse for his leaving and say a warm feelingful good bye to him. It would be worthwhile if such a short and emotional speech is concluded within 100 seconds. The speech should motivate him to respond with similar emotions. Since the atmosphere prevailing on such occasions is generally serious, and emotional it should be kept dignified as far as possible.

Presentation Speech: The presentation speech is given at a time when a gift or an award is to be given to some one at a public function. The purpose of this speech is to express recognition for his performance, achievement and to celebrate the occasion. One must be objective or sincere in appreciating the performance of the awardee. Since the audience is in mood to celebrate, such speech should be to the point, crisp and not bombarded with heavy vocabulary. The person who presents the speech is supposed to be an important person, so he must express gratitude and pleasure for being invited to present the awards. He should also inform the audience about the significance of the award and inform why it is being presented or awarded. The story of the achievement of the winner must be told briefly. It would be in fitness of things if the details of the gift be handed over to the winner. The presentation speech should be between 2-3 minutes and should also highlight the happiness and the joy of the occasion.

Speech of Acceptance: This speech is given after you have accepted the award, gift or a post in token of having received it. Basically it is a speech of thanks and appreciation. This speech should be delivered with all humility with a smiling face and to the briefest possible, not more than a minute. Dramatically, the award, the gift or time and certain cases a certificate, should be shown to the audience with full view and tell the audience how much you welcome and appreciate this. If in the presentation speech any remark or a compliment is given this may be humbly and respectfully replied thereto. You must say something about the gift or award highlighting its beauty, workmanship, wherever possible and the significance of the award. This is also an occasion where you come and thank all those who have contributed to your success in winning the honour. Please don't forget to thank the audience for sparing their valuable time to be associated with the celebration and their warmth of applause.

Ceremonial Speech: This is a very emotional and personal speech for the selected audience on the occasions of birthdays, marriages, parties, social functions and condolences. In the celebratory speeches like birthday parties, marriages and social get together, the speeches should be very light, full of humour and joy to create an atmosphere of celebration. However, the condolence speech should be very solemn, full of emotions to create a serious atmosphere. While making condolence speech the sad demise of dear one is condoled and the bereaved family is given a feeling of association to share the grief of his friends and relations. Before speaking in condolence meetings, please verify from two to three different sources of information about the authentication of the death about which the condolence meeting is organised to avoid embarrassment and anger of the person involved. The speech must tell the source of information, the name and the position of the person expired, cause of the death, place of death and the details of cremation correctly. During this speech never speak ill of the deceased since he is not there to defend your comments. Speak highly of his virtues, values and achievements in life and his contribution to his family, organisation, society, country in general. After making a speech you may request the gathering to keep silent for two minutes so that you can pray to your God to give peace to the departed soul. You can also communicate to the members of the bereaved family that all his friends and associates have expressed sorrow and grief on this occasion either by writing or by the word of mouth.

Political Speech: Political speech is a class by itself. These speeches are delivered by the politicians at their party meetings, public meetings, election meetings, wherein they inform the policies and programmes of their parties to the public for keeping in touch with the public to promote their ideologies to win elections and to contradict the views of the opposition parties. Since these speeches do not form the management studies, we would not elaborate in this chapter.

1.4 Good Communication Improves Inter-personal Relationships

Aristotle said that man is a social animal. By nature and necessity he is bound to live in a civilised society. The moment an individual comes into contact with another human-being or any living-being, relationship starts. Men are seen talking to men, women, children, animals, birds, plants and all their pets. These communications become relationship which become basis of intimacy.

The best of the man's life is spent at the place of work where you come across with your superiors, colleagues and juniors. If you know your men you must build up relationship with them without which you can't exist.

Friendliness: There is an old saying that, "A friend in need is friend indeed". Somebody else said, "Friend is another thyself." But to have a friend you have to be a friend. Real friendship takes a sacrifice. It is an emotional inter-dependence on each other. There is a wrong notion that any acquaintance is also treated as a friend, which is not true. Friendliness and friendship are two different things. For instance when you board a fully crowded train the passengers inside the train don't allow you to enter. Once you enter, you also become a part of them and then you don't allow another person at the next railway station.

During this period you interact with the people inside the train and try to know each other. This is friendliness. But when you are in trouble or you want a guidance, an advice, support - moral or economic, social or political, then you go to a friend. He will not only give a patient hearing, but he would solve the problem considering it to be his own.

In office you may not have a friend in every section or a department, but friendliness is a must to interact with various sections and departments for smooth running of your work. Friendliness is a means to friendship, it's not an end in itself.

I had a pen-friendship with someone in Mauritius for over 15 years. The very first letter informed me like this, "I do not know whether you are a boy or a girl, Hindu or Muslim, something within is compelling me to write to you. If you accept the hand of my friendship, I would write to you regularly." I replied and this friendliness grew into a very intimate friendship during the next fifteen years. Due to some technicalities this friendship could not mature into an everlasting relationship, but that is all a different matter. The feelings of friendship still remain afresh.

Friendly Co-operation at the Work Place: Friendly co-operation is a must. Relationship should never be taken for granted because people make friends for different motives. Sometimes the motive may be financial, personal, political, sexual or any other purpose, but in true friendship the motives are absent. Even if a person is against you professionally, personally or having professional jealousy and criticises you in private or public, the spirit of friendliness must be shown. Even when you make mistake and apologise to others it makes you look big in his eyes and you don't lose anything, but win a friend.

How to Make Friends? I am no Dale Carnedgie to advise you how to make friends and influence people, but it is very easy and pleasurable to make friends and it makes you more thrilled to make difficult people as your friends and maintain the friendship.

Pleasant Communication is the Answer: If you are always humble, suave, docile, reasonably kind, sympathetic and smiling, you can enrich your communication which becomes pleasant if you use the appropriate words, appropriate language and the intelligent use of body language you make a friend. The best example is use this communication in toto while addressing an infant. You use all traits of communication by addressing a child or an infant and win his attention either by showing something or smiling at him or shaking his hands or giving him a toffee. You use all modes of communication to attract the child's attention because this is necessary since he does not know the language. As he grows and learns the language, your communication with him becomes easier, and if your communication is devoid of any infirmities or ambiguities, your communication becomes pleasant. Communication is an art and a lethal weapon which wins all battles of life. The role of communication in establishing and maintaining inter-personal relationship is very significant.

Social Skills: A man being social animal is full of social skills, some of which are your etiquette, mannerism, education, family background, your attitudinal behaviour, your perceptions, your talents, your ability as a sports man, your friendliness - all these make you a skilled social animal. If you are presentable and can skilfully handle all situations at any time you can be not only popular in your circle, but people around would crave to make friendship with you.

After having noticed the pink faces of film-stars, some selected leaders and public figures, I asked many of my learned friends and even my elder brother, who is a psychologist that how the cheeks of these people become red. I wanted to know whether it is due to some special diet or some tonic these people take. The overall response was that the people who are liked and respected by public, the warmth of admiration glows on their faces. Therefore, they look red.

You would have noticed yourself that the persons who are socially very popular in your circle, they glow better than other people. In our society, generally, people understand by being social is to attend parties and invite persons to your parties. That is not so in totality. A person should be sought after because such people are intelligent and have values. They are knowledgeable, well informed, well read, well understood, quite communicative with pleasant and positive outlook, such people improve their own social skills in all situations.

Sense of Humour: It is said that he who does not live in a society, is either a God or a Beast, but it has been proved scientifically that all living creatures have in-built sense of humour. I have neither met God nor a Beast, but I am quite confident that I can, if I meet God or beast, make them laugh. I had written several humorous skits, articles and poems, which sent the audience rolling into laughter.

While in the Railways, I had participated and won prizes regularly in the Railway Week celebrations held in the month of April. I recall when Babu Jagjivan Ram was the Railway Minister, I presented a skit called Tarlok Sabha where Minister like him were presented humorously which had won the Northern Railway prizes. While in Indian Oil Corporation, someone challenged me to produce humour out of petroleum products. I could not rest till a piece was written the same night, about the ghosts of petroleum products coming out of their tanks in a moonlit midnight holding a conference and yelling that each one was the best of the mankind; and finally Dr Mobiloil guides them to hold a conference and each product told its values and virtues in blank verse. The piece was later staged live and thrilled the audience. The children and ladies shrieked in panic while several adults fell down from their chairs when this was enacted. The person who had challenged it demanded further that humour be taken out of the petrol tanks and the same was done when the romance between the petrol pump and the consumer pump was enacted. There are several incidents where the sense of humour was displayed at various times.

The sense of humour can be defined as a capacity and capability to make others laugh or to compel others to enjoy laughter. Even a child has a sense of humour. The animal and birds, they also have humour although they do not have capacity like human-beings to communicate in language, but everybody wants to laugh or hear a joke. A good joke is that which is told correctly, but if a persons does not have a sense of humour he would generally ask at the conclusion of the joke saying, "What happened next?". A person not having a sense of humour kills the joke. In every gathering, be it a political gathering, a social gathering, club gathering, office gathering or even a small birthday day, the persons with the sense of humour carry the party. A cheerful person is liked by every one. Therefore, if you have a sense of humour, it would help you to establish and maintain inter-personal relationship.

Exchange of Individual Talents: When you see a movie, you want to become a hero yourself. When you hear a speech of a great leader, you want to become the leader the same way. This happened with me also when I first saw and heard Netaji Subhas Chandra Bose, Jawaharlal Nehru in Lahore, just after the Second World War. I had even heard the creator of Pakistan, Mohammed Ali Jinah, but at that time the political atmosphere was different so I was very much impressed, and I wanted to be a leader and an artist.

In day-to-day life we come across persons who are either sportsmen, singers, painters, speakers, dramatists and so on, which act as motivators and source of inspiration. We want to become talented person like the ones you come across. We can certainly exchange such talents if we have a positive attitude and willingness to do it. The process of exchanging such talents helps in maintaining inter-personal relationship.

While at Nasik, we had an opportunity to arrange 'Mushaira'

(Urdu Poets Meet) regularly. There were several Urdu poets who would compose pieces and recite their poems, ghazals and hazals (ghazal is a sad song addressed to someone whereas a hazal is a humorous poem). One such poet was nicknamed 'Papad' (made of dal with masala, flattened thin and round by rolling pin - crispy and tasty snack after deep frying or barbecued on live fire). Mr Papad used to read his poems repeatedly at the mushairas. He was requested to read something new at every Mushaira. So much so that I promised to read something new for each occasion and I nicknamed myself as Jhapad, which means "slap". The nickname Jhapad rhymed with Papad and the series started with a new and newer poem in every Mushaira that followed. We both became very popular and sought after. This led to our climax when my Hazal became famous by the name of Machchar wali poem, which won the first place in an Annual Mushaira.

The purpose of telling the story is that exchange of such talents help in maintaining inter-personal relationship not only with the poetic fraternity, but the general public at large. In a similar way an acquaintance of mine painted my English poem on canvas by the name, 'The Witherings. The painting became popular when the name of this poem became the name of my next book, "The Witherings." This poem was earlier published in my first publication, "Buds & Blossoms", which was published by my class-fellows while doing my Master of Literature in 1961. These incidents strengthen inter-personal relations.

Give and Take Attitude: Attitude is everything in life. In order to lead a successful life one must have a positive attitude. The biggest influence on job satisfaction is relationship with others, like colleagues, seniors, juniors, visitors and anybody connected with the job. It is really a hard task to deal with individuals. In order to maintain the friendliness with others you have to have some sort of positive relationship in order to initiate positive interaction because a positive interaction would give a positive reaction and with this approach you will improve your image right along with your attitude substantially turning into magical results.

It is well known all over the world that give and take is the most effective tool to solve all issues. Without this attitude it is difficult to solve even an ordinary matter. Typical example is this; when small kids exchange their belongings in return for the better. Though they do such exercises innocently, but they have a goal to achieve. Even in major national issues or international affairs without give and take you cannot solve your problems whether they are bilateral or unilateral. The best example of give and take is the relationship between husband and wife, who make the home atmosphere conducive by sacrificing their personal egos and comforts.

Set Personal Examples: Leadership is always attained by setting personal examples before the followers. You cannot expect your followers to tread the path until you know the passage yourself. Lead by your own example is the key to leadership. In a cricket match if the captain does not perform well in all departments of the game, like batting, bowling and fielding, he cannot expect others to perform well and win the match. The great cricketers like Steve Wagh, Kapil Dev, Garfield Sobers, etc. led their teams from the front by their personal examples.

After winning the first prizes consecutively in the Railway Week, the Railway authorities asked me to take the team to any hill station of our choice on their account. We picked up Dalhousie and included hiking in our programme. The same year I picked up the first prize in the camp fire in the All India Railway Scouts Rally held in Delhi and the prize was given by the Chief Justice Vivian Bose. With the team of, perhaps, 5-6 colleagues, we set out for Dalhousie. We went for hiking from Dalhousie to Khajjiar and then to Chamba. On return the night had fallen and people at Chamba, whom we enquired about the return route to Khajjiar, advised us not to undertake the journey in the dark. We had kept our belongings in Khajjiar where we had established our camp. It was cold and night had fallen and we had to return to Khajjiar. Even our colleagues seemed reluctant to undertake the journey. Physically I was the smallest in size and figure than the rest, but I insisted that we must reach Khajjiar and stay the night there. My determination encouraged them to agree to undertake the journey. It was about 6 p.m. when we entered the thick forest. We had only three torches and two of us had a match box each. The path was very narrow and we were marching in a single file – me being in the lead of the line and the tallest at the rear. Suddenly I saw a huge bear standing in the middle of the path about to welcome me with open arms. There was no room for manoeuvre either to return or to take sides. I kept my torch on and signalled the colleagues to stop and keep the torches on without getting panicky. The animal slipped away, but the aftermath was very fearsome. We all were cautious that we were chased by the bear. Immediately thereafter one of the torches went out and the second torch was also dimming. Suddenly we heard rustling of the bushes behind and we saw one bear and few other animals, perhaps, monkeys trailing us. We turned our two torches and suddenly in one voice started singing loudly. The animals withdrew and after a short scare we marched ahead. The second torch also went off.

And then came a deadly sight - a six feet cobra - lay across the path right in the middle and I was about to step on it. Suddenly I stopped and stepped 3 or 4 feet reverse. My colleagues were also aghast. At the spur of the moment I used my club placing it fast under his belly and flung it in a flash. We could see the cobra hurtling in the air, then falling at a distance. We heaved a sigh of relief. After this we did not have any torch working and both the match boxes were emptied and we had still 3-4 km to go, and it became the middle of night. The chilling cold started shivering us. The colleagues looked scared. I told them to follow what I do and I started singing at the top of my voice. All sang together. Chorus vibrated the valley far and deep breaking the stillness of the night. Song after song we marched together through the narrow path-way, which is generally called pug-dandi. While engrossed in the activity, we could neither think of the animals in front or rear nor we could see any. By one O-clock in the morning we reached Khajjiar, opened our wooden crate type hut, took rest for some time, discussed our 'long' journey from Chamba to Khajjiar. We started preparing food and took our 'dinner' at 2 a.m. and then we went to the world of dreams.

This episode was a clear example of setting personal examples before the colleagues. Had I not done so, we would have been stranded at Chamba and this example encouraged the colleagues to be more enthusiastic through the remaining part of the journey.

In the inter-personal relationship trust is the basic factor. All such relations are trust relationships. We shall discuss various factors that build trust:

Reliability: You cannot trust anybody until he is reliable. Reliability comes from commitment. Any person who is not committed cannot be reliable. I remember many characters in my life who were committed to the core and they were very reliable. You just give them a job and it is done. I recall one such story:

Govinda was one such character whom I met in Nagpur. He was a self-starter. He used to perform his duties like a computer. If anything, was asked to be performed, he would do it immaculately. Once I told him to conduct a fire drill. It was scorching heat. During summer Nagpur is the hottest point in India. During the fire drill of the employees at the location were assigned various duties. Govinda was assigned to ring the alarm bell and supervise the entire operation. As designed, one fellow was asked to operate the fire extinguisher. Since that particular unit was of very old model, it was decided to be operated, but the cap would not open and the staff wanted to abandon the exercise. Govinda came forward and cajoled the colleagues saying the exercise had to be completed. He himself took upon to operate. He pressed that lever very hard and in the process the nozzle slipped off and with the accumulation of the gas the extinguisher's cap burst open in his face throwing all the dry chemical powder into his eyes and nose injuring him seriously.

While he was bleeding the incoming flight had landed which was to be refuelled by Govinda. Govinda had to be rushed to the hospital. The flight was refuelled by the substitute. After the operation was complete, we all rushed to the hospital and we were glad that his eyes were safe and the first line he spoke was, "I am sorry I could not refuel the flight".

The commitment and the reliability of Govinda was always remembered throughout my stay with the aviation department thereafter.

Consistency: Commitment and reliability is not a one time affair, it has to be consistent, only then it is reliable. Consistency builds confidence. Govinda was not only committed and reliable, but he was very consistent in his attitude and approach. The reliability of a sports man becomes doubtful if it is not consistent and if it is consistent it strengthens the confidence of friendship and hence relationship.

Respect: With the commitment, reliability and consistency of relationship you develop respect for the individuals, whatever may be his age and grade. This is by his consistency and reliability that he won respect from all his colleagues, seniors and juniors. He was respected even by the customers. I always cherished to have more Govindas in all departments of all companies.

Fairness: Any person who achieves respect from others tends to be fair in justice and integrity. His fairness multiplies his respect and reliability. Fairness begets fairness just as respect begets respect, love begets love.

Openness: In establishing relationship, you will have to show the spirit and give and take which establishes two-way traffic. In relationship you can't afford to have a close-ended traffic. Openness is the sign of strength of the relationship. It strengthens to friendship. The openness of each other brings the friends closer.

Competence: The commitment creates reliability which builds up strength to give way to respect with which he becomes fair in his justice and open to communication and this develops into the highest level of competence which comes through the attitude and the service in the relationship.

Integrity: This is the key ingredient to trust. It is said that ability without dependability, responsibility and flexibility is a liability. The true friendship always rests on the integrity of the friends. This is the touch-stone of relationship.

Acceptance: In establishing relationship the acceptance of each other is a must. The acceptance can be developed through give and take, respect and emotional integration of each other. Without accepting the totality of friendship, the relationship cannot be strengthened.

Character: One who lacks character cannot be accepted. The character of individuals is the biggest casuality in the 20th century in the history of mankind. The characters of individuals affects the character of the country. That is the reason the people have lost faith in themselves and each other. We have to build up the character in order to build up all other ingredients discussed above without which the inter-personal relationship cannot be built.

Congruence: This is a stage where action and words of relationship are harmonised. The fair-weather friends can easily be identified if they are not congruent. Start talking to people in a positive way and the attitude of others will change as well and you will find that something is in common that can be the final of positive interaction and this positive interaction would lead to more frequent interactions which will make you start to be liked by others.

Quite often the inter-personal relationship get marred by misunderstandings which keep on piling if not defused in time. This ultimately affects the relationships. We list below some of the methods as to how to defuse explosive situations.

1. Whenever a misunderstanding or break in relationship takes place try to refuse to take things personally. Sentiments

are the pillars of friendship, but if these are injured or corroded get demolished. If things are not taken personally it can be discussed immediately to clean sweep the misunderstanding.

2. Always understand the others point of view keeping yourself in his shoes. This would help understand the misunderstanding better. The only hurdle in this is ego which you have to set aside for the time being.

3. Listening is another antidote to misunderstanding as is known the communication is in-built in the absence of listening. Listening is important part of communication. If you sharpen the listening it will help the explosive situation to cool down. Keeping cool is the tonic of the treatment. In the heat of arguments the explosive situations can be controlled if both the parties keep cool or even one of them keeps cool. Keeping cool would enable you to understand the other persons point of view.

4. Seek agreement by down-playing disagreement. This should be done by valid statistics, logical conclusions and openness of discussions without taking the things personally. A workable agreement can always be attained if there is willingness to arrive at a decision. This helps the inter-personal relationship and in turn good relationship enables reach workable agreements. Arguments can be settled if the principle of fair play is allowed to play. If the relationship is allowed to function in a fair way any dispute or negative argument can be defused.

5. Admit mistakes if you think you are wrong or you are convinced that you are wrong. By admitting a mistake you are not losing anything, but gaining a friend and establishing and strengthening relationship. Inter-personal relationship is the need of the management of the century.

1.5 Consequences of Poor Relationships

For having a good atmosphere in offices good inter-personal relationship is a must. When we talk about how to make the job interesting the very first idea comes to mind is the atmosphere prevailing at the working situation. The work culture is established by maintaining a very healthy inter-personal relationship. The consequences of poor relationship are listed below:

Stress: Strain and stress in the office affects the health of the employees. Stress may be due to lack of facilities, inadequate furniture, uncomfortable work-stations, shabby tools and machinery, low quality stationery, uncomfortable working hours, heavy burden of paper work, absence of systems and above all unhealthy relationship with the colleagues. I have a long list of bosses who do not maintain healthy relationship at work places. I have a story to tell which runs like this:

I was posted as a trainee at one of the locations. Since I was new to the department, I was very eager to learn the systems and working of the office fast. The location in-charge was neither more qualified than me nor very keen and committed to the job and his presence in the office used to be a huge amount of tension. He would not only use harsh words but he would involve the staff in very unproductive work. He would neither do his own work nor allow the others to complete their work. This resulted in lot of embarrassment and firing at the time of inspections. I had taken the initiative to keep him at home due to one reason or the other. I would tell him to take the office jeep and take his wife for sightseeing. Some time I would tell him it is too hot to come to the office. On cloudy days I would tell him to go and enjoy the weather and so on. In his absence the office work went on very smoothly. For 21 days he did not come to the office. Then suddenly one day the boss had come for inspection; perhaps, the news of his absence had reached him. Though he came running, but he didn't review and sign the Quality Control documents which as a location in-charge he had to do as a part of his duty. The boss had fired him so much, little short of suspending him. This caused too much tension amongst the colleagues. So much so one or two persons had to be hospitalised. So much stress in the offices should not be allowed to happen and healthy inter-personal relationship must be maintained at all times.

Distress: Lack of communication at work places causes distress among the employees. The relationship gets distorted and reaches the breaking point. It hampers the smooth working of the organisation. It is said that communication is the blood-stream in an organisation. Similarly, the lack of communication is a death knell for the organisation.

Anger: Lack of communication and tension in the office spreads anger which leads to irritation. This irritation and anger boils down to inefficiency.

Prejudice: When the communication is cut off and anger and irritation crops up, it results in close-mindedness leading to prejudices. Under this atmosphere the senior personnel get biased and staff become irritated and stressed.

Breakdown of Morale: From the above story all these elements brought down the team spirit at the station and the small stations were divided into three groups, i.e. the boss, the trainee and the two regular employees who were mostly coming in the night. They were always at cross-purposes and the morale of the team was down which was bridged by the trainee who was sandwiched into two groups. This situation invariably happens when there is no responsible person who could control the situation.

Lack of Credibility: When the relationship are affected and prejudices prevails all over, the lack of credibility of individuals as wellas collective leadership is affected adversely. It also affects the attitude of the employees who become uncooperative in behaviour.

Conflict: Poor esteem of the employees creates conflict which becomes difficult to eradicate because of so many elements prevailing due to lack of leadership.

Frustration: Conflict and prejudice creates suspicion in the minds of the employees and the element of frustration looms large all over.

Loss of Productivity: When there is suspicion, frustration, conflict, low morale, anger and irritation, the work culture of the organisation is adversely affected leading to unhappiness and isolation, which is very painful.

Thus you would realise that the inter-personal relationship are very essential for the general health of the organisation in absence of which all the above elements would be clearly visible which would bring down team one day.

1.6 Managing Confrontations: An Interesting Issue

The confrontations open the gateway of conflict management. There are millions and millions of species of mankind living together on this planet who differ from each other in shapes and sizes. Although the limbs and bodies are identical, but they differ from each other in ideologies. Different people in different countries present different ideologies. These differences have led the human races into several battles and two world wars. The planet is ready for the 3rd world war any time. The League of Nations and the United Nations could not prevent the wars. To discuss these issues even the United Nations General Assembly is not adequate. However, the problem as the human- beings face can be debated in the form of a subject for training programme.

Man Conflicts Himself: Every individual has his own personality, his own style, his own growth based on his attitudinal environment and educational developments over a period of time. As he grows his inner conflicts also grow. What he desires when not achieved translates into conflict. It is said that all problems have solutions. It is only the method of finding that solution, which is not evaluated with dedication and sincerity with guidance and experience. The solution can be found for any problem. It is the in-built conflict which restricts the movement of efforts to find a solution. The individual should reason with himself to identify and sort out the solution.

Conflict with other People is Inevitable: When a man is in conflict with himself, the conflict with other people is inevitable, it is natural. No two people can exist to go without conflict, because they are the products of different built up. Though the conflict negates progress, it helps motivating people for analysis and finding a solution. A think process gets started. The think tanks of more people get activated till the conflict is resolved.

Take the example of husband and wife relationship. You may tally the horoscopes, you may bind them in some nakshatras, they are bound to conflict with each other in their lives, come what may.

It is Natural: Conflict is neither unnatural nor a dirty word. In fact it is very important and useful for relationships. When conflict occurs it is not an indication that those involved are bad people. After all debates take place in schools, colleges, panchayats, assemblies, parliaments and the international fora. The very essence of debates is conflicts of ideas. When you say that debate is a healthy exercise the conflict also proves beneficial. The management of conflict is a very useful exercise.

Reasons For Conflict: The reasons for conflict are manifold and thus can take several forms. The key to identify conflicts is your capability to recognise a variety of conflicting attitudes and your handling such situations. In man's life there are millions of situations where two or more people differ with each other due to their inherent conflicts. This is inevitable in mother and father, father and sons, mother and daughter, son and daughter-in-law, neighbour to neighbour, friend to friend, employer to employee and so on. The problem comes when we don't have the conflicts. Once it is recognised it can be resolved, then purposeful efforts are made to resolve it.

Establish the Source: Just with a little effort you can pinpoint the source of the conflict and when you identify that source efforts can be made not to repeat. If a small kid keeps a candy, the other kid would try to grab it from him. Both will fight to get that candy. Now the candy is the source of conflict. The children may not analyse the conflict, but the grown ups can analyse and prevent that source to recur again. Despite their education, experience and maturity even the grown up people and even world class statesmen fight for their 'candies'. Only candies may differ, i.e. in the form of political power, land, sovereignty, governments and the like. All other conflicts are the smaller 'candies'.

How to Contain Conflict? The conflict gets complicated when attempts are made to explain it. The conflict should be described and not explained as to what happened and how happened. If it is explained, the arguments come into play. These arguments are counter-productive and more arguments are enforced to justify the conflicts. A competition takes place. In the competition emerges the war of words, conflict of theories, the battle of bias and fire of frictions, which burns all logics.

Keep the Conflict Localised: When fire takes place the first step is to cut or eliminate any of the three ingredients. The three ingredients of fire are the combustible materials, (oxygen/air), and temperature (heat). The second step is to localise the fire. Similarly, when the conflict is established and identified, it should be localised. Then it should be described and misunderstandings resulting in hurting each others' pride and ego be eliminated. Emotional language often fuels fire. Problem can be stated as clearly as desired. Let the issue wait for some time. Time is a great healer If the smouldering of all burning passions cool down the mutual agreement comes into account and then the outcome of the situation affects positively to the conflicting parties.

Kill the Flame of Ego: The biggest hurdle in building a relationship between the individuals is the ego. Ego is so intoxicating that no amount of alcohol can match this. It is a negative pride resulting in arrogance. Most conflicts of human-beings are originated from ego. All of us are suffering from this. If we can control or camouflage this distracting element, we may not win, but we cannot be destroyed or defeated. It is sad that healthy pride is a feeling of pleasure of accomplishment of humility. How true it is that ego gives a swollen head while pride gives a swollen heart. This results in a big head giving a big headache and big heart giving humility.

I was confronted once with a number of officers who were posted after the annual promotions and posting session, who had ego problems and they were not acceptable at their previous assignments. They were proclaimed difficult persons. When so many difficult persons are kept together at one location, one can imagine the variety of conflicts emerging therefrom. Just as you give a bottle of whisky to an alcoholic, he would be pleased, you give a better intoxicant to an egoist, he would be soothened. All these so-called difficult persons were given difficult, but responsible assignments. They were individually proclaimed most responsible persons. Each of them wanted to do better than the other and a situation of grand competition took place. During this healthy competition I kept myself aloof without disturbing their actions and activities, I monitored them closely, the results were fantastic. It surprised many persons that how such difficult persons could deliver such astonishing results, but it was very true example of managing conflict in the work-place. I endorse and agree and prove the statement, "One of the most difficult and distasteful tasks that managers face is the need to make judgements about or confront difficult employees, specially when personality issues are involved and I proved this statement umpteen times". I cannot forget those people who were involved in this exercise and I am sure that they will not forget it either.

1.7 Discussions Yes, Arguments No

The management of conflict originates from the elements of discussion and arguments. Both these elements form different faces of the same coin, but their implications are far and wide. All over the world the decisions come out of discussions and debates. The modern method of selecting employees also revolves round discussions, hence several groups are formed into small batches, different topic is given to each group and discussion takes place. One or two persons from each group are shortlisted and the total number of shortlisted persons are formed into more and more groups and the process goes on till you get 7-8 finalists. In discussions it is not necessary that the candidate who speaks more wins, but the yardstick is that what the candidate speaks and how. The discussion throws light on the subject matter by providing statistics, details, the tried and tested procedures, the decisions arrived at culminating successes, whereas in argument the tempers are exchanged.

When there is conflict the matter should be discussed in a very cool and calm atmosphere rather than in the atmosphere of heated arguments because argument throws heat while the discussion throws light.

Argument is the product of ego and closed mind. The best example is a straight fight or quarrelling kids. They exchange heated words, harping the incidents with a closed mind, displaying lung power at its best and you often hear, "You don't know who I am", without explaining himself. A closed mind can't discuss smoothly. Discussions always come from an open mind. You never come across high dignitaries arguing the points. You must have seen on electronic media several discussions which culminate into arguments. In solving the conflicts in the management the parties concerned must have open mind.

Argument is an exchange of ignorance whereas discussion is an exchange of knowledge. The people who are not well informed they only argue their point of view because their knowledge is limited whereas the knowledgeable people discuss each and every point with logic and accepted principles and norms. Argument is always an expression of temper. In order to resolve conflicts the distinction between argument and discussion must be made and kept in mind always.

When two persons express their views putting their heated

arguments, it is generally believed that the person who has got authority, some power or majority of persons behind or with greater lung power is considered to be right. But if the same topic is discussed without the use of elements of arguments then you can reach a conclusion as to who is right and what is right. Thus argument proves who is right and discussion proves what is right.

The problem is that in the day-to-day management the matters are generally argued out and not discussed, but our experience is that in top managements or in the big organisations the key decisions or the vital decisions are always taken in the meetings of the heads of departments which in some organisations it is a must at the beginning of the working day. The same principle is applied in the discussions of the armed forces whenever a vital or a strategic decision is to be taken. Arguments can't or don't decide the strategies, but the strategies are always formed out of discussions. I have a very interesting episode to elaborate this point:

There was a time when I was provided with a team of difficult people. I called them difficult because they were proclaimed unmanageable individuals at their respective postings. They were unmanageable because they were more intelligent and educated than their superiors who wrote their annual appraisal reports. Perhaps, because of the inferiority complex of the reporting officers, they always argued their point of view with these characters and developed permanent conflicts with them. At the end of the year they were not given good reports and hence missed their promotions. This strengthened their conflicts further which resulted in their being discarded and transferred. The biggest damage was that they hardened their attitudes.

When the time for writing the next year's report came, I called them to my cabin individually on different dates. I came to know their backgrounds, their stiff attitude, rough language used in heated arguments. Their attitude was so tough that they didn't want their reports to be written or even read to them. According to them the whole exercise was a trash. I was convinced that the argument with them would be futile. The counselling was done on individual basis on several occasions before they were called together.

Thus one day I called all of them at the same time and place, they were six or 7 in numbers and me all sat together over cup of tea in the VIP room of our location. The same issue which I discussed with each individual was thrown open for discussion. I was quite aware that they represented the majority of opinions and I was alone to defend their point of view. I turned the arguments into a discussion in such a way that the point of view of one was opposed by the majority of others. After a very lengthy debate the consensus was arrived that the adverse reports given to them were due to the unjustified attitudes meted to them. It would not be repeated. The results were startling. All of them individually and collectively brought a remarkable change in their attitudes and the results thereof. Due to this in the next 3 or 4 years all of them got their promotions in their next grades to the utter surprise of the senior managers who had a chance to handle them earlier. This was indeed a very tough job, but it was performed.

1.8 Characteristics of Difficult Employees

The so-called difficult employees are generally aggressive persons who lack sensitivity to others. Some of the common traits are as under:

Autocrat Type: In our day-to-day life we often come across some individuals who have very autocratic approach and style of

working. They always dictate. These types of people always want to do everything in their own way with utter disregard to others. The autocrats don't discuss the matter with their colleagues to evolve an opinion. Whenever an idea or thought comes to their mind they want to implement and impose on others. Quite often even the failures of their decisions and implementation don't correct them. History has thrown off several personalities of such type who were though brilliant but failed to achieve their goals.

Rebel Type: It is generally presumed when a person does not get what he deserves or believe to deserve he counter-acts and rebels. The majority of such people cause revolution, but in management style you come across some people who are denied certain concessions like promotions, increments, etc. They become furious and rebel against the company rules and they become anti-authoritarians. Their negative approach adds to the conflicts of the management and finally land them in trouble. The rebels generally don't get over with the organisational rules. At the end they get themselves alienated by the majority of the staff.

Aggressive Type: Man by nature is an assertive. This assertion when over-played becomes aggression. The captain of a team has to be assertive. The moment he becomes aggressive his leadership is in danger. The aggressive person invariably plays the game of one-upmanship. Generally he is not a team player. The story of these seven people given above were aggressive, the rebels and the autocrats. They had to be tamed very carefully. But when tamed well, they become assets because such characteristics are generally considered to be in the above-average people. Because a lazy uneducated, a foolish and stupid person cannot become aggressive. If he does, he is generally sent to lunatic asylum.

Destructive Aim: Such person resemble a bull in a china shop. These people don't have any regard to the sensitivity of other people. Can you imagine when such employees tear the important documents when given to them for execution without imagining the consequences thereof. Such employees generally communicate in a very devastating way. If you visit any jail you would find such characters in abundance because this is the ultimate consequence of their harsh behaviour.

Unpredictables: We often come across some persons who are not consistent in their action and inter-actions. Some persons would be very consistent to give all care and attention to their seniors, but not to the juniors, e.g. they would be very respectful, be very kind, polite and good towards their seniors, but they would be very hostile and rough in handling their juniors. Some time conversely they would be very good to the juniors, but they are very bad to the seniors like rebel types. Such employees are inconsistent and unpredictable. It is risky invariably to handle such characters, because they can tilt either way.

The above characters are generally observed in employees who are major causes of conflicts in the management.

2

Art and Science of Management

The Simple Meaning of Management is to Manage Men. Every Human Being is the Most Important Student of Management.

In the early stages of primitive man he lived like an animal devoid of home, family education and even language. He lived in caves, killed animals and ate them raw. When he raised a family he felt the need of nursing his offsprings, taking care of mate, felt the need of shelter from sun and rain, needed security, built dwellings. He felt the need to feed the family and look after. From that day the **'management'** came into being. He managed all those activities which were required to cater the needs of that small family. The evolution of management progressed at every stage of development of man.

Today; management is a subject which deals with setting, seeking and meeting objectives. Each individual manages his own life covering every facet of activities like education, service, participation in government, armed forces, commercial establishments or any activity.

For a layman management is to manage men or getting things done through other people, but for a student of management it is a process consisting of planning, organising and actuating, controlling and accomplishing the set objectives with the use of human beings.

There are several factors which constitute management. They are Men, Material, Machines, Methods, Money and Markets. Some say management is an art because it gives pleasure. Some say that it is a science, with-set inputs and outputs. Some further say that management is an art leading to become science. We would not like to debate all these factors for the time being.

Our aim is to tell what is managing and who manages, what

manages and where it happens and how! Time has changed. The 21st century manager does not have time to go through the traditional textbooks to study the art or science of management. Today he does not need spoon feeding. The time has come, if we adopt **yesterday's** methods **today**, we would be out of business **tomorrow**.

While we don't discard the traditional methods which are good for students of **management** in schools and colleges, but we have to tell about the experiences of management and how they will be useful for implementation in future. The basic need is to produce results through human beings and the subject becomes crystal clear that it is the manager who produces or who is required to produce results. Let us identify that phenomenon called the **manager**. The manager is a huge personality, like an elephant in the jungle of management. The following characteristics are the essentials of a manager:

Managers Must Have a Huge Head: A Manager must have a big head, not that of a buffalo or a wild pig. To have a big head means he should have a store house of knowledge in his head, like information, skilled technology, should have the will to learn more, manager should be innovative. With all these characteristics, he would inspire others and lead them. The people around will come to him to share a pinch of knowledge from him. It is well known that an average 7% of the man's brain has been used so far in the entire scientific development on Earth including sending a man on moon. Imagine what would have happened if 100% on average human brain was used. We all know it cannot happen, but manager must have more information and knowledge than the persons he is managing to store such an information a huge head is required.

Managers Must Have Large Ears: Listening is an important factor of communication. Manager must have ears to hear every one. He should listen to any advice, complaint, information, problem, grievances - official as well as personal to win confidence of the people. While listening he must have empathy, assurance, affection, feelings, without which the listening exercise will not be complete. A manager should not hear only the pleasing music, but he must have the capability to hear noise. A good manager should identify the words of flattery and unwanted praise and the subjective comments. In the process he must probe, if required. He must listen to all types of information relevant to the objective. He shouldn't listen to biased or one-sided version. He must have complete information of his department, company, publics, internal as well as external. His ears should be so sensitive that even the falling of pin must be heard amidst the noise of the churning machines. Successful manager must have very sensitive ears, that is why it is necessary for him to have large ears. He should be capable of hearing anything audible.

Managers Must Have a Long Nose: Nose is for smelling. It is used for all kinds of smells whether very foul objects or the fragmented ones. There are people around who are nosy about all matters. To be nosy is also considered poking nose in every pie, but the term used for subjective managers is that he should have the information as to what is happening in his organisation. It often happens when you come across a very sensitive information or news and you break it to the manager. A good manager would simply say, **"I know it."** He may not know it, but he says he knows it so that the informer feels that manager is not ignorant.

Managers Must Have a Big Belly: It should sound not that the manager must be a glutton, but the term is used that the manager must have the capacity and capability to digest everything which he has been asked to swallow. While managing men the manager gets bouquets and brickbats. For his good work he is rewarded in cash and kind. He gets increments, promotions, incentives, foreign tours, bigger assignments etc. For incompetent work he gets memos, charge sheets, punishments, transfers, suspensions, dismissals and sometimes imprisonment. Thus he gets both types of treatments. The managers must be capable to digest both types of these treatments. One does not expect that the managers dance around when he is applauded or to cry in public when he is criticised. Not physical but philosophically he should have big belly to digest everything.

Managers Must Have Small Eyes: Small eyes signify concentration. During the training of Pandavas each one of them was asked as to what they saw while aiming the at eye of the bird. All the four Pandavas described everything about the bird, the branch on which it was sitting, the trees, the clouds, sky, etc., but Arjun said that he only saw the **'eye'** of the bird. His aim hit the eye only. Manager must concentrate on his job, on his goals, on his results, on his achievements only. It is always taught that managers must have the only paper on his table on which his concentration is required. A Manager has got many assignments; he must have concentration on each assignment, proportionately depending upon the importance it deserved. While aiming during shoot, he closes one eye and reduces the size of the eye to have the optimum concentration before firing a shot. This means the ultimate concentration. Concentration is very vital for making all decisions. It is so vital that even a dot has to be placed on the drafted letter with full concentration. In the 21st century communication **.** (dot) has to play a very significant role in the e-mail. Concentration is the key in the 21st century management.

Managers Must Have Sturdy Legs: The manager must have a very strong support to stand on. The support is provided by his academic qualifications, professional skill, technical attainment, his vision, his speed and efficiency, his commitment and dedication, his understanding a man. All these constitute his solid support. If he has got all these legs to stand on, he cannot be uprooted or defeated at the time of crisis. He then becomes the strength personified in an organisation. Just as a man with strong legs walks majestically, the manager's solid support makes him look majestic in each marathon.

Managers Must Have Sharp Teeth: The big bellies need well chewed food. The successful manager always has very sharp teeth to chew everything that is pushed in his belly. The teeth should be visible to scare distracters. They are not only ornamental to beautify the facial personality, but they are well kept armaments.

Managers Must Have Wide Back: A Manager is very responsible phenomenon in the organisation. He has to carry several responsibilities on his shoulders and also hold a heavy luggage on his back. Like in the war the generals have to carry their wounded and casualties, the managers have also to carry the casualties on their back. Since there are more people, more casualties and more load, hence wider back is required.

Managers Must Have a Swatter: Most people have swatters to kill flies in the office because these pests disturb the concentration of the managers. Even a single fly entering the cabin disturbs the peace of mind of the manager. There are several pests in the form of obstructions, nuisance and other foreign objects which are called the organisational insects. The small tail of an elephant swats the nuisance so that the elephant is not disturbed. This little part of the body is very symbolic to the composite elephant.

Managers Must be Intelligent: The 21st century manager must have equal proportion of LB and RB traits. He should be self-organised, methodical, sincere, analytical, innovative, imaginative, philosophical and a practical person. All these traits can be had if he is well educated, professionally qualified and extremely intelligent having updated his knowledge about everything at all times. He should be beacon to others.

Managers are Not Poor: All these traits mentioned above will attract the Goddess of Wealth, i.e. Lakshmi. The man with so many qualities cannot be poor in any respect. The person who has responsibility for so many activities has to be paid well. Lakshmi resides at such places.

If you substitute all these qualities in one person the immediate image that would emerge in your vision would be that of **Lord Ganesha**, the **Ganapati**, He is truly a symbol of a true manager. Imagine the contrast that such a huge personality is transported by rat. This is also significant that a manager does not need a huge BMW or an executive aircraft, he can traverse all the distances in open and into the holes of the earth by rat, which means he is accessible to each nook and corner of the mother earth. Perhaps that is the reason that Ganesh is worshipped at the beginning of all ceremonial functions.

You have heard the story of five blind men who were taken near the elephant and each one of them described the form of elephant to the extent they could feel with their hands, but if all the five men had opened their eyes and seen the elephant in toto then they would have analysed all the qualities of an ideal manager in him. True, Ganeshya (Ganapati) is the personification of an ideal manager.

Activities of Management

Management is a distinct process consisting of activities of planning, organising, actuating and controlling to achieve objectives. It is the "Art of Arts", because it organises it through human talents.

Planning: In any activity of an individual or a group of individuals, one important thing to be decided is the objective of the group as well as of the individual, which is to be achieved. Once the objective is identified then the individual or the group makes effort to accomplish it. In order to achieve this you have to serialise the task to be completed one after the other. In doing so, you have also to identify as to what are the essentials to accomplish the task. These essentials are people required for the task, place at which the task is to be performed, the materials required for the project or the task and all other paraphernalia which becomes necessary for its achievement. It is also to be identified as to what manner or method the projected task is to be performed. In other words a complete plan of integrated function of all these activities are to be assembled. This requires the total involvement of the managers to foresee the plan of activities and visualise the consequences thereof. This entire sequence of events is called **planning**. The basic function of management is to plan.

Even if an ordinary activity of a marriage of your ward is to be performed all these components are required to achieve the objective. To start with you are to identify, requirements of the boy. Your aspirations about the girl to be married, family background, where, when and how the marriage is to be performed, what are the various customs and formalities to be completed, preparation of guest list, arrangement of other accessories, jewellery, clothing, household goods, music, band, photography, flowers horse, etc. etc. All these constitute planning. Even the budgeting is also planned. In the same way the managers are involved to plan for the start of an organisation and list out all the components.

Eisenhower had said, "Plans are nothing, planning is everything".

Without planning no one is sure how far he will be successful in achieving his objectives.

To quote a recent incident of planning, the United States of America planned to find out and take the terrorist groups to task who had smashed the American properties on 11th September 2001. The USA contacted almost all the countries including United Nations moved the entire naval flotilla, the air force squadrons, the army units and sent diplomats to contact various governments and attacked Afghanistan after a month's planning and that too on top priority basis. In this exercise all the pros and cons of national and international consequences were discussed and debated. Materials worth thousands of millions of dollars were planned, arranged and transported to the strategic locations. The consequence of Third World War were also discussed with all the alliance partners in this campaign. The success of any project lies basically on the efficiency of planning.

Organising: There are three important words, viz. to Organise; Organising and the Organisation. To organise is an activity which has been planned taking all the components into consideration, whether it is a picnic, marriage function or an attack. Organising is a process to undertake the activity. This process is generally a lengthier than to organise, but temporary till the objective is achieved. Organising is a prominent feature of the activity which is in the state of organising which is generally directed to the future activities. In this process the task to be performed among the group members are distributed to various individual members and seek the co-operation of other members in completing the task. The work is distributed amongst its members in order to complete the task methodically and within the stipulated period. The work of allocating the assignment and monitoring the progress and the interaction with the group members for analysing the progress is called as **organising**. This is the basic function of the management.

Take for example a small commercial establishment whose function is to manufacture and sell them in the market through the network of vast distributorship. This main task is distributed to several departments like the personnel to arrange the manpower, the marketing to appoint distributors and dealers, the production department to produce the items, the operation department to replenish stocks and the accounts department to keep the income and expenditure records, service department to run services and serve other departments like engineering, stores, legal, despatch, etc. etc. and the monitoring of the function of all the departments is meticulously done so that no department suffers for the lack of communication on the part of any one of them.

Actuating: The meaning of actuating is the moving of action. In order to perform the activities emanating from planning and organising, it is necessary to initiate actions to accomplish the task. All the steps which are necessary to be taken for the action to take place or taken by the managers depending upon the competence of each group or individual, the manager has to take a leading part to advise, to guide and to train the members of the group to improve their productivity and **creativity**. The entire process is called actuating. It is this process that activates all the instruments of management like planning, organising into real action when the performance takes place.

Controlling: It is the essential duty of managers to monitor, control and measure the progress at each level of activity towards the set goals. While performing tasks several impediments come across like inter-personal relationship, inadequate manpower and funds, governmental rules and regulations, labour problems, internal and external conflicts, all these are required to be established, identified, controlled, monitored and followed up at each level of the activity. Unless it is done the management activities are not completed.

The above are the salient features of the management. Besides, there are other functions of the management which are carried out by all levels of managers and staff during their day-to-day activities, some of which are as under:

Decision-making: Decision making is the most important function of the management. At each level of planning, organising, actuating and controlling process the decision are required to be made. The People generally are not decisive. The effective managers succeed because of decision making quality. The lack of decision making delays the action and encourages red tapism. Red tapism is itself a term which denotes that the file has been bound with a red tape because no decision could be taken on it. It has become a big disease in most offices, especially, public offices.

Why This Phenomenon? Why people hesitate to make decisions is a common phenomenon in our society. The very first reason is the fear of making mistakes. Any person who has to do any job is afraid to decide because of fear of making a mistake. He has perhaps decided in his mind that if he makes a decision it is bound to be incorrect and if that be so what would be the consequences. That fear holds him back to take decision. Generally people are afraid because of, **"What would people say?"** This constant fear prevents anybody to take a decision.

Most politicians, ministers and the men in authority are

affected by this fear of making a mistake. It should be known to every one that those who work make mistakes. One should not be scared of making mistakes. The very definition of experience is number of mistakes a man makes.

Lack of Confidence: Self-confidence is built by the experience, knowledge, skill, training, motivation and leadership qualities. If any one of them is missing, the confidence is missing. Lack of confidence multiplies fear. More the fear less is the confidence. Any person who is lacking in confidence cannot be a good leader and cannot make a decision.

Courage of Conviction: The managers who are full of confidence, knowledgeable, develop a courage of conviction. Courage of conviction comes from experience. The managers who don't have adequate knowledge, experience and confidence, lack the courage of conviction which prevents them to take decisions. In our traditional cultural conditions the decision used to be taken by the head of the families in our joint family system. Now when the unitary type of systems are prevailing the decisions are taken by husband and wife either individually or collectively. Even the youngsters in the family take decision these days. It is not only matters of taking decisions, but the implementation of those decisions which matter most.

In the initial tenure with the Indian Oil, I was the Secretary of the Indian Oil Club and we had to organise a very big cultural evening for which we had to bring out a beautiful leaflet. On some reference I had contacted a printing press in Daryaganj, Delhi and asked him to print out a leaflet. The proprietor of the press was highly educated who was involved in printing business just for the love of it. He designed a couple of leaflets and presented it for approval. It took hardly few minutes to select one of them and print order was given on the spot. Next day when he met again he brought the printed leaflets and said, "In my entire life of printing business I have never come across a person who had taken decision so fast in the matter of printing. I am so elated that I would not take the printing charges of these leaflets as a token of my appreciation towards your decision making". While I thanked him for his bold compliments, I compelled him to take the payment towards the bill and told him that it was a sheer courage of conviction which made me take decision without fear.

Fear of Objection/Opposition: Man by nature resists change, but constantly preaches that a **'change is spice of life'.** Whenever a new change is brought in a system it is objected. From my experience while working in private organisations, the managers at middle level, and higher level generally gave the opinion that the decisions to bring the changes will not be welcomed. They always resort to one line opinion, **"This Cannot Happen"** - nothing can change. This fear of resistance prevents the professionals to bring change for effective management.

I recall the incident of marking attendance sheets. The traditional system of marking attendance sheets, was the signing of attendance register. Senior managers and the habitual late comers would not sign the attendance register. With the result it became difficult to tabulate the salary because details of working days of managers were not available. We brought a change that attendance be marked by the watchman on the attendance cards which were in vogue for the labour class. The white collar staff objected to it. We again switched over to the new system of keeping a blank sheet of paper at the gate and all staff were required to sign as and when they entered the office by putting signatures against their names with time. This also was objected and late comers naturally did not want to be reflected by signing and putting the timings. We brought out the latest change by installing a time punching machine. Some officers had some reservations on this also, particularly, for those who come late and go early.

From the above you will find that this is one of the several decisions which is quoted as an example otherwise every change is generally opposed and resisted unless and until the employees are first mentally prepared to accept such changes.

I quote yet another example in relation to the stitching of

uniforms. The prevailing system was that the cloth of the uniform was distributed to the employees every year and stitching charges were paid in cash. On record the system was working smoothly but the staff were not wearing uniforms and those who were wearing it got stitched as per their own style, with the result that all staff wore the clothes, no doubt, but their pattern of stitching were different, for instance some had long sleeve, some short, some had one pocket while the others had two pockets, few people had flaps on pockets and others had no flaps, the name-plate and monogram were not in line with the uniform pattern. We wanted to set this right, but most of the staff generally the youngsters opposed the idea of having uniform system of uniforms. A meeting was called and the purpose of uniforms was explained to them convincing them that uniform was given from safety point of view, that the clothes should not result in static electricity and the shoes should not create a spark while handling petroleum products and the most important point was the presentation of officers and staff at the Tarmac. The good uniform builds up the image of the organisation. We had repeated meetings till the staff were convinced that we must have proper uniforms. The decision was made to call quotations from best tailors available who were advised the standard pattern of uniforms and the measurements were taken at the location itself and the uniforms were stitched and the turn out of the staff was far better than in the past. Had we not taken the decision just because we anticipated opposition or fear of objection, we could not have implemented the decision. The fear of objection certainly prevents the weaklings to make decisions.

Scare of Criticism: The managers who have the courage of conviction are afraid of being criticised. Glaring example can be cited of the service support department who are to provide services to the staff, like disbursement of salaries, grant of leave, grant of other favours like sanctioning of loans, recommendation for holiday trips or medical reimbursement, etc. You can be serving them, they will be friendly to you but when you bring in rules and regulations and their interests are not served, those very so-called friends start criticising. It is these biased reactions which cause scare for the managers to take decisions. It is, therefore, necessary that the managers and the top management particularly, must be very fair and square in making decisions to avoid criticism. The professionalised managers don't; rather should not bother about the decisions taken in the interest of the smooth functioning of the management systems.

Decision Makers: Let us analyse as to who makes decisions. In reality all of us make decisions in one way or the other. Even a small child makes a decision as to what type of ice-cream he likes to eat. From management point of view the people who are in command take decisions. At the front in war, the commanding officer takes a decision as to when and where to attack. In organisations the people in authority take decisions. The hard task masters are not influenced by the blockers in the management. For them 'no' is a 'no' until it is 'yes', and the disciplined managers should not say yes if they want to say no. At times you have to learn the art of saying no.

Committing Mistakes: Just as making decisions, committing mistakes is also a very significant part of management. Decision making is a compulsion in itself, whereas the mistakes are not compulsive. Those who work are bound to make mistakes. Mistakes are committed either through ignorance or through communication gap, through an oversight, through inefficiency, through habit, or through rush of work. Generally mistakes are not committed deliberately. If the systems are allowed to work, function effectively, the number of mistakes are reduced. My personal experience has been that the mistakes are committed in haste. Most people have habit to keep the pending work piling up and suddenly when they are asked to complete the assignments at that moment out of hurry and worry the mistakes are committed.

It is my firm view that experience comes through the number of mistakes a person commits, but the problem is how many times he accepts the mistakes. If we have the courage to accept the mistakes and don't repeat it again, it is part of the learning. But if we commit the mistakes again and again then it becomes bigger mistakes.

In my previous company the senior executives were given small printed diaries on which they were required to note down the number of mistakes they made, the consequences of the mistakes and lessons learnt from such mistakes and then reactions of the management/staff. Most of the senior executives kept their notebooks generally blank because it is a natural tendency that every one would like to hide his mistakes. As I had been a learner throughout I had recorded a number of mistakes which I committed while making decisions. One such mistake was that once the union approached for certain concessions to be given to them failing which they would resort to work to rule. The demands were very genuine, but the way they asked for the demand was not correct since the union leader was not educated enough and he was rash in putting the demand in an irresponsible language, therefore, the decision could not be made on the spot. Consequently they resorted to work to rule, e.g. at lunch time they would break for lunch irrespective of the fact that 2-3 aircrafts had to be refuelled during that time. In that situation the officers present in the shift had to double up and stretch themselves to drive the refuellers themselves and attend to refuelling simultaneously single handedly. This created lots of operational problems though the situation was handled perfectly well.

The lesson learnt thereof was to sit with the union, discuss the matter in a healthy atmosphere, and not to react in the same way as leader of the union reacted and another lesson leased was that all such demands which needed to be made should be settled in time.

The reaction of the management was very commendable that the mistake had been identified, accepted and corrective action taken, and this had a very favourable response from the union leaders as well in the days to follow.

The committing of mistakes is necessary part of the management which all managers make at their work stations right from simple mistake of incorrect spellings, not attaching the enclosures, despatching wrong material to the very wrong destinations.

From my personal experience, I would recommend that the staff should be open and frank to notify the mistakes and once in a month or quarter the recorded mistakes must be discussed in open and remedial measures taken to eliminate such mistakes. This would help the management to make their task most effective and successful.

Communication: Communication is the blood stream of the organisation. It is the most important function of the management. We always communicate with our internal publics as well as external publics. Gone are the days of my time in the Railways and other sundry departments when we used to write memos, letters and reminders to government authorities and private parties without much results. The use of telephone was a luxury at that time. Today in the 21st Century the management has been blessed with the fastest means of communications' through fax, e-mail, telephone, pager, mobile telephone, tele-conference, that the total globe has become a small village where any incident or information originating from one part can be communicated to the other part of the world in a matter of seconds. Science has gifted this boon to the people of 21st century which is very effective and helps to speedify all the functions and operations of all managements.

In addition to this, most managements have various methods of communication through circulars, in-house magazines, seminars, conferences, tele-conference through which they communicate to their publics. The most effective method of communications with their publics is the printing/circulation of a house magazine. It not only reflects the culture of the organisation, but it reflects as a mirror of all the activities and profiles of the persons working for the organisation. While the subject has been discussed elaborately, separately the mention of this topic is listed here as a part of the management function.

2.1 Managing the Boss is Essential

All Mighty God is the Master of the universe. Every one worships Him. Had it been some individual, he would have been obeyed as well. I have asked several Bosses to define what is boss. I have gone to some houses of my friends where there is a placard hung in the drawing-room on which is written, "I AM THE BOSS OF THE HOUSE AND I HAVE THE PERMISSION FROM MY WIFE TO SAY SO". You again do not know as to who is the boss of the house.

Lucky is he who gets a good boss. In reel life the BOSS is generally shown as big bad bully, generally played by film actors, Prem, Pran, Ajit, etc., but in real life boss is a person who can make or mar the career of his subordinates. It is very tricky and sometimes funny and many a time dangerous and difficult to handle a boss. It is said that don't stand behind a horse and in front of a boss. You can be kicked any time.

Boss is a powerful individual who enjoys tremendous powers - if he wants to use it, tremendous knowledge, if he is highly educated and trained, a great teacher, if he has values and virtues, a great artist, if he has a talents, great scientist, if he has wisdom and techniques, and the biggest nuisance if he is stupid and insane. All these types of bosses I have the privilege to have worked with.

Notwithstanding the stories of all of them, I would not like to ignore one instance where I had a tiff with my boss who had developed a kind of complex while dealing with me and a number of times I had to report to his boss, i.e. who was two stages senior to me to solve my functional problems. My boss was my departmental head. Once his Boss called him and counselled him in my presence.

During the course of our discussions I told him, "If I have to come to you to solve my problems every now and then, then this man is not required. My boss heard this quietly and sat still.

After the episode the Regional Head talked to me on phone telling me that he had seen me handling of union leaders, customers, difficult colleagues, bosses in other departments, and asked why I could not handle this particular boss. In reply I told him, "A good boss need not be managed. A bad boss can be managed with some tact and diplomacy, but you cannot handle a mad boss and you know that". The Regional Head laughed heartily endorsing my view.

There is another story when I joined Indian Oil in the early stages of the company's journey. During those days the company had just started and we had to push our products forcibly to increase sales and compete well established foreign companies. Coincidentally, there were two dealers of the same name-one being a big dealer and the other a small one. I despatched a large tank wagon of Kerosene to a small dealer instead of the big dealer of the name-sake and he had no paraphernalia to unload the wagon.

I rushed to the boss saying that a serious mistake had been committed. His immediate response was, "Those who work only can commit mistakes. What for I am sitting here? Don't worry for the mistake. Now tell me what happened?"

I explained the matter in detail and he said, "That's all? Inform the dealer telegraphically to make necessary arrangements to unload the wagon in time."

While the wagon was unloaded without incurring any demurrages, but I was loaded with the kindness and greatness of my boss. All people who worked with him made their careers, me included.

Boss is just an individual like you and me having some extra responsibilities and powers to lead an assignment. He is a human-being with all the qualities and frailties of man. He can be handled emotionally, diplomatically, tactfully and professionally.

It is said, the most important duty of a boss is to motivate people. Build them up when they are down, and pull them up when they begin to rest on their laurels. Here are some of the levers which can be used to handle the boss:

Know Your Boss Well: Physiognomy is a science which teaches you about the structures of the body of man with specific characteristics. I recall Shakespeare play, Julius Caesar, where Cassius says, "Yond Cassius has a lean and hungry look: He thinks too much; such men are dangerous." Physically apart you can know about your boss about his educational qualifications, family background, mannerism, habits, style, tastes, likes and dislikes, etc. well and then meet his requirements. Every boss wants that he should not be let down. If you do a lousy job your boss gets the discredit. But if you accomplish a difficult task and you are rewarded for that, the credit goes to the boss. In war the soldiers die on the battle-fields, the generals take the medals. But the generals have to carry their dead and injured. In civil the same pattern decides whether the boss is a reel general or generally a boss.

It is mandatory for everyone to please a boss. Some people resort to flattery. Again, recall Julius Caesar when it was being discussed that Brutus would go to Caesar and tell him that he hates flattery and he would say, "Yes", thus most flattered. Some people resort to please their bosses by gifts and presenteries and other personalised services, but a good boss does not need all these extra boons. What he needs is an efficiency and a professional accomplishment. If your boss values punctuality, you should be punctual, if the boss is honest you have to be honest, if the boss is professional, you have to be professional. The qualities of the boss should not be compromised.

I once complimented my secretary saying, "Anita you are looking damn smart today". She replied, "I am the reflection of my boss". If you feel your boss and know your boss well, you have used the first lever perfectly well to handle him.

Know What You Want: While handling your boss you should also know what your expectations are, what you want from him - a promotion, a pat, a good increment, a reward, a firing or a stick? If you meet the requirements of the boss you would get what you deserve.

I was sent to a Naval station where we had a huge installation at Goa. My brief was to set the station in orderly fashion in all respects like housekeeping, stock loss control, discipline of the staff, maintenance, repairs of the installation, discipline and upkeep of staff, proper accounting and PR.

On the very first day, I noticed that the housekeeping was in very bad shape. So much so that the three windows curtains of my office were not only torn, but of different shades and colours giving a very dirty look. Similar was the condition of the staff rooms and several other aspects which I had observed in my taking round of the location. I called a meeting of the officers in my room. At the outset I asked as to who can replace the curtains by the next day. They all laughed in unison. I replied this was not a laughing matter. I told them that one of them take up the responsibility of getting the curtains changed. The second in command of installation replied that this could not be done even within a week as markets were very far off and they close twice in the day - one after the lunch for a siesta for four hours and the other at 6 o'clock sharp. I again insisted that this had to be done the next day only. They again expressed their helplessness and very casually retorted that this was not Bombay where this could be done at leisure. I asked one of the staff to take measurement of all the windows and doors including the staff room to which they all were surprised as to how so many curtains could be provided so soon.

In the evening I took one of the local boys in my jeep and went straight to the market into the best shop of tapestry. After exchanging pleasantries and introduction I made the shopkeeper friendly and bargained the price of the best curtains available in the shop after selecting shade and texture. When the shopkeeper looked pleased with the proposed sale I put a condition that the curtains would be stitched by his tailor and delivered it at 9 p.m.

the same day. He called his tailor and he also showed some reluctance at the scheduled delivery, but when I advised him that the job was very minor one as he had to stitch only ready-made tapes and the corners. The ready-made tapes had arrangement for hooks and the job was not very demanding. I assured him to pay his price as well as extra tip for the fast job. Right on dot at 9 O'clock about fourteen curtains were delivered while I was taking dinner.

My driver came to pick me up at 7 O'clock in the morning to reach office. By 7.45 all the curtains were put on all the windows, doors before all the officers arrived. They were startled to see the new look of the office and choice of the curtains and the speed with which they were arranged. Thereafter, the entire team of officers and staff realised that a job when demanded had to be done.

So, therefore, when you know what you want, the assignment is completed. Then throughout my stay in Goa, the local officers were made aware as to what I wanted and how I wanted the tasks to be accomplished.

Express Yourself: If you know your job well, you need not be afraid of anything and when you are not scared you must express yourself clearly. Another story of expressing self comes to my mind again at Goa. The condition of the station came to this pass because of so many factors which were not brought to the notice of the Regional Head on two accounts. Firstly, the then location in-charge was not committed to the location because of lack of responsibility from the local staff which he could not manage well and secondly he could not express himself properly. The staff realised that I had come all the way to perform and I meant business. Secondly I made a list of goals required to be done by the regional office and flashed to Bombay. To follow up I expressed myself very frankly justifying whatever I had written in my report and got the response very quickly. Immediate response brought three additional officers by the next flight next morning and three staff members were rushed by train.

This manpower strength was very essential to complete the tasks ahead. Similarly, I gave freedom to all the officers and staff working there to express themselves and advise all the difficulties experienced by them. I made them sit in a closed room to discuss the problems and in a matter of few hours they came out with a long list of local problems which were very trivial like keeping a soap and the wash-basin having dusters, oils, etc. The water-cooler needed repairs for a long time, the fans and the lights needed repairs and many other such things. All these facilities were provided very fast and whatever they demanded in their list were fulfilled promptly. This acted like magic and they all rose like a one man team overnight. The results were quite obvious. The station gave a new look within seven days. After another seven days when the buildings and the equipment were painted, the premises were made spic and span, we were ready for inspection of any standard. This was the great demonstration for all of them to put their efforts one hundred per cent.

Look for Common Points: While negotiating or handling any individual, the agreement cannot be reached if you do not have something in common. In fact, my three months in Goa was a matter of exemplary case study. I made a common cause with my boss that the location is to be set right and similarly I made a common cause with my staff and team of officers to develop the station and in the process all of them worked together. A new enthusiasm was sparked and the results could be seen within days.

Ideas in Terms of Benefits: If you share a common cause with your boss your ideas can be presented as benefits to the boss as well as to the organisation. The benefits can be realised if there is a deep understanding between you and the boss without which you cannot see eye to eye with him. My inspecting boss did not see eye to eye with me, particularly, during his periodic inspections, but when the common differences were explained to him clearly the terms of benefits to the location were clearly visible. This not only endeared me to the boss, but he came closer to my thinking.

Get a Fresh Perspective: It is very essential to get clarification of your boss's perspective. Every employee must know as to what his boss requires and the expectations vary at different situations and change from time to time. Therefore, in order to match the understandings, it is necessary to get fresh perspective of the boss, e.g. you are doing a routine kind of job over a period of time. Suddenly, the responsibilities got elevated due to additional assignments given to your department, it would alter the perspective of your boss. Therefore, the perspective of your boss has to be updated.

Mind you, the boss is not robot, he is also a human being, fallible to make mistakes, an emotional being, a social person, logical one, a well-known individual. Therefore, it is not difficult to handle such an individual provided you conduct yourself in the way it is expected of you.

Characteristics of Ideal Bosses: Good bosses are always liked and respected because they are SIMPLIFIERS. They not only simplify complex matters, but they simplify complicated ones. In my early stages of career I had taken some problems to my bosses.

The good bosses didn't make me feel that they are complicated, but the average bosses made those problems look bigger than I presented them. In the process they not only made my working difficult, but embarrassed themselves in the eyes of their superiors.

Bosses as Informers: Good bosses always look like beacons from where you can get guidance. They always inform you, they give more and more information and education. They share the knowledge with staff that gives confidence to the subordinates. It is well-known that information is knowledge and knowledge is power and if this knowledge is shared you become a teacher and teacher is always respected.

Boss Need not be a Star: It is not necessary that a boss should be a popular person. You may not be as popular as a star, but he must be a star performer. A star performer is he who is committed to the task and a team's man. His performance always shines like a star.

Lead by Personal Example: Good bosses always lead their teams by their personal examples. They catch the bulls by their horns. I was once asked by the Director as to how I maintained punctuality in the office. I replied, "By personal examples - I never come late." Once or twice in a month, I would stand at the gate casually and shook hands with a smile and met the employees who came late, without asking them the reasons for their late coming. This was enough to make them punctual. This method has been tried at several locations/offices where I was posted The results were very positive.

Allow the Employees to Grow: Good bosses who share knowledge with their staff always encourage their employees to grow. Wherever you find that you have an extraordinary employee who has the urge to improve in academic and professional qualifications he must be encouraged to enhance his skills. A good boss must encourage his employees to improve his standard and style of working. I recall my secretary Murli, who would learn one new word every day, record in his diary and used it frequently in his day-to-day correspondence and at the end of the year he told me with pride that he had learnt more than 360 new words that year which he has used them invariably. This elated me.

Bosses Inspire and Motivate: Good bosses are the source of inspiration. This inspiration becomes motivation. Dull and inefficient bosses do the opposite. They demotivate and discourage their employees to the extent that they become useless. In the organisation where I worked for 30 year, our culture had been to develop at least 2-3 persons who could occupy your chair and if this was not done, we didn't deserve promotion.

No Confrontation: Good bosses always keep their employees at ease. They do not confront.

I had a strange coincidence that majority of the officers posted at my location were discarded in their previous places of working. They were considered as difficult persons. They were publicly known as trouble-makers. When I interacted with them I found them very intelligent and above average persons. The problem had been that they were con-fronted by their bosses at their previous locations. I understood them from close and they became my most efficient team members about which the top management was surprised. The simple reason was that I didn't confront them. All of them earned their promotions in due course.

2.2 Motivation Keeps You Going

"Motivation is a pre-disposition to act in a specific goal-directed manner." Hellriegeloslocum

"Motivation may be defined as the state of individual's perspective which represents the strength of his propensity to exert effort towards the same particular behaviour." Gibson

"The term motivation refers to goal directed behaviour. Goal directed behaviour is characterised by the process of selecting and directing certain actions among voluntary activities to achieve goals." Chung

"Motives are expressions of a person's needs: hence, they are personal and internal." Davis

"Motivation phenomenon is an internal need energises and activates human behaviour."

"Motivation is the need or drive within an individual that drives him to goal-oriented action."

Many people argue that traditional "carrot and stick" method of motivation still works today. The carrot has been money and the stick has taken the form of physical, financial or social punishment.

The growth of mankind is the result of motivation. It is a will to do things. It is a compulsion to act. Motivation means to turn on or ignite a spark or to propel the feelings or action.

It is said that motivation is like fire, until you feed fuel to it, it dies. We have seen that people will do lot for money, more for a good leader and do most for a belief.

Take for instance the incident of 11th September 2001 when a group of terrorists hi-jacked four aircrafts on a single day, two of them dashed in the twin towers of World Trade Centre at New York, one into Pentagon, the highest base of world class security centre and the fourth one crashed because of struggle inside the aircraft. Throughout my long life I don't find a better incident of extreme motivation. It must have taken a very long time to train these people as to how to fly the aircraft, how to hi-jack it and the plan of mass destruction killing thousands of people in the action and the surprise is that the intensity of motivation was maintained throughout this period. This motivation is the result of too much money, command of the leader and a very strong belief in the cause. This may cause now or later the start of third World War.

Coincidentally, I had the occasion to visit New York and go on top of the building of the World Trade Center in 1987. After having a breakfast in the restaurant in one of the floors and the moment I reached the top it was difficult to stand there because it was windy and I had to hold the railing to have a glimpse of the city. The immediate thought that flashed my mind was that if an aircraft hits this tower because of its height how much havoc it would cause to this building and its surroundings and see the things I had imagined and had seen with my own eyes on the TV screen the aircraft hitting the first tower. The second aircraft hitting the second building as well and immediately the words blew out from my mouth spontaneously, "The Third World War has started."

Motivation is powerful urge, it can persuade, convince and propel you in action. Motivation comes into action to satisfy your needs, your tasks and group needs. There are three types of needs:

1. Individual needs.
2. Group needs.
3. Task Needs.

Individual Needs: Every person has to satisfy individual needs to survive. These needs are classified as under:

a. Self-actualisation.
b. Ego.
c. Social needs.
d. Security, and
e. Physiological.

These needs if not satisfied create tension and that tension produces a drive which cause behaviour which builds up personality and temperament. In order to achieve the goals you have to play your values and attitudes. While achieving such goals sometimes you may feel aggressive and sometimes demoralised and if the goals are not achieved, you become unsatisfied again. To satisfy these needs you are self-motivated to achieve such goals. The motivation needs you to grow, to get educated, get employed, raise a family and start a home.

Group Needs: When more than one individual are grouped together they form into needs of the group, e.g. the family. Individual needs are multiplied into the family needs. To achieve the goals in a family the members of the family get motivated individually and collectively to achieve such goals.

Task Needs: Each individual or a family or a group has to perform a task. All the communities have defined their tasks. In offices your task is to perform specific job and the collective jobs for all the members of the organisation developed into task needs of the organisation. For example marketing, finance, operations, PR, HRD, etc. For the time being we emphasise upon the two factors which are required to be understood for use of the managers of the 21st century. There are two types of motivations, viz. positive motivation and negative motivation. Positive motivation makes a man to grow or to climb the ladder of success, and negative motivation is for destruction, like the activities of the terrorists who are motivated to destroy. These can be further divided into external motivation and internal motivation.

External Motivation: Fear and money are used for external motivation. Money is generally paid to individuals or groups to motivate to do action. Several impossible jobs are done by the exchange of money and muscle. At your work places you are paid salary and perks, facilities and several allowances, bonuses, incentives - they are all motivational gifts. Those who don't perform they are punished, victimised by transferring them or dismissing them from service. It is said that fear is the biggest motivation.

Internal Motivation: Pride, sense of achievement, recognition, rewards play the role of internal motivation. A student works hard to top the exams and when achieved it is recognised by the family members, friends. Photos are published by the media and this internal motivation gets general reaction for other students to get internal motivation to repeat the results. The following example would prove the external and internal motivations:

At one of our work places there was a piece of uneven land on which nothing could develop because of stones and gravel. Except for this the entire area had been developed into green gardens. All the staff and workers were called near the piece of land and each one of them was asked as to how much time it would take to clean that place so that the same may be developed into a Badminton Court. The minimum period announced was three days and the maximum seven days. All of them after discussing came out that the piece of land could be developed within 4-5 days. I told them to play a game; and the game was that each one of us would pick up the stones and put them in bucket turn by turn for five minutes each. The others would count the number of stones collected by the earlier player. The person who collected the maximum number of stones was to be rewarded Rs. 200/-. The person who would collect the minimum stones will have to do double duty. We emptied a bucket and I played the first round in order to lead them. In five minutes I collected 130 stones in the bucket. Each member of staff followed thereafter and started collecting the stones in five minutes each. While one was collecting stones the other players were counting the stones collected earlier. We were seven in all. Can you imagine that the entire piece of land was cleaned within forty minutes. In fact the last player could not get sufficient stones, only pebbles, within his stipulated time. Within an hour we played a game of badminton at that very spot. You can't imagine the pride and the sense of achievement on this success glowing on the faces of all the persons involved.

From the above, you would find that the money was involved in the shape of Rs. 200/- as prize, the fear was there for doing the double duty, pride was there that we played the game in a unbelievable short time and the sense of achievement was there for completing the job within forty minutes. This was promptly recognised when the event was celebrated by enjoying tea and snacks thereafter the game. This was a small but a compact example of motivation. The successful managers keep trying such methods in one form or the other, day in and day out.

These are some of the experiences which cannot be sighted in the traditional management books because the experiences of success differ from man to man.

How to Motivate? The 21st century managers and members of staff in offices do not have the patience and time to go through management books and literature. However, the following tips can be given to motivate the employees and staff working under them which have been tried and tested tips:

Thanking Employees: All good human-beings should develop the habit of thanking people. If you thank even a younger and junior member of your team for any job, for instance, bringing a file or posting a letter and thereafter you thank him, he would be pleased and motivated to do your job again.

At Ozar our location was situated at the extreme end of HAL factory. For all matters of maintenance/repairs, catering, etc. we had to depend upon the HAL factory and we had developed a culture that whenever a job is to be done by the factory, we must send them a letter of thanks after completion of the job. The senior manager maintenance was pleased on this unusual compliments. During the course of our chit chat, we had reiterated that letter of thanks would reach them before their team returns to base after the job. He promised to defeat me on this issue. On the next assignment, we wanted to get some electrical repairs and he sent the staff by jeep. Now it became difficult to send the letter of thanks because our employee had to deliver the letter only on bike. After getting the job done, we typed the letter of thanks immediately and sent the boy on foot running short cuts and crossing the boundary wall and delivered the letter of thanks well before their jeep returned. Shri Singh, the senior manager of HAL telephoned me back saying, "You win."

Listen to Employees: Whenever an employee brings a complaint or a problem, personal or official, generally a manager does not listen to him seriously if he is occupied. If the employee is listened to seriously, he develops confidence in the boss and becomes closer. This coming closer to boss motivates the employee, while a good boss always calls his employees once in a while to enquire about their difficulties and problems. This becomes the part of the job of the manager, but when an employee goes to the boss he has approached the boss specifically to solve his difficulty. The manager or boss must give time to listen to him.

Once an employee was hauled up for his habitual absence. He was too uneducated to reply. By nature he was shy and quiet, but his habitual late coming became a problem so much so that he was to be charge-sheeted. I called the employee and the shift manager and asked him to explain as to why he was absent regularly. He related his story very pathetically. He and his wife who were permanently sick. His four children were also very sick. The youngest child was on milk only and there was no one to bank upon and he had to take care of his wife and his ailing children, particularly, the youngest one. His regular absenteeism affected his salary because most of the time he was on without pay. He was compelled to come to the office very rarely just to earn some money to survive. Even while telling the story he collapsed. We comforted him, accompanied him to his house, saw the condition of the family and consoled him. We offered him some money as a loan to treat his wife so that she can take care of the kids. He was happy to have this assistance, but he was more jubilant that at least his problem was listened to. Earlier, all his pleas were brushed aside and he was branded as a habitual absentee. After this incident he become the most regular employee. This also set an example for other shift managers to listen to the pleas of the employees, because listening to them was itself a balm.

Create Healthy Environment: Work quality is very important to motivate the employees. Work culture depends on so many factors like the working conditions, comfortable timings, facilities, interpersonal relationship and systems. To add to this is a fantastic house-keeping.

At one work station the working atmosphere of the location was very pathetic. Most of the employees were alcoholic. They would either remain absent or come late and could not concentrate on the job. Besides, for any absence there was no substitute, the work suffered badly. The importance of work culture was innovated. We started planting trees, flowers, peanuts, where everybody started taking active part. While the station improved and the staff were occupied always. Their drinking habit also were checked and they looked healthier than before. We started games in the office when free, particularly, playing cricket with rubber ball. Whenever the cloud would come, we would cook good dishes in the evenings and enjoyed eating together. A stage came when the first shift staff terminating at 3 O'clock would not go home, but to play cricket because it was mandatory that the losing team shall have to pay for the sweets which everybody enjoyed. This small innovation improved not only the inter-personal relationship but their health and environment and reduced their drinking habits. The families of some of the staff personally came to see for themselves the work environment. This innovation was repeated at other locations as well bringing remarkable results.

Keep the Employees Informed About Policies: The employees must be kept informed about the strategies, policies, products, incentives, allowances, new schemes and all other new facilities given to them from time to time. This creates sense of belongingness and any new incentive or allowances keep them motivated.

Involve Employees in Decision Affecting Them: There are decisions which the management takes relating to employees. All decisions which bring change are generally resisted by the staff, but if the employees are involved in making such decisions affecting them, become part of the decision making. The implementation of the decisions is neither resisted nor opposed. There are so many occasions when the management wants to implement some decisions, e.g. the change of shift timings, working late hours, punctuality, discipline on wearing uniforms. All these decisions can be implemented successfully if the staff is taken into confidence. The best way to do is hold staff meetings periodically. The new policies and strategies be explained and their views invited for implementation. The minutes of such meetings should be recorded so that they become part of the decision.

Encourage Employees: Most managers in most companies don't pat their employees or speak word of encouragement to them on their achievements. If the staff is encouraged to improve his academic qualifications and is rewarded by giving an appreciation letter as and when he does some commendable job, he gets motivated. When we issued a charge-sheet to an employee, he would hide it from his colleagues, but when you issue a letter of appreciation, he would show it to everyone. I have made it a habit to issue appreciation letter to all employees who complete their jobs efficiently and promptly. Wherever I worked this act of mine kept the employees motivated. It is a natural instinct of man to be complimented and be applauded. Encouragement given from time to time creates a sense of belonging to the organisation.

Give Chance to Learn: The man by nature is a learner right from his birth. As he grows, his skills grow. All good parents and managers give chance to their wards and employees to learn new skills whether they are technical or attitudinal or other skills. Send them for training or institutes to learn new skills. Any knowledge gained through these trainings would be useful not only to the employee, but to the organisation. In most companies the managers are given rotational assignments so that the employees learn more and more skills in more than one department.

Celebrate Success: The management teachings recommend that one must celebrate one's success either individually or in the company of others. It is generally recommended that if you have achieved something unique or completed a difficult job you need a reward for self and such success must be celebrated. It is recommended that one should buy himself a gift. To celebrate such success either buy yourself a new suit depending upon the type of achievement. Similarly, if your department or section has won a competition or in the quality performance programmes or won a trophy in a game or won a drama competition, the entire team should celebrate the success.

We at Sahar won the QUALITY points 100 out of 100 for three consecutive years and we won British Council Safety Award for five consecutive years and also this was celebrated with the participation of all the employees. Twice we presented a table clock and a gold coin to all employees. This was the motivation at its peak. On an other occasion our batch of five scouts won the first prize in drama in the Railway Week celebration for the fourth consecutive year and the Railways awarded us to celebrate this success to go to any hill station and we went to Dalhousie. Those who accompanied us were very happy, but those who heard about it were motivated, more.

Performance to be Considered: While rewarding staff his performance should be the paramount criteria for the award and not for his personality or individuality. For rewarding on the basis of meritorious performance, it motivates others who come to know about it. When every one is aware that performance is always rewarded, the results are bound to yield good dividends in motivating the general staff. The classic example of this is when the medals and other monetary benefits are rewarded to the Defence Personnel for their contribution in war. Posthumous awards are given even for the contribution of the soldiers who die in action. Any award/prize/reward cannot be measured in terms of money or monetary benefits. The very recognition in presence of others when applauded is itself a reward. A small pat on the shoulders of staff for doing any exemplary job is a motivation in itself.

Set Personal Examples: A successful leader is he who motivates his staff with his personal examples.

The best example could be given about punctuality of the staff. Wherever I have worked I motivated the people to be punctual by my own punctuality. Throughout my career I have never been late under any circumstances. Often in a while I would stand at the main gate of the office and receive the persons, those who come late with a smile. I didn't have to tell them or ask them about their cause for late coming. My presence was enough to motivate them. This worked at most locations. This would certainly work at your office or set up.

Make Them Feel Important: Every individual in the organisation had its own importance which he would like to get recognised and acknowledged. By word of mouth or giving him an important assignment you can make him feel important. In the earlier chapter it has been made out that by handling difficult people at Santacruz the main motivation for getting them working was giving them responsible assignment and making them feel more important. This worked and it can work everywhere.

Consistent Training: Right from the birth till death each individual requires training, whether it is academic, mental, physical, professional or technical - in all fields the training is necessary and it has to be continuous process. Constant hammering of knowledge is a must. If it is not done man begins to forget. You have noticed the mighty blitz in the advertising which is hammering the brand name of the product again and again till the consumer is compelled or motivated to buy. Training of the staff motivates them to learn more.

Highlight and Use Talents: Talent cannot be hidden whether it is fine arts or sports or any hidden quality, it comes out in the open some how. Each individual is talented in one way or the other. It must be highlighted either by giving him chance to perform or the talents should be used for his individual betterment and for the over all growth of the organisation. The recognition or use of talents motivates staff at every level.

I was adjudged the best scout and my one act plays won consecutive awards in the Annual Railway Week celebration. The Railways not only asked me to go to any hill station with my team, but encouraged me by permitting me to publish my first book, "BUDS & BLOSSOMS", which earned me immense publicity in the Railways.

Need Them: Every staff must feel that they are needed by the organisation. This can be amplified by respecting them and seek their services on very important occasions so that they can get motivated because of their skills, talents and achievements.

2.3 Attitudes: Passport to Success

It is said that great organisations are not measured by wages and working conditions, they are measured by feelings, attitudes and relationships. Mahatma Gandhi has said, "Study as if you were to live for ever. Live as if you were to die tomorrow."

All of us have to die one day, but how you would like to be remembered after death? Have you ever imagined or thought whether the life was worth living? A purposeless life is a living death. purpose bring passions. It is the passion that gets you going. Therefore, we need to find a purpose to live so that we may make life meaningful and then work hard to achieve that purpose.

The story of Alfred Nobel is well-known. He invented dynamite. A false story about his death was published in a newspaper which announced that, "Merchant of death is no more". He happened to read his own story and lamented that he would be known as the merchant of death there after he made up his mind to do something good for the society. He started doing things in that direction till he was claimed noblest person and today the Nobel Prize is attached to his name. This is how he is remembered. "Human beings can change their lives by changing their attitudes" William James.

Nothing can stop the person with the right attitude towards achieving his personal goals in life. Mahatma Gandhi's book, "My Experiments With Truth", has proved the success of attitudes towards life. This also supports the view that the right attitude directs one to use his abilities to gain the maximum from them.

Great People Leave Something Behind: Socrates taught Plato; Plato taught Aristotle; Aristotle taught Alexander the Great. "Knowledge, had it not passed along, would have died". Our greatest response is to pass on the legacy with the coming generations could be proud of.

Human Brain is Creative: The creative potential can be realised on the positive attitude towards freedom of ideas, whether you paint a scenery, compose a poem, compose a musical tune, whether you write a literary piece or a public speech, whether you organise a social exercise, whether you manage a good commercial office or whether you organise a marriage party or any other even in life, the positive attitude is required to maximise the creative potential. The influence of these creative potentials is not depending on any criticism or any unfavourable reaction. During the process sometimes premature judgement, biased reaction and other cultural blocks can kill the seed of an idea.

The ideas and the creative potential are the results of the knowledge and experiences. Ideas cannot be created out of a vacuum. Ideas come like a dot of illumination which gives birth within the idea to a new idea till the illumination of creativity starts glowing. It is observed that the illumination frequently takes place when least expected.

I recall the success of my poem which was read in a mushaira attended by the noted Urdu writers of Indore, Mumbai, Nasik and several other districts. All the creative artists were asked to compose on one line, "kiski gali se guzar ho raha hai" (in English it means, "To which street you are passing through"). Most scholars wrote as if they were passing through a street dominated by temples, mosques, churches, gurdwaras, etc. Some wrote about their journey from the street of their beloved one. Some wrote that they passed through a lane inhabited by pickpockets, thieves and robbers. Some wrote that they were going through the lanes of various houses of politicians. Few of them wrote that they were passing through a graveyard. Some said that they were passing through the red-light area enticed by the sex workers, etc. etc. When my turn came, I wrote that I passed through that lane after taking several rebirths, i.e. human-being, a mosquito, a crow, a dog, a frog and a bed-bug and being a bed-bug resting on the seat of a chair in the theatre on which my beloved sat, thereby I Clung to her legs and kept clinging to the body. When she passed through the street then I saw through her clothes the outside world I was most intoxicated. This was how I passed through the street.

This creation was done with the very positive idea that how to make a successful poem from a very trivial idea of passing through the street and to describe as to whose street it was. This creativity was so effective because the need for this idea was identified and recognised because it was new and fresh. There was freedom to express the idea, there were no reservations and no public reaction was anticipated. The birth in each life was an idea illuminated from one birth to another and the idea was kindled when I was a mosquito in my previous life, I could suck the juice of her lips and enter the clothes of my beloved uninterrupted till she killed me as a mosquito, the way a mosquito is killed and takes rebirth again. Kindling of this idea illuminated new ideas till journey through that street was completed.

That is why it is said that the attitude is learning to find enjoyment in your work. Therefore, one should allow incubation of an idea to an unconscious brain so that the action could take place.

The conscious mind is but a small part of the total mental power. Medical science has proved that there are many memory cells holding an infinite number of facts and associations and this unconscious mind gives a chance to find a solution to the problem.

Left Brain: Right Brain: Biologically human brain consists of left and right hemispheres that perform different physical and mental functions. These hemispheres are the LBs and RBs, that is left brain and right brain. The left brain functions for logical, analytical and systematic thought processes, that is how we read, write, calculate, plan, execute and analyse with this human sphere. The RB, i.e. right brain functions for creativity the product of, subjective thinking, spontaneous thought processes. All artists, poets, dramatists, writers, thinkers are product of this hemisphere.

It is essential that every one should be well organised, but it is not possible for every one to do so because it is ongoing continuous process and it needs lot of efforts. The successful persons are always organised. The organised managers keep their tables free of papers at all times and they don't appreciate others who don't come up to their organised standards. Such people never face problems in their day-to-day working. LBs are very organised, methodical, neat and clean, punctual, well maintained. On the other hand there are people who face problems at every step. Their papers are not organised, their items of daily use are not properly kept, they are not particular about their clothes, they don't bother for shaving regularly or even taking bath daily, they will never feel committed on commitments and they lack concern about the commitment of others. If they use the tooth-paste, they would press it from the middle or top and they will never close it after use. After shaving they never clean their brush. These are the traits of RBs, i.e. the right brain dominated persons. They are creators, thinkers, the poets, artists and philosophers.

Both these traits are present in all human beings. Some are right brain dominated and some are left brain dominated. It has been found that all human beings use both traits simultaneously, but the hemispheres function differently. The people who use both sides of hemispheres equally or judiciously in a balanced way are the successful managers. To highlight the point the right brains are the creative persons and the left brains are organised persons. The dominance of these hemispheres produces the type of attitudes which guide man's activities.

Look around yourself, you will find that you are surrounded by RBs and LBs. During training courses we have conducted tests which are prescribed in some books which determine the influence RBs and LBs in each individual.

Positive Attitude: The very idea that you would like to live and live comfortably, peacefully, without any worry, is the internal trait of positive attitude. If you love life you are sure to do any job. Any person who believes that he can do his job and he likes his job, makes a positive thinking. I have been telling in most of my training lectures that people who have positive attitude they have the capacity to enjoy even the sipping a glass of water. If you develop the capacity and capability to enjoy any activity you will not only derive pleasure in doing so, but you will be successful in doing so.

Always Think Good: It is said that nice people always think the other people are good. The persons with positive thinking are optimist, full of enthusiasm and they always think good about future. They don't care for the negative things.

Use of Common-Sense: While all other five senses e.g., smelling, seeing, tasting, hearing, touching are invariably used in our activities; the sixth sense, i.e. common-sense is more predominant, both for LBs and RBs in their respective spheres. The well organised managers will use common-sense in making decisions in their managerial assignments, RBs would also use common-sense in using appropriate notes in music, appropriate words in poems and appropriate colours in painting. But the very use of common-sense tends to make the whole attitude as positive. It allows the incubation of an idea though it may be a small part of the total mental power.

Don't Think Negatively: There are people around who always keep telling that "this cannot be done", 'that cannot be done'. This creates a chain reaction between the LBs and RBs. Any person who is determined will always think positive and he will get it done. There are people around like Shiv Kheras, Promod Batras, Chopras and the likes who teach the art of positive attitudes. Negative thinking is not associated with these names. It is pleasure to work with persons having positive attitudes. They always teach you how to adjust your attitude before some one else adjusts for you. It is the negative thinking which hardens the attitudes which makes most managers fail to learn and they fail miserably.

Keep Calm: All times are not equal. Situations differ from time to time. Successful managers always adjust their attitudes. They keep calm when the tides are rough and when times are difficult. Persons with negative thinking or negative attitude would always fight against the waves and perish.

Be Alert: Positive attitude always keeps you alert. Such persons are always tuned in, they are never out of tune, they are always alive to any situation, they are always bubbling with enthusiasm. Such persons are aware that their positive thinking would always make them victorious.

Make Mistakes and Forget: Every one who does a job is

liable to make mistakes. Some accept it, apologise it and try not to repeat it. Some forget the mistake, but commit again because they have forgotten the earlier one. Very few people make mistakes, acknowledge it, admit it, but never repeat it. Such people are successful. This trait of accepting a mistake and to learn a lesson is a positive thinking. I firmly believe that the definition of management is number of mistakes one makes.

Receptive Mind: During our usual training classes, which we conduct on Sundays, we defreeze the thinking of the participants either by making them laugh for 2-3 minutes or to close their eyes and imagine something beautiful or to chant "Aum" for three times or to do any such activity which deviates from their normal working so that the container of their mind is emptied of the negative or contaminated thinking, anger, worry, depression, jealousy, pain, etc. so that their minds are fresh and their thinking faculty is open to have new ideas.

The above traits of positive attitude reminds me of a story of three pairs of sparrows. Although these cannot be compared with the lives of human beings, but they are certainly the best examples of different traits of attitudes of living creatures.

I had a two bedroom flat and a lobby. In each room there used to be a pair of he-sparrows and she-sparrows. Each one was so committed to each room that in each season they would land in the respective rooms as if they were allotted to them. In my room the couple would bring straws and other material to build their nest in a corner of a loft, settle down, rub their beaks, cajole each other, copulate, lay eggs and incubate them till the off-springs would spring out. Both the parents would feed the offsprings, give them company, fly with them till the offsprings would fly out independently.

The couple in the children's room would also repeat the same sequence as in my room, but the parents would depart before the offsprings could fly themselves out. One of them invariably would die either eaten by the cat or falling out and injuring himself, but one of them could survive. The parents would not be seen till the next season. The couple in the lobby was the noisiest, they would never build a nest, they would always fight, they would lay eggs at the end of the loft which always fell down and broke. This couple never had an offspring but they always made the maximum noise which affected our peace and sleep.

This continued for six seasons regularly. One day the she-sparrow of my room was hit by the moving fan, fell down on the ground and was injured. My first-aid and all comforts could not revive her. She died. I still remember the shrieks and cries of the he-sparrow. The ferocity which he showed his anger agony continued for six continuous days. It was a very pathetic situation. After few days he brought another mate and started living thereafter normally.

Now all the three 'couples' of the species had different attitudes towards their lives, responsibilities, thinking same commitment. I normally observed the feelings and the movements of birds and animals, but lives of these three pairs of sparrows always remind me of the sensitive examples of attitudes.

From the above story you can easily place the couple of my room was well balanced of LBs and RBs traits and the couple in the children were LB and the one in the lobby was RB.

Benefits of Positive Attitude

Attitudes always lead you in the direction of your activities. The results of the activities or the successes thereof depends upon the attitudes with which these activities are performed. When we say you must have positive attitude, it would definitely be accepted that the positive attitudes must be beneficial. What are those benefits, we would like to list below:

Enhances Productivity: Each one of us has some amount of in-built productivity which enables us to complete our tasks, but if we have a commitment and enthusiasm or a motivation and above all a positive attitude wherein we believe that we can do it, it would certainly increase or improve the productivity which would get the results faster and better.

The glaring example of positive attitude is reflected by the efforts of the freedom fighters who won freedom for us. All of them individually and collectively had the positive attitude to work together, increase their productivity to make the movement successful that won us freedom.

Strengthens Team Work: In all the activities of man, he has to work in a team. There are very few activities where he has to perform individually even there he has to be part of the team whether it is a home or a section of a department in an office or a sportsman or a club. A person with negative thinking and negative attitude is kept poles apart by more people. They are kept away in social circle. The people with positive attitude make a winning team. Their positive contribution strengthens a team. Take the example of cricket teams of South Africa, Australia. It is the positive attitude which enables the team win matches. The teams where even a single player with a negative approach tends to overdo or undo the performance the team is weakened. If you are in a position to change the thinking of persons into attitudes, you can succeed at all levels.

Eliminates Problems: Negative attitudes always create problems. Positive attitudes eliminate problems or if the problems are complicated the positive outlooks solve the difficulties and the problems thereof. If the student is having a positive attitude to be successful in the exams his teacher with the similar attitude would not only eliminate the difficulties, but solve his problem to enable him get through with flying colours.

Quality Improvement: We are all prisoners of habits and attitudes. We have to change, viz., knowledge and attitude. In the 21st century it is the individuals who matter. These individuals would bring new revolution - the attitude revolution. We have to change ourselves, even the change is changing. There are good people but that is not enough. We need people who would like to improve, who would like to change, that is important. In this century everything could be duplicated, e.g. brands, machines, the systems, the management principles, but not the people.

Therefore, change in attitude is required. In this century a new mind is needed. The century does not need managers, but leaders who could change the mind-set of people. New leadership is required. When the leaders bring change the quality would also change. The attitudes, the new mind-set, the new leadership will bring quality of the people. The science has given too much power to machines. The quality of machines have improved, human being is being ignored. In any organisation only the 20% bring the 80% results. It is the 80% people who are average and an average is always below average. In such a situation, the quality improvement is not feasible.

The managements will have to bring change in the attitudes of people, to bring total quality improvement not only in the human investment but organisation as a whole.

Congenial Atmosphere: Positive attitudes create very healthy relation-ships which brings a total congenial atmosphere in the organisation. With the positive attitude the talents are encouraged, the talents are used, talents are enjoyed, people meet each other for entertainment, get-together and they also inter-change the experiences. I noticed a typical exercise which build up a congenial atmosphere at work stations.

The Russian specialists had been staying at HAL Factory at Ozar. Most of them had brought their families. Because of the language barrier and security restrictions, they did not mix up with the Indian families, but they had fixed one day which was presumably Thursday on which they used to invite their families in a hall and during each session one of the managers would explain in details about his work in the hanger. They would explain about the MIG aircraft, its working, its refuelling, its maintenance and their day-to-day working in such a way that each member of the family would have the basic knowledge of their spouses working in the factory. While sharing knowledge they would also mix up with each other and this attitude of families created a very congenial atmosphere. Once I invited the ladies club member to our location when the aircraft fuel was shown to them, even the wives of senior most officials of HAL Factory were not aware that the aircraft fly with kerosene, that is aviation turbine fuel. Their only impression was that the aircrafts fly with some kind of white petrol.

Most of the organisations have their clubs or associations where the employees meet together for some musical evening or sports events just to create a change from the normal routine work to create a healthier atmosphere and relationship.

Positive Attitudes Breed Loyalty: Although the science has given importance to the machines, it is the man who matters when he operates the machines. The man is becoming professional in his approach, in his skills, but the attitudes which are developed through the consistent trainings bring change in behaviours and this change breeds loyalty. You compare the employees of the government departments, public undertakings and the private enterprises and you would find that the loyalty differs from these categories of work cultures. The training, the behaviour and the quality of human beings selected for the private entrepreneurs is mostly depending on the commitment. The traditional entrepreneurs used to bring their own family members, kith & kins and known relations to position them at the strategic posts. Now in the change of time, the attitudes have also changed and this change has brought commitment of the employees towards their employers.

Increases Profits: Change of mind brings change in the behaviour of the work force and the change of attitudes enables the work force to become result-oriented. These results are measurable. When the tasks are set, goals are achieved, the results are the increased profits. It is assumed that 19th century was an era of knowledge and information, the 20th century was an age of organisation and 21st century is the century of individuals who would bring change in the attitudes and they bring results and the increased profits.

Reduces Stress: The most important factor of the positive attitudes when creates congenial atmosphere it is bound to reduce stress. I am always reminded of this event.

Bundhs are organised in various cities as a mark of protest to settle scores with the authorities. Of all the bundhs and hartals, the Mumbai bundhs is most effective. When there is a Mumbai bundhs nothing can move. The taxies, the auto-rickshaws, the offices and even the lifeline of Mumbai, the suburban trains, they are also stopped and stoned. During one of the bundhs our staff also went on strike because they were already in the process and this coincided with the bundhs. All the officers and managers of aviation department at the national and international airfield resolved that not a single flight would be delayed. They all worked in twelve hours shift round the clock. This attitude helped in carrying out the job to such an example that not a single flight was held up during the bundhs and the staff strike, and the overwork fatigue was not felt by anyone even working long hours. When the bundhs was over, we celebrated the occasion and everybody realised that it was the positive attitude, a commitment and willingness to rise to the occasion which didn't affect the normal working and on the other hand it didn't tire anybody physically and mentally. This fact was acknowledged warmly by the management.

Assets are Built: In the 21st century the employees are termed not only as human beings, but human assets rather human investment. We have already discussed that it is not the good people who are important, but the people capable of improving that is important. Everything can be duplicated but not the people. The individual becomes an asset, it cannot be duplicated.

Personality Development: If you happen to come across a successful human being, be he a marketing salesman, a PR executive, advertising man, you would find a change in the totality of his personality. The positive attitudes are reflected when you talk to him, shake hand with him and exchange smiles, you would see the cheerfulness personified. The net result of positive attitude and his each movement reflects purpose, commitment, result, relationship - all these are outcome of the attitudes.

In conclusion it is said, "While what constitutes a 'good' attitude is different for different people, a positive, friendly, willing-to-help perspective makes life for us enjoyable and makes job easier". Therefore, forget yesterday's failures and mistakes by the enthusiasm of today. Always remember tougher the problem, the more enthusiasm is needed. The success will knock at your door if you always think enthusiastically.

Consequences of Negative Attitude

We have enumerated several points highlighting the benefits of positive attitudes. From these it is easier to derive the consequences of negative attitudes. You can converse all the advantages of the positive attitudes into disadvantages of negative attitudes literally. However, we would highlight some of the consequences of negative attitudes, which are as under:

1. Bitterness
2. Resentment
3. Purposeless Life
4. Ill-health
5. High Stress Level

Bitterness: You come across several people in your circle, whether at home, on the street or in office, who would always express their views negatively. Suppose you organise an event, the person with negative attitude will not allow you to have the event on one ground or the other saying that this could not be done because of being busy, because of time constraint, because of transport problem, because the people will not participate and so on. He would not participate himself, but he would discourage others to do so. Such persons in life create bitterness. The result of negative attitude is amply established when your jobs are not easily done in various public offices, mostly because of the prevailing corruption, generally because of the negative attitude of the employees. The end result is bitterness in public. Even in departments of normal commercial offices, the persons with negative attitudes create functional problems as well as image problems of the organisation. It is, therefore, necessary that the persons with negative attitude must be identified and efforts be made to develop their mind-sets as far as possible before they pollutes others.

Resentment: Negative attitudes often result in resentment. Most glaring examples could be found in homes, where it results in conflicts between the husband and wife, between father and son, between relationship if one of them or all of them have negative approach towards life. It is difficult but not impossible to change the mind-set of people at large, but these must be developed right from the childhood of tomorrow's work-force. Efforts must be made at the education level to develop attitudes, in schools, colleges and other institutions.

Purposeless Life: A suicide is defined as a permanent solution to a temporary problem. Most suicides take place because of the extreme situation of negative attitude. The victim gets convinced that the life had become meaningless because he failed miserably. For him it is purposeless to live, so he decides to commit suicide. Negative attitudes can create havoc with anybody.

Ill-Health: You are aware that the healthy mind in a healthy body and the healthy mind is the product of positive attitude; negative attitude cannot be part of healthy body. It has to be a part of ill-health which culminates the extreme step taken by the patient in the society.

I recall an individual whose name is not necessary to identify as he is no more. He was a man with negative approach in life. All his colleagues would make a fun of him because besides his attitudes he had a peculiar way of walking, talking, style of moustache, hair-style and everybody would jeer at him. At all such jeerings and taunts, he would pick-up quarrels to the amusement of others. This continued for months together and one day I counselled him as a friend. He used to listen to me because his father was a friend of my father. I used to advise him that he should not pay heed to the jeering of others. It used to work for few days, but the provoking of colleagues increased day-by-day and one day I heard that he went home and killed a small playing child in the street. I didn't go after the details, but he was in the hands of law and what happened at the end was not worth recording. Everybody declared that he was sick, but he was sick because of negative attitudes. No medicine could have worked on him, but change in mind-set could have worked somewhere.

High Stress Level: A person with negative attitude is always capable of creating problems for himself and others around, so he would always be under stress. The above example is quite clear to explain this.

In conclusion, I am of the opinion the creation of negative environment at home and at work is becoming a liability to the society as well as to the managements.

Action Steps for Improving Attitudes

After going through literature and management experience, I have come to know that with the consistent training and constant hammering, the mind-set can be changed to produce positive attitudes. Some of the following steps may be tried at your door step:

Be Good To Yourself: A man cannot bc called selfish if he thinks himself the best human being in the world. Every one in his humble way tries to project himself as a good person. Because if you are conscious of being good you would try to be good in making friends, establishing good relationships, reading good books, forming good habits and be a member of good association and all your activities would tend you to be good. Even then it is said, "It is good to be good, it is not good to be too good". A good mind-set would grow positive attitudes. This will enable you to think good, act good, the results are bound to be good.

Be Decisive: Most of our problems in the management circle are caused because of indecision. We keep postponing things, we don't take quick decisions, as per T.S. Eliot, the nobel laureate, a man in this century has become a Prufrock, a character who keeps things postponing. In one of his poems, these lines have become the best three lines in the modern literature on which hundreds of books have been written. These lines are:

"Let's go then you and I
When the evening is spread out against the sky
Like a patient etherised upon a table."

Modern man is a patient who is unconscious but living. I would personally prefer a person who can take even take nine correct decisions out of ten than a person who can't take a decision. At least a persons has made mistakes in nine decisions but he has taken one decision correct. The successful managers are decisive, make it a habit to take a decision and, "Do it now approach". This will go a long way in making you a successful person.

Attitude of Gratitude: Most persons are thankless ones. They don't even thank God that have been blessed with this life. God has blessed, just remember life, i.e. human beings. If you consider yourself lucky each one of you is much better than thousands and thousands of others who are more miserable than us. We must thank for whatever we got from wherever we got. You would recall the story of a man who was worried and painful because of the pinching of his shoes, but when he saw a man cheerfully walking on the road who had no feet, then he realised that he is far better than that person and still feeling miserable. We must be thankful to any kind of kindness showered from anywhere. A man with a positive attitude does not forget the attitude of gratitude.

Positive Self-Esteem: Self-esteem is one of the basic needs of a every man. Each one of us is important in one way or the other. Each one of us needs to be respected, loved, recognised, applauded and rewarded. If you build up a positive self-esteem it will lead you to be a successful human being.

Discard Negative Influences: Please ensure that negative influences don't change your mind-set. In most offices the management of politics plays havoc. In fact this needs a separate chapter to elaborate, but a good manager understands the management of politics and other negative influences and he would always stay away from such influences.

Continuous Education: Mind-set needs to be reset at every level. Continuous education, knowledge, training updates the mind-set. If there is no set education programme at least a manager can involve himself in serious reading either about his profession or on any subject like philosophy, spiritualism, yoga, politics, history, etc. Any reading is a good learning. Books are considered as man's best friends and companions.

Start with Positive Note: When you get up you feel relaxed after the last day's fatigue and worries. A new day dawns on you. Start the day with a positive note. Morning Walk is always refreshing.

There are two pigeons who are present in the morning near the window of my bed-room. When I get up I see them cajoling each other necking each other, communicating beak to beak presenting a very enjoyable scene far away from the madding crowd. While I observe them seriously I plan for the day's activities at those moments. These 5-10 minutes of the day are the most enjoyable moments. Without any hurry or worry I plan my activity for the day and act upon that plan and implement it by the evening. Before going to bed I again take the inventory of the events of the events planned in the morning and feel contented about the successful implementation thereafter. The two pigeons are not seen at night.

3

Role of Managers in the 21st Century

The role of managers in 21st century in most organisations would be different from their role in the 20th century and before.

The Confederation of Indian Industry (CII) conducted a HRD Summit last year. The top speakers of various industrial houses of the country and abroad made presentations to 250 delegates drawn from all over the country. I also attended the same on behalf of Jaquar & Company Limited as a delegate.

The Theme of the Summit was "The People"

The Summit resolved that people are important everywhere. It is the people who have to change and keep with the changes. Several speakers wondered as to where we were going. Where the Information Technology would lead as to? What would be the nature of the people in future? The future seems to be uncertain. "Change" should be the only constant factor and therefore the change of technology would bring knowledge and opportunities. Thus, we all have to change with the march of time.

The management of all organisations be it Private Enterprises, Public Undertakings, Young Technologists shall have to be involved in the management for charting future course of action. It is the management; it is the people who would make the work globally. It was dwelt upon with values of companies which reveal through the behaviour and the quality of the people. It is the quality of professionals involved in the company which determines the quality and the growth of any organisation. With the incoming of NRIs and the Foreign Investment, the new Managerial Personnel System have come in this country. With this, several new factors have emerged.

The implications of globalization are as under:

- Movement of managers from different countries into India

and from India to overseas locations whether the companies are indigenous or foreign. The movement of the managers from/to would have been a compelling impact on the performance of the companies

- The import of system, practices and procedures from the transnationals. This would play a significant role to change and developing working culture of the organisation.
- A change in work, practices, culture and the way the work is organised. This would also bring in new style of functioning for which the general behaviour of the management will have to be moulded.
- With the larger number of organisations in the same industry, there is an enhanced competition and consequently there would be pressure on prices, quality and productivity. Since customer would have choices, there would not be any guarantee of any sales.
- With the implementation of these policies, there would be immense pain and pressure on the whole lot of indigenous corporates.
- Because of the increased globalization of management functioning, the cross cultural relationship with the foreign managers has become major issue.
- The global manager must be aware of the cultural difficulties and he must study what are the strengths and weaknesses arising from these variations in personal values and how these can be harnessed to realise the objectives of an organisations.
- In the words of Rai Bahadur M. S. Oberoi, their organisational "Dharma" was "The idea was never merely to make money". The compulsion was to **think big**; offer the best and let it happen. The profits will automatically come in.
- According to Oberoi - Dharma, they could clearly distinguish between the shareholders, employees and business partners.
- In this century, we are in the age of employees, stockholders and entrepreneurs. We are convinced that the boundaries are blurring . We do not know where would it lead to?

- In the knowledge-economy, success depends upon creative application of knowledge and the knowledge resides largely in the employees. So the issues arise as to why do people perform? What are the ideal conditions? These basic issues are the crucial concerns of the 21st century managers.
- The managements of this century, therefore, must pro-actively look at the successional planning in terms of development and the retention of thc employees. At present, it is difficult to get a right man for the right job and when we get that right man, it is difficult to retain him. The answer to this problem is the managements must recognise the talents of the employees immediately and set milestones for creativity and teamwork. It is observed that in this war of competition, the brand name is the criteria flashed across the Media Blitz, the talent of the employees has often been over looked.
- The key responsibility of the managements is to spell out the values that the company stands for. The values of the company are revealed through the behaviour of the people and converted values into actual behaviour is the key to Profit, Reputation and Sustainability.

According to the organisational Dharma, the conduct of the managements and the people:

- Should be of the highest ethical standards.
- Should build and maintain teamwork and put the customers first.
- Should exemplify the care for the customers.
- Should demonstrate 2-way communication
- Should safeguard the safety and security.

Another key speaker of the Summit cautioned that the war for talent has been intensified. There is greater competition for the 'BEST' Executive Talent. Small competition always excrts powerful "PULLS" to get the best talent to promote their growth.

The entrepreneurs have felt that there is increasingly difficult to attract and retain the best talent because the supply of the executive talent is shrinking day by day and the talent has become very elusive. Because of this, the managements try their best methods of motivation to retain the best talent.

One entrepreneur categorically announced in the forum that the talent is more mobile across the companies. Several placement agencies are resolving to headhunt this primary job of the management to retain the top of the talent

Winners Make Commitments, Losers Make Excuses

The success of every Corporate Joint is the quality of people working together especially at the "TOP". It is the top people in every organization whose behavior, discipline, culture, style of working, percolates down the line in an organization. To keep top people in the organization and retain them, the key principles were identified which are as under :-

- Create a compelling vision.
- Ring "fence" key talent.
- Provide real tops.
- Flexible career templates.
- Invest in people development
- Institutionalise a "mind set for growth".

The following steps should be taken towards talent value proposition.

- Open a transparent communication on performance and potential.
- Early and feasible differentiation
- Fast track growth based on demonstration, leadership and team work capability.
- Tailored career tracks for specialists and general managements.

To sum up the above, if the management had to retain the executive talent, the vision of the company should be so transparent that it can compel the executive to remain where he is the top executive in any organisation, he must be identified, especially those who are real professional and give them adequate security, comforts, perks and flexible career progression. The management should invest in the development of the top executive by sending them for career developmental growth abroad or offer some positions or rewards to their wards and institutionalise in their mind the future growth of the executives.

All this can be achieved if there is a mutual understanding and transparent communication on the performance vis-à-vis potential of top executives. HR Deptt. should draw their career path for specialists and professionals so that they are also kept on the right track for which the growth be assured.

Contribution of HRD

The traditional role of the HRD in the organisation has gone and rapid transitional change have come. In the 21st century, HRD role in the organisation would be to have :-

- Enough people
- In the right place
- Organised in right structure and system.
- With the right skills, experience and competencies.

A question was raised as to what is the meant by 'mind set' and how we do recognize it?. It was answered by the speakers that

- The 'mind set' is an aligned individual way of thinking - as expressed in behaviour, in respected pattern of action.
- We are most affected by a shared mind set – by how people think in a collective way is part of a team.
- A shared mind set aligned with business strategy and the market place – an essential component by HR strategy

The key employees can be retained if they see themselves as creating a dream with a group passionately committed people stretching their performance and exploiting their potential.

In these days of talent war, the best way to keep your 'STARS' is to know them better than they know themselves and then use that information to customise the career of their dreams.

Retention of key employees is a perennial issue. The management has to create a permanent, sustainable atmosphere in the organizations that the employees should enjoy working. This is not difficult if the employees are given "business class offerings".

With the emergence of a new industrial culture, the entire environment has become competitive where the customers are more enlightened with growing aspirations. This has further raised the aspiration because of ever growing multinationals. As the competition grows, there is a greater mobility of professional cadre. Thus the knowledge based industries are seeing global opportunities. The liberalization is posing both opportunities as well as threats.

Retention of Employees: The Broader Perspective

It is easier to select the key executive from the competitive market either through the placement agencies or through the advertisements or through the contacts but retention of this is a difficult proposition. Several speakers in the Summit came out with several suggestions. Some of which are enumerated here :-

- Motivation is key agenda – retention is a integral part of motivation.
- Record wisely – select them right ….. cultural fits.
- Retaining valued employees is a strategic issue and not a mere composition point.
- Aspiration/business dynamics employees, flexible formation for effectiveness.
- Teams run organisations – Do not miss bigger picture, Energising key resources is an organisational task - not just HR dashboard.

Creation of Right Ambiance

- Nurture a culture that inspires employees to take care and share .
- 3 magical words – **"I Trust You"**.
- Consistent rewards – Do not penny pinch on performers.
- Make the stay hassle free – fringe and service support.

- Development/training focus – imperative for individuals and organisations.
- Bring in community service bit - corporate citizen role
- Smart organisations breed payment uniformly.

Nurture a Culture

Every organisation has a culture of his own. The 21st Century Managers will adopt the culture that inspires them to take care of themselves, their customers and their management. They should share not only the obligations but also responsibilities as well. The managers must contribute their talent and skills for the development and nurture culture of the organisation by their own talent and performance.

The key players must be involved in this through and through so that they should not peak through the exits.

Trust

Trust begets trust just as love begets love. These are 3 magical words which keep the organisations bound together. If the managements do not impose trust in their employees particularly on the top level, these organisations are likely to collapse or the top executives are likely to run away. The management must bestow confidence and trust in the employees which would be extended back with the same trust. In this country, most of the private companies are owned by traditional families and the key functioning is in the same fashion as per their traditional outlook. They do not share their responsibilities with the new comers. The trust becomes a casualty and whenever casualty takes place, it has to be treated.

Consistent Reward

It is well said that the management should not save pennies where the performance of the employees are to be rewarded. Human being by nature needs pat and the top performer in the company deserves reward. Management should not save the money or reward wherever performance of the employees deserve to be awarded.

Hassle Free Stay

Each employee in a company wants to have a hassle free stay. If the employees enforced to run in circles for completing formalities to make his work conditions comfortable, he would not like to stay. Top executives must have a hassle free freedom to function.

Training

With the Information Technology coming into focal point of the standards of working in the globalized management, the training must be encouraged for the developmental growth. The training programme whether inside in abroad, has to be intensified. It must be remembered that when an employee grows, the organization grows. The management has systematic training avenues for the development of all.

Corporate Citizen Role

Throughout the globe, you not only have COLA WAR wherein the film & Sport Stars are running neck to neck to advertise the goods but the Advertising Agencies are also involved in the bitter Media Blitz of their products. Far from this, few organisations offer community services like rendering assistance in a earthquake hit area, providing jobs to the poorest of the poor, taking responsibilities of drinking water in the drought hit area. The managers should come forward to ensure that the services to the customers are given promptly and corruption free so that the community at large is benefited from the organisational goal. Naturally, the executives who would take lead in such activities would be rewarded and this will not only act as reward but also will be a specimen of motivation for others to follow.

Uniform Payment

The payment in Government companies is based on traditional value system of salary structure and fixed norms for increment and promotions. In the multinational companies, the payment of the employees is confined to set principles and rules as per the technological skills. In the private companies, the wages are given as per the whims of the company owners and the employees involvement is not visible with utter disregard to the hierarchy of the organisation.

The speakers at the Summit suggested the following tips to retain the Talent, at the top :-

- Distribute "ownership". .... It produces wonders.
- Recognise celebrations .... Do not miss them.
- Career pathing – reveal the future .. Let them identify with it.
- Establish psychological contract…Bond with leaders.
- Label free appraisals................. Increase job challenges.
- Encourage cross functional alliances ..Rotational assignments.

Most of the above practices have been discussed in respective pages of this book.

Put High Performers on Victory Stand

Talent must be encouraged, sincere, hardworking, dedicated and potential employees must be rewarded suitably and consistently:

- Key employees look beyond HR practices in deciding their destiny; this is a leadership agenda.
- Retention is not the real mission – individual satisfaction is the goal.
- Some key employees will always leave – corporates should actually encourage induction and "creation" of key employees.

Training Gives Growth to the People and the Organisation

- The goal of training is growth, development, enhancement, maturing on continuum.

- Development is foregone conclusion during and after training.
- This development has latent advantages for the organisation.
- To understand and to harness goal direction is important.
- All employees are expected to reach a proficiency level where they can train others.
- Competency that can be developed need to be identified and nurtured.

Benefits of Training and Development are More Visible, When

- Superiors believe in the potential of their subordinates.
- A crucial role of function of management is to provide appropriate environment in which expectations can be fulfilled.
- An opportunity to use what is learnt without much delay helps.
- Development depends upon the environment.

Guidelines for Effective Management

The concept of spending additional time for analysing the pros and cons of objectives from all different angles and clearly defining them results in a bigger success. Ensure clear and committed responsibility and personalise it. Have fixed days for communication, coach your PEOPLE.

Always Keep Your Focus on the People, People and People

Targets can move mountains. You must have a very clear goal in mind, not only for official work but in personal life as well. Strive to do things right the first time.

Avoid rectification, but mistake is a good teacher. Ask yourself what you have to change to avoid this mistake in the future. Failing this you have already committed the second mistake.

You are stronger together rather alone. Find managers and colleagues to multify your thinking and strategies.

Work Like an Entrepreneur

- Give more responsibility to your managers so that they are as far as possible responsible for the whole process just like the owners or entrepreneurs. **This Independent Working Motivates.**
- Each department leader must function as an entrepreneur. Give him your TRUST; give him a free hand. Lead through yearly target agreements which appear in the form of a contract. Maintaining targets is a matter of TRUST, TRUST and TRUST.
- Your team supports you if it is a well informed and involved in the decision making process.
- Avoid top talk-down decision. If you often make important decisions on your own where your managers disagree they would be demotivated.
- Team work is essential to reduce errors. In a "round table" for decision making the information level should be the same for all members. In a team work every person has the same importance.
- Every problem encountered is an opportunity for training and development.

Peter Drucker Says, "There are no Under Developed Nations. There are Only Under Managed Ones."

- The need of the hour for India is management.
- The science of creating change and adding values.
- Stop managing people, lead them – show them the way.

Manage Our Non-Human Resources So That

- Dying of thirst and drowning in water are not simultaneous.
- Management is a process and not a body.
- Management is a force that binds for the time.
- Training together binds for much larger.
- A family that prays together stays together.
- Employees who train together stay together.
- Training be seen as a time and opportunity to build

friendships which go beyond the call of duty.

We Can Hire a Human-Being Who Has Knowledge, Skill and an Intellect That We Would Like to Put to Our Use. It Will Happen Wholeheartedly Only at the Instance of the Employees :

- So it is question of heart.
- Popularly we know that heart is where home is.
- The managements must bring homes right into their works to organise family, charts, family visits and celebrate family days.
- This has helped many organisations in the development of greater heart felt participation.

In conclusion, the trainings help organisations transform strategies into results through people.

Thus it is the PEOPLE, the PEOPLE and the PEOPLE, who matter most in the art of managing the people, which is termed in the modern scenario as the human investment of the investor, for the investor and by the investor – THE PEOPLE.

The above material has been re-produced from the speeches delivered at the Summit by so many noted and well professionalised top executives of top companies. Since time given to each speaker was hardly 15 minutes each, the points noted above are not elaborately deliberated because these are the key points for the 21st Century Managers.

3.1 Housekeeping Builds up Image

Housekeeping is an art to keep the house in order. Whether it is a house, office, factory, airport, railway station, hospital or any other place , it has to be in order. It not only enhances the aesthetic value of the place, but it has lots of other advantages, some of which are as under:

1. Improves appearance.
2. Prevents accidents.
3. Visible inventory.

4. Build up image.
5. Good working environment.
6. Improves quality management.
7. Motivates innovation.
8. Cleanliness is next to Godliness.
9. Improves work culture.
10. Improves productivity.
11. Timely disposal of unused material.
12. Regulates the maintenance/repairs.
13. Very economical.
14. Stimulates visitors.

Improves Appearance

Even a dog sweeps the place where he sits. Man is aesthetic by nature. He has very deep-rooted aesthetic sense, e.g. he has the capacity and capability to admire beauty. As John Keats has said, "A thing of beauty is a joy for ever." Anything that gives you joy is beautiful. Man has got five senses, viz. seeing, smiling, tasting, hearing and touching. The sixth sense is common-sense, if all the five senses individually or collectively derive any pleasure the source of such pleasure is beautiful. By this yardstick the beauty also appeals to the common-sense.

The army parade looks very impressive because the soldiers are well dressed, marching pace by pace, arranged height-wise, presenting a good appearance, the shine and colour of ribbons and medals, their name plates, their ranks, they are all thrilling. Since they are organised, they look beautiful. You iron a piece of cloth or garment, all its threads and wrinkles get pressed and even. They look smooth, regular and organised, that is why a well pressed suit or garments look more attractive than the freshly washed clothes.

On the above pattern if all the paraphernalia of the house is properly placed, it looks organised and orderly on the above principles and hence it looks beautiful. Same goes with the office. General cleanliness is the first principle of housekeeping.

This includes sweeping, swabbing, rubbing and removing dirt and dots from the tables, window-glasses, telephone, etc. and then arranging furniture, like tables, chairs, stools, racks and almirahs in a systematic order, they give an appearance of the army unit. Wherever I have worked I have given the topmost priority to housekeeping because it gives a visual aesthetics. I will relate incidents and achievements on this issue while working in the oil company. Later, I would like to relate incidents while working in the private companies.

I was the general manager of a plastic moulding company. Within the first three days I changed and removed only a few things here and there like shifting of the watchman's cabin to the appropriate place, putting some paint and colours to the walls and entrance, the factory gave a distinct look within 3-4 days. The work-force had stirred up like the crowd on the railway platform when the train steams in. Such was the enthusiasm.

When I joined my present company, i.e. Jaquar & Company Ltd, I was made to take a round of all the factories and the first thing which came to my mind was the housekeeping. Since I was not aware as to what assignment I would be given on having been invited to join this company, I made up my mind to give my first priority to the housekeeping.

I took off with the idea of organising a "Housekeeping Week" in the first week of my joining Jaquar. I identified some critical areas and took pictures. I invited one man each from various departments and formed a committee to take active part in the housekeeping week for the next seven days so that area throughout the factory is made spic and span. I also called the meeting of the sweepers and their supervisors to detail them about the "House Keeping Week" and declared suitable incentives for those whose areas would excel. After doing all these preliminaries issued a notice to all employees of all sections of the factory that a "Housekeeping Week" would be organised and during the next 7 days everybody would make efforts to participate in the cleaning process. All the team leaders and the committee were activated to follow up consistently. After the completion of the week the pictures of the same critical areas were again taken and the significant progress was visible in each segment from picture to picture. The results were quite obvious, both the sets of pictures were pasted on the notice board side by side for everybody to view. A small function was organised and those who made contributions were awarded suitable prizes by the Directors.

While the shape of the factory showed improvement, but the biggest task was ahead to maintain the same standard and improve it further. For this we invited some prominent housekeeping agencies and selected one to undertake this assignment professionally. Unfortunately, most of the agencies called for this assignment didn't know the meaning and purpose of housekeeping. The common understanding amongst them was that housekeeping means cleaning of place.

Much more significant efforts were made at several other places where I worked in the past; like Nasik, Santacruz, Goa, Sahar and other places. The appearances of the locations were changed by cleaning and sweeping premises making small path-ways by slanting the bricks and painting them white, by painting the equipment like pipelines, filters, etc. with their coded colours, replacing or maintaining office curtains, planting plants and flowers, advising the staff to improve their turn-out, and above all putting flags at the entrance in different colours and with the inscription," QUALITY, SAFETY AND SERVICE". With all these significant changes the appearance of the locations and offices improved. Any one of you could try these methods and you would see the results yourself.

Prevents Accidents

A good housekeeping prevents accidents. Start from the minor activity at your residence. The housewife after stitching the button does not keep the thread and needle back to its place which pricks a child or a visitor who steps on the needle.

Similarly, the master of the house after shaving does not keep his blade or razor back to its place. In the factory if everything is not kept at its place some heavy items like tools or an Axe or barrel may fall on you and crush your limb. But if all the tools and gadgets are kept at the proper places after its use the chances of accidents, if not eliminated, may be minimised to a very large extent.

The petroleum installations are notified that they should keep their locations spic and span to prevent accidents. I recall one incident without mentioning the name of the location for security reasons that the location in-charge kept the location very spic and span, but outside the boundary wall which was nothing but barbed wire. On one side the wild grass was not cut which had dried up and a stray cigarette butt thrown by a passer-by sparked and inflamed the entire grass and the flames topping the wall. The flames were so high it crossed the boundary wall and reached the office. Due to the alertness of the staff and well maintained equipment and timely help from the fire-brigade it prevented accident which would have resulted in an enormous loss. This incident made the company issue directives to all the locations storing fuel to eliminate the growth of dry grass or remove the grass at least ten feet away from the boundary wall. There are several instances some of which may come to your mind as well where the good housekeeping prevented serious accidents.

Visible Inventory

Let us take an example of a house. In well maintained house all the items would be individually visible. The wide space would make a mark in highlighting each item, but in any messed up house everything would come in your way and you are not in a position to identify individually as to which item is clearly visible at what place and why. If you search such a house for some investigative purpose you would find that 75% of the items were not required to be kept. But in a well maintained house you would easily remember 75% of the items visibly placed there. In a clean environment a small dirt or patch would look magnified, but in a dirty house even a bunch of flowers could not be noticed significantly. I recall the housekeeping standards I maintained at Nasik installation.

I was posted at Nasik Aviation station where the housekeeping efforts were at the highest ebb, which would be discussed at relevant points The popularity of the station was so highlighted that the general manager of HAL who became my very close friend would visit regularly to see if I had done something new. During his visits he was once very much jubilant to see the shine and glitter of the station, took a round and applauded at every nook and corner, but when he reached the office a small wire of telephone line was seen hanging and spoiling the entire show. He remarked, "Look! had this wire not visible, there was not a single comment worth mentioning about any lapse on the part of the housekeeping." He further remarked that the most attractive portion was the 'Kachra Corner' where the entire waste was dumped. We had dug and used two fluorescent tubes and hung a glass panel with the sign, 'Kachra Corner' and the portion was surrounded by bricks and painted with white and even the Kachra thrown in was looking attractive. So you see a small portion of a wire was spoiling the beautiful location. Similarly, if the entire office is kept neat and clean with shining windows and office tables a small spider web in the corner if not removed would be clearly visible and would destroy the beauty of the entire housekeeping.

Builds up Image

Good housekeeping builds up the image of the organisation. The classic example is visit to the armed forces offices whether it is Air Force unit or an Army Mess or a Naval installation, the very name recalls of housekeeping. You visit various Embassies and other multinational firms, particularly, the Japanese offices and they would stand by the image of housekeeping. I take pride in improving the image of stations where I was associated, although the house-keeping at all the Aviation stations was always a thing to be proud of. The standard of housekeeping keeps up the image of the organisation. With the incoming of MNCs their offices and their surroundings present very good environments to maintain their images.

I went abroad in 1987 for the first time. At San Francisco, the residential areas had the identical houses and colour schemes which cannot be altered by owners. In front of the houses the residents have to maintain their lawns. If the lawns are not maintained well and the grass is not watered or mowed periodically you are slapped a fine, and challaned by the authorities. The roads, the streets and the houses presented a beautious sight. I am carrying on this image fresh in my mind and I wonder whether municipal authorities in this country could ever dream of such things in order to build up images.

Good Working Environment

The good working environment in a house can be seen with the management of a kitchen. The happy and successful housewife keeps her kitchen in a very professional way. Every item in the kitchen from spoon to stove would be immaculately kept. At times when the lights would go off, the hands would pick up the match-box without search whereas in disorganised houses you may not get the hand fan even during the day time. It is well known that a bad workman quarrels with his tools, because he cannot find an appropriate tool at the appropriate time. If you have visited a workshop to get your vehicle repaired you would invariably find that the mechanics would waste lot of time in searching their spanners attending to the vehicle returning to the shop to get another spanner, search the third one and try the fourth one and a small nut which is to be attended is fixed in a matter of second would consume two hours of your agonising time. The working condition at such repair shops is an example of bad housekeeping.

But if you visit a well organised office or factory you would find the working conditions not only comfortable, convenient, clean and cosy, but pleasurable, you are pleased to work at such places. The working condition should be hassle free. This can be done if there are systems and there are people willing to adapt those systems and which are implemented in all its seriousness. Once the systems are regulated the working conditions improve automatically. The ideal working conditions provide, less paper work, lesser rules, more productivity and top class in personal relationship, a considerate management and a very committed work-force.

Improves Quality Management

Just as a quality is a way of life, housekeeping is a way of quality. Both improve each other. A good housekeeping motivates every one to produce quality people, quality work, which is achieved by quality efforts which are made in a quality commitment consistently.

Once a visiting quality control manager from the head office came to inspect my location at Nasik (Ozar). Our relationship with the HAL Factory were very intimate and outstanding. Just by a small tinkle you can get anything from the factory. If we knew about some visiting inspector, we would just give a tinkle, we would get a truck-load of poles, colourful flags would arrive at the location from the factory and flags would be installed on the boundary walls within 30 minutes. The painting of boundary bricks and all other gadgets was a daily routine because we had motto, "EVERY DAY IS AN INSPECTION DAY".

When he saw the location, he was baffled and he remarked, "Is it a Disney Land or a filmset or a United Nations office". When he saw the trees with their name plates, the fountains, the bridges and the placards here and there he came to a stop at the tank farm under which the storage tanks are buried. It is a matter of practice for all the quality control managers to draw a sample from the storage tank and see for quality and clarity and record their observations. When I got ready to draw the samples of the fuel he merely declined saying, "When the quality of the station is so outstanding, the quality of the fuel at least has to be good". I insisted to show the samples, he was astonished to say, "How can the colour of the ATF (Aviation Turbine Fuel) is brighter than the samples inspected at other locations". I replied that it was the quality of the sample bottle as well; through which the colour of the sample was so clearly seen. This incident was time and again mentioned at various quality control meets.

A good housekeeping improves the quality of everyone. We had kept a brush and polish at the watchman's cabin where the shoes of the staff used to be polished by themselves again as and when they got spoiled. The good out turn of the staff in shining shoes made them a quality work force. Bridges, fountains, trees, name plates, fire extinguishers etc. added to the beauty of the station.

Motivates Innovation

Good housekeeping creates cleancr, comfortable and compact situations at work. At such places the man is at peace, his thinking faculty compressed into concentration and he is in a position to think better and innovate new things. A cleaner environment provides concentration and motivation to try something new. You are always in a thinking process and this is a situation where innovation springs up. Suppose you have arranged your belongings in a decent order it gives freshness to your eyes. To quote an instance, my wife who is not in job these days keeps innovating things like changing the position of the households, e.g. shifting TV, sofa, chairs, fridge here and there, so after 3-4 days you get a new look to the same drawing room. To quote another experience when the station was beautified to give a new look because of housekeeping, a new innovation came into play.

There were five workers at Nasik. Though the station was spic and span, it was desired to maintain and improve it further. We had divided the premises into five sections. Each section was allotted to an employee after mutual discussions. We had put the names of the in-charge of each section on a beautiful glass board depicting as, Sodhi Gardens, Sheikh Bagicha, Bajirao Udhyan, Patel Path and Pandu Park. All the first names of the areas were the names of the employees. Each employee was to develop his own area and the competition started. Can you imagine that each one of them had a fountain and a small bridge as we used to make when I was a scout. Within a very short period the entire area looked like a botanical garden that any film-maker would have liked to hire the premises for the film shooting.

Not only this they planted fruit bearing trees and grew peanuts. The general manager of HAL, and all the senior officers started visiting our place to relish the cheeku, papaya, pomegranate and guava. Besides we planted 400 trees and each tree was named and a name plate was hung to identify them. Some of the names were Birbal Akbar, Shahjahan, Guru Nanak, Einstein, Shelly, Shakespeare, John Keats, William Wordsworth, Hitler, Nehru, Gandhi, Prithviraj Kapoor and many. These innovations gave birth to more and more innovations which would be discussed separately.

So you see that it is the housekeeping that had motivated to go for the innovations which got multiplied as the time passed.

Cleanliness is Next to Godliness

It is said that Gods live in clean environments and Goddess Lakshmi which is worshipped by Hindus all over resides at clean places. Naturally, therefore, house-keeping prepares you to invite the Gods and Goddesses to come and stay at the cleaner places. You must have noticed that the shop-keepers pay respects before opening the shop and clean their premises not only inside, but outside the shop as well to invite the customers to their establishments. For them the customers are their Gods. Same goes for factories, offices, residences and they sweep and clean the premises before they start their activities because it is the over all view that their Gods whether in terms of deities or customers or visitors they like and love to visit only the cleaner places. A good housekeeping brings your "Gods" to your places.

Improves Work Culture

Every organisation has a work culture of its own. Every household has a work culture of its own. For households the work culture can be measured by the standard of their bathrooms or their dust-bin which is cleaned by the sweepers daily. This would indicate as to what are the items which are consumed by the household. The work culture in the offices can be measured by the quality of men working there, the dresses they wear, the language they speak, the standard of communication they adopt either by correspondence or on telephone or orally and above all the condition of their table drawers and the content of their brief cases of the executives. That is why it is said that executives must keep up their drawers, their wallets and hand-bags updated. Just open the drawer of any executive you will find the standard of professionalism. The amount of papers and the way it is kept by the staff denotes the standard of the work culture. The efficient executives would keep their tables spic and span and only that document shall be kept on the table which is required to be seen by him. If there is only one document at a time on the desk you can imagine the height of concentration the executive could give while dealing with the document. House-keeping plays a major part in keeping the standard of work culture. I would like to share with you my personal experiences of this by the following example:

During my last working assignment, I spent major portion of my career at Santacruz installation and Sahar installation. While I was at Santacruz my table used to be neat and clean except for a daily newspaper or some magazines. Top people of the organisation frequently visited our office either before boarding the flight or occasionally after landing and they would find my table always without any official document Whereas whenever I used to visit my counterpart at Sahar, his table used to be loaded with papers and papers, contrary to the fact that paper work at Santacruz was much more because we had to handle several small time domestic airlines. After some time, I was promoted to the next grade and I had to be shifted to a bigger location that was Sahar and the person at Sahar was shifted to Santacruz. The work culture at both the locations also shifted. My table would have only the newspapers and the magazines and as and when I would visit Santa-cruz for some work or reason, his table at Santacruz used to be loaded with papers.

The director of the company when visited me, he asked me this question, "How come that when you used to be at Santa-cruz, the table used to be clean while your counterpart at Sahar loaded with paper work and now when he is at your place, his table is again loaded with paper work while your table is clean." My reply was, "It is only due to housekeeping." Housekeeping does not mean the cleaning of the table only. If you tackle the papers immediately and take appropriate action the accumulation of papers will not take place. If you maintain cleanliness daily the accumulation of dirt and waste would not take place. Housekeeping is a constant process, should be undertaken every time, every day, so that the accumulation of waste does not take place. I am of the firm opinion which is tested and tried at several places that a consistent and constant housekeeping improves work culture.

Improves Productivity

Productivity is a term used for optimum level of functioning of an individual in his sphere of work. Suppose a person is capable of meeting 200 persons a day, but he cannot meet more than 70 people because there is no space for them to sit, no chairs, no drinking water, no one to receive them and he himself is attending to telephones, documents, other incidental works so his productivity is naturally hampered. His capacity and capability to handle 200 persons is badly affected.

To elaborate, take the example of a scooter mechanic. If he

can attend 20 customers a day and he can't do so because his tools are not properly organised because the workshop is not neat and clean, so instead of 20, he only attends to 5-7 customers. Now if you go to a well organised workshops where the systems are in force, the premises are kept in order, the workmen wearing uniforms and keep their tool kits ready, they would certainly attend to more customers. If the capacity of a works manager is to attend 20 customers and in healthy environment he attends 20 or more his productivity gets improved. It is, therefore, essential that the executives must be aware of their productivity level.

After retirement I approached an NGO to be associated with them to keep myself occupied and do some social job. The NGO was involved in publishing consumer buying guides. A concept where the consumers are advised as to what type of equipment to be bought. In doing so they would buy all the items available in the market got them tested and then published their observations. When I took up the assignment there was a big confusion as nobody had thought of working to clear the old pending records which was not arranged properly for years. The cupboards and racks were full of dirt and every one had to search for references, which would consume lot of time and in return we used to cough and breath heavily after the dust emanating from the old records. Since I was the chief co-ordinator, I called the other co-ordinators and told them that for the next three days we would not take up any work except to clean up the old records and destroy whatever was not required. We all worked as one man team and for three days, we read and sorted out all the documents and by evening we would look like ghosts due to the dust settling on us. We destroyed the unwanted stuff with the result was that our cupboards and racks had lesser paper and files and from then onwards it became very comfortable and convenient to trace out any document or file whenever needed and this pleased all the members working there. This method should be tried at homes and in offices by allotting one day in a month to take stock of the situation, items of inventory and dispose of all the old stuff to make room for the fresh ones and your house will look more spacious and appearance improved. Whether you believe in Vastu Shastra or not if you adopt this method you would certainly improve the productivity. Just give it a try.

A small exercise in housekeeping improves the productivity of all and working becomes a pleasure.

Timely Disposal of Unused Material

The serious activity of housekeeping gives you an opportunity to dispose of unused and unwanted items at your homes and in offices. The above example though a small one would certainly improve the working condition.

I give you another example on this issue, "Whenever I took up a new assignment house-keeping had been my first priority. This enables you to bring a visual change at the work-place and your presence is acknowledged at once and this visual change pleases the eyes of every one which creates greater impact to last longer.

When I was posted at Sahar International Airport the housekeeping was already a regular feature, but new efforts had to be taken because of the vast area involved. During the housekeeping exercises in the main stores alone, we found lots of items like pumps, pipelines, valves, etc. which were lying unused for a pretty long time and they were required badly in other locations, the value of these items ran into crores of rupees. We made out a list and sent the same to our regional head for information as well as for disposal. The surplus stores were shifted elsewhere. The after effect of this was that we created lot of space in our stores which looked neat and clean, and inventory taking process became very easy. Keeping of unwanted stuff prevents you from bringing new things. You would find the results startling if you spare one day in a month for this exercise".

Regulates Maintenance/Repairs

Maintenance and repairs is invariably ignored by habit by most people, e.g. servicing of vehicles, air-conditioners, electrical gadgets at homes, typewriters, computers, fans, clocks or generally left unattended with the result they not only occupy space, but present debris in the house. Regular house-keeping makes you aware of this responsibility.

We had a culture in the Aviation department that everything which has been installed must be in working condition at all times. At homes this activity is limited only to few items where as in offices and big factories where the inventory is very large and if the systems are not generated or implemented the accumulation would be unmanageable. Thus a good house-keeping regularises your maintenance and repairs needs. The working of vacuum cleaner is an example in itself that if it is not in a working condition how can you clean your premises, but regular housekeeping would ensure that at least your vacuum cleaner should be in a working condition at all times. This applies to all other items which are being utilised in your day to day use. By all standards housekeeping must be a part of your life.

Very Economical

Any activity in life, if carried out regularly it becomes well managed and anything which is well managed is economical. Suppose the cleanliness of a premises become neglected and start deteriorating. At that moment if you arrange cleanliness and repair it would involve a substantial sum for this job. I recall an incident:

While working as a general manager of a plastic manufacturing factory, we had hired a works manager, who came from Bangalore. Since he was to join us on emergency basis we had to provide him accommodation also. A vacant flat which was not occupied for years belonged to the owners of the factory. It was decided to give the flat to the incumbent for the time being. When we went to see the flat it could no be opened because everything had been jammed right from the lock to the door bolts. With some concerted efforts; 3 to 4 of us opened the door and we were aghast to see the sight of the three bedroom flat. It was observed that hundreds of pigeons had occupied the premises and when we opened the door the pigeons in hundreds flew out all at once hitting us on the face and body all over. It was difficult to open the windows even to make way for others. The entire house was full of so many droppings that the doors, windows, wash basins and all fittings were not visible When we brought the team of cleaners, they refused to start the work. It took us at least ten days to get the flat cleaned after spending a huge amount and even after ten days the smell of the birds was there along with the droppings here and there. It was difficult to sit there and finally the works manager had to go back as he could not continue the job. Had the flat been cleaned regularly, this much damage would not have been caused. The entire walls of the house had to be plastered and painted again. This is only a small example because it was visualised in person. The fact remains that the regular housekeeping maintains your equipments and items economically.

Stimulates Visitors

Several situations occur when you visit a place you would like to visit again and again because of its beauty and grandeur. The ready example is Taj Mahal. While you see it you would like to visit again and again. I have the pleasure to write here that wherever I had worked I had made all out efforts to keep the place very attractive whether it was Nasik, Santacruz, Goa, Sahar, Plastic Factory or even at Jaquar, the place compels the visitors to come again and again. We had put up a board at the gate at Sahar which read, "YOUR VISIT WAS A PLEASURE, PLEASE COME AGAIN". A number of airlines made repeated visits not just because of the board but the beauty of the place. Several of them confirmed that whenever they came they got something new.

It is quite evident that housekeeping plays a very prominent role in the development and so many factors in man's activities at home, at offices, at factories, at hospitals, at jails, railway platforms, bus stands, airports and other places, and it creates visual impact on their minds and the mind 'which is intelligence in action' percolates down to the other sensory perceptions to create impact on all other activities, which are visible in the ultimate results thereafter.

3.2 Cost Effectiveness Adds to Profits

In management activities, cost consciousness plays a very important role. All commercial organisations work for profit. Money saved is money earned. Money earned goes to profits.

In the normal management functions, profits are bound to take place but if the employees become cost conscious, the profits are so increased. There are two types of items on which expenditure is made, which are as under:

(a) Non-controllable items

(b) Controllable items

Non-controllable Items

Non-controllable items are those which are fixed and no control can be effective; such as Wages, Taxes, Government Fees, Licence Fees, Municipality Expenses or any other expenses, which are bound to be paid.

The management cannot have any effective control to reduce these costs. Of course, the management should monitor these expenses because these expenses are mandatory.

Non Payment of such expenses creates lot of complications like strikes, cancellation of the licences, fines or penalties.

Controllable Items

Controllable items are those where the expenses are borne regularly but they can be controlled with some effective monetary measures. The list of such expenditures is as under:

(i) Communication

(ii) Telephones

(iii) Electricity
(iv) Maintenance & Repairs
(v) Stationery
(vi) Entertainments
(vii) Transports & Fuels etc.
(viii) Canteens
(ix) Consumable Stores
(x) Furniture & Fixtures
(xi) Overtime
(xii) Miscellaneous

The control on the expenses on the above items can be and should be maintained if effective systems are evolved and implemented. The managements would be surprised to see the graph on savings going up and all the savings would add profits. We would take up the controllable items and discuss how to monitor the same.

First of all, develop a proforma, listing these items and note down the expenditure of the last month and then compare with the current month and any unusual difference, if noticed has to be investigated. If this system is monitored carefully and regularly, it would effect lot of savings. We will discuss the salient features of the items of the Controllable sources as under:

Communication

The communications have made a tremendous change from the traditional past. Earlier, the communication was confined only to writing letters. In the 21st Century, the communications can be had through letters, fax machines, e-mails, couriers etc.

The system has developed lot of complications because the old habits die hard. You would often see that the employees write letters then send the same message by fax, followed by e-mails and then the letter is sent through courier also. Quite often the same communication is repeated all over on all the channels of communication and then it is often passed on telephone also. This exercise is a sheer waste. Only one of the channels should be used for communication which would save paper work, filing, records, multiplicity actions and money.

The addition of photocopiers in the modern office is also a source of expenditure while its utility cannot be mined but it has been seen that the staff and the managements quite often keep on making copies of the documents without any planning and justification. The proper use of this machine can save lot of expenditure. Some companies are affecting a very strict control on this.

Similarly, the concept of sending mails through courier is also an additional source of expenditure. Although, it is useful for delivering the mail faster than the postal services, this can be monitored by clubbing together various letters or mailing instruments going to the same destination. A very strict exercise of vigilance is required on this subject. This needs constant review in the organisational set up.

Telephones

In the last century, the use of telephones was a rare phenomena. I remember when I was a child, any incoming telephone would invite lot of embarrassing situations. All family members and friends would gather together and showed anxiety and worry on the receipt of telephone. In the same way, whenever a telegram was received by any person, he used to start crying before reading it, thinking that this is a message of somebody dead. Now the times have changed.

Now in this 21st Century, times have changed and telephone has become an extreme necessity than a luxury. Mobile phones/car phones have taken place of telephones as the fastest means of communication. This is certainly the fastest mean of communication. You can communicate from any point to any point on the globe. Even, the school children are seen carrying mobile phones to their classes. This has become a status symbol these days.

This facility should be used very-very cautiously. No

communication on telephone should exceed the time limit of three minutes. If the managers are misusing this facility for a longer period, it is over expenditure and must be curbed. Earlier the trunk-calls and now STDs have enhanced the expenditure on this element but mobile phones operated throughout the world, though convenient, add to the costs. For the convenience and the quick action, this facility must be used but very sparingly. There is no point of making so many telephone calls a day to the same location again and again. It can be monitored by clubbing together all the messages on a sheet of paper, could be conveyed through one or two calls in a day, covering all the points which would save a number of STDs or trunk-calls.

Electricity

21st Century is the period of Push Button Technology. It is said that even the world war would be an electronic war, based on the Push Button Technology.

If you see around in any modern office, most of the fixtures or electronic gadgets, from OHP (Overhead Projector) to computers are being used. Most of the offices are air-conditioned, electricity is rare commodity in the Metros, it is either not available easily or over used. The air conditioners, fans, electric lights, computers, electronic typewriters, all should be switched off when not in use. It is not only the conservation of energy but also reducing the cost thereon. Overuse of this energy can cause accidents like, short circuits or fires or electrocutions. The effective use of this energy can save considerable cost.

Maintenance and Repairs

The maintenance & repairs is another important expenditure which any management has to bear. Ideally, every machine which is installed, must be in working condition at all times whether it is a generator or table fan. If any machine goes out of order, it must be either repaired or replaced. If the system of getting the machine in working condition is maintained, the cost of maintenance & repairs cost goes down considerably. For instance, if a machine is not working and not repaired in time, it gets rusted and a stage comes when it cannot be repaired. After a period of time, the cost of repairs or its disposal would be much more. Maintenance & repairs are also be done economically either through a manufacturer or through an authorised dealer or it should be contracted through competent persons so that the maintenance & repairs be carried out regularly and periodically.

To make it a systematized, a master plan may be prepared for all the machinery items in the office. Their schedule and repair & preventive maintenance may be chalked out and implemented. The over expenditure on this item takes place when preventative maintenance or the timely repairs are not carried out.

Stationery

In spite of scientific development, the items of stationery are used and consumed considerably in all offices with advent of computers. The computer stationery has been added to its inventory which is also expensive. The overuse of pens, pencils, erasers, staplers, stapler pins, clips, card boards, files, pad, note book etc. is invariably over-used or misused.

Once I noticed in one office that lot of stationery items were lying scattered on the floors in almost all the departments. I organised a team of two persons and deputed them to pick up the various items of stationery lying scattered in the office premises at least for two weeks. To my utmost surprise that the team collected more than 10 Kgs. of stationery items like clips, pins, tags etc. which were lying scattered. This is only for two weeks, imagine the cost of these items in a year!

From the above, you would find if the management and the employees take effective measures to control and monitor the use of stationery items, the managements can save considerable amount of money on stationery alone. This also includes the issue of stationery which must be monitored effectively.

Entertainment

Entertainment in the modern age of Public Relations (PR) is the need of hours and the managements. We have to maintain excellent relationship with the internal as well as external publics. For the internal publics, the maintenance of PR is not expensive at all but to maintain relationships with the external publics like the government authorities, dealers, distributors, customers, general public, costs money. The expenditure on entertainments are made regularly but it should be done in a systematic way so that expenditure on this vital issue is well controlled and monitored.

Transport

Transport has become a very important gadget with the management for the movement of employees from one place to another. Fuel has become costlier year by year. The company transport, if there is, can be pooled effectively and the use be economically organised so that expenditure can be reduced on this item.

Furniture and Fixtures

The outlook of the modern office has gone into a rapid change and development and each establishment has got the latest designed fittings and fixtures which can be installed with justification.

Overtime

Overtime is another item of expenditure. From my personal experience, I can categorically declare that overtime is a disease. The reason being, the worker gets fixed salary as wages whereas overtime depends upon his labour done during extra hours which are not consistent because it depends upon the work requirements. But it increases the salary of worker who look after his family than the stipulated wages can not run his family expenditures if and when the overtime is either curtailed or stopped. His way of spending remains the same while the income is reduced. So he becomes the sick person finally. Hence it is a disease.

I have several cases in my previous company where overtime earned by an employee was more than double than his normal salary. Quite often, the income of the worker was more than the salary of the Shift Manager. Therefore, the management should avoid putting labour on overtime as far as possible. The job on overtime must be carried out in rare cases where the need of customer has to be met in order to maintain the production or other exigencies.

Consumable Stores

All items which are not added in the above list but they are regularly used like soaps, toilet papers, phynol, teas, coffee, milk, sugar, snacks are all consumable stores.

These consumable stores are often wasted which can be monitored by effecting strict measures.

From the above, you would find that a great amount of money can be saved and added to the profits of the organisation if effective controls are monitored and implemented.

3.3 Training is a Must at Every Level

Right from birth till death training is a constant companion of man. The consistent training not only educates individuals, but it helps in improving the ability and competence of the employees. The professionalist companies even train their employees at the time of their retirement as to how to lead a retired life. And even after retirement a man has to be trained as to how to die in a dignified manner.

Some top companies rather all top companies have a systematic and well organised department of training, which is generally a product of HRD. department. The concept of HRD (human resources development) was initiated in the late sixties or early seventies and the propounder of this system led by Prof.

Athreya made big strides when this concept was made known to the progressive companies. With the rapid growth of this concept the human resource development has become a human resources investment.

Most companies have developed their evaluation system of annual appraisal of their employees and they identified the needs of training to be given to the concerned staff in a systematic manner. In a routine manner the staff gets acclimatised with the regular training and given him a break or variety he is often sent to outside agencies like CII, Assocham and other such institutions, who conduct seminars, conferences, trainings and this has also become a professionalised trade by some professionals who train the staff as advisors and specialists in management. If a systematic pattern is set in the annual appraisal forms and strictly adhered to this, it would become easier for the training department to conduct such trainings. In doing so it has to be planned, organised and implemented. The following steps are necessary:

Identify the Training Needs: It should be established as to what are the training needs of the employee. Could it be performance, improvement in his present work, knowledge-oriented, systems information, product knowledge, his temperament, motivation, communication skill or attitudinal development. Should he need the skills on the inter-personal relationship or to improve his over-all knowledge about the organisation, its competitors and the marketing strategy, etc.

Training is also important to the employees to enhance their knowledge and capabilities in view of their added responsibilities when promoted. It is also observed that most of the time the lacking skills of the employee are known until he is tried on a higher assignment or even in rotational assignment in the same level. In order to improve the performance in the new job, the training needs must be identified and imparted training suitably.

To systemise the training activities the following steps are required:

Training Task: Once the training need of the employee is identified, the method of training has to be planned. The plan should indicate whether it should be a time-bound training through lectures either conducted in-house or outside or skilled training on the spot or professional training on the job. If other methods are required to be planned like suggesting a professional course or sending him to professional seminars the same be provided.

Training Period: Before putting the plan into effect, it has to be decided what would be the time frame of the training, i.e. when should he be trained, what should be the period of training, what should be the sequence of the period, fixing a target date of the training, how much time is he required from his normal work so that the existing work is not affected. All these have to be understood and chalked out for each employee.

Follow Up: The detailed follow up method is to be designed or formulated to monitor the growth of the employee and the progress of the training at every level. He should be counselled periodically or he should give a report of his progress or his reporting officer should give the performance appraisal report as to how much he has picked up from his new training and how much more is to be done.

Methods of Training: The most important method of training is through lectures, which are generally held for a short duration of 2-3 hours. Generally it has been observed that they are not very effective because the employees don't give due concentration on the subject howsoever the lectures may be interesting. It is well known that training of any kind, needs consistent hammering.

From my personal experience it has been proved that the lectures given at the regional level or at bigger stations to a large audience were not as effective as to the training given at smaller places to a fewer staff without lecture. At such locations the results of the personalised training were more effective and the results achieved were very fast.

On the Job Training: This can be amplified by adding some new elements to the already existing job in order that the knowledge about the on the job training is enhanced. It is more objective when on the job training is explained by adding something new. It can be illustrated by the following example:

The training was imparted to the front office person as to how to improve his presentation, communication and behaviour with the visitors. He had attended lectures a number of times, but they were not very effective. One day the most presentable officer was made to sit at the receptionist desk in the presence of the receptionist in the room. Whenever visitors came this officer welcomed them with a smile, shaking hands, requesting them politely to take a seat, offering them a glass of water, followed by a cup of tea and enquiring from them about the purpose of their visit and guiding them to the concerned person with warmth and grace. In between he attended the incoming telephone calls with courtesy and audible communication in flawless language. While talking on phone he received yet another visitor, yet another call and he attended to all with same poise and promptness. This continued for two hours and it had a telling effect on the trainee receptionist. Next day another experienced employee was made to sit at the reception and he repeated the entire exercise in the presence of the receptionist, again for one hour. This had a telling effect on the receptionist and his job profile improved thereafter considerably.

This method of on the job training is generally given to more employees working in the factory, nurses in hospitals, air hostesses, pilots, army, police, etc.

Training for Specific Assignments: When a man is appointed afresh he is given preliminary training on the job assigned to him whether it is filing of papers, preparing a memo, writing a report, correcting and analysing data, compiling statistics or the actual work on a shop-floor, the tools required to perform the job and other systems prevailing in the organisation. This training is also given by lectures to a group of persons or to man to man discussions for specific jobs or to the group attached on the shop-floor of factory. This cannot be done in a matter of days, but it is a continuous process which is normally to be picked up in the probation period itself if or when it is specified in the appointment letter. The employees who attend and can't pick this training in the probation period are not liable to be confirmed. The employees who pick up such jobs well before time are confirmed earlier as well.

Learning by Observation: This is a method with the children who pick up fast by observing others around him. In offices or factories the new employees are made to sit with the veterans and they learn the work by observing others. In exceptional cases, particularly, in factories the trainers are required to induct better methods at the time of students learning by observations, because the veterans may be proficient to in their stalls but may not be good teachers. The employees though intelligent may not be good learners. Therefore, the involvement of the trainer becomes significant.

Job Rotation: Most progressive companies rotate the jobs of the employees from one department to another to increase the efficiency of the employees by inducting freshness in their assignment. Each new job adds more enthusiasm in the employee. The purpose of the job rotation is to make more and more people all-rounders and the churning takes place among the dead-wood. In bigger companies job rotation has become a must because the induction into the company does not take place at all levels. Therefore the growth of the employees takes place from grade to grade on the ladder of success. It is therefore necessary that an employee who reaches the top must have a fair working knowledge of all the departments. If any small company resorts to job rotation it is a very healthy sign but the scope is less because number of employees are less. The efficient HRD department can project the career path of employees for 10-15 years hence. In this relevance the inter-departmental interactions also form a job rotation assignment.

Succession Planning: A good manager is he who develops through training at least 2-3 persons to take over his seat. It gives opportunities and avenues for the employees to get ready to take over his boss's seat. This kind of training involves through involving the immediate juniors in all your activities including decision making exercises.

Inter-Departmental Meetings: Most efficient companies have a system of HODs meetings (Heads of Departments) where a review is taken of the previous month's performance and planning for the next month's programme. During these exercises the HODs or the participants of the meeting get sufficient inputs in respect of learning and training about the working of other departments. These inter-departmental meetings also minimise, if not eliminate interdepartmental communications like the memos, etc. which are churning out into an avalanche of paper work.

Attending Seminars and Conferences: Most companies conduct seminars and conferences where the representatives of other companies are also invited to share experiences. Even CII and Assocham and the like are doing great service by conducting seminars, conferences involving national and international personalities to share their experiences. This is the most modern method of training people and professionals from all walks of the industry.

Delegation: Down delegation of responsibility has become the need of the hour because of the added responsibility at the top. When the responsibilities are passed on to the next in line a training is imparted to them to carry out the responsibilities like those of the head. In major companies the down delegation of powers are well defined in writing either through circulars or manuals.

Through Games and Case Studies: The professional trainers have come out with interesting games and exercises and case studies through which the employees get trained by observing others taking part in the exercises. During such games the participation of the fellow employees is very useful where the opportunity is given to all to express their views and interaction.

Through Competitors and Audio Visual Cassettes: Science has provided wonderful means in the garb of competitors audio-visual tapes, CD Roms, etc. where the individuals can get training sitting in drawing rooms. These can be played and displayed at any hour of the day or night subject to the convenience of the user. The impact of these gadgets is very spontaneous and effective because of visual glamour.

The 21st century would take us to longer horizons where the human beings visualise to go forward to the unlimited barriers through various methods of training. Training is the ultimate vehicle of growth to achieve goals. Never miss a training programme and never miss a goal set by you or your organisation.

3.4 Decision-making: 21st Century Requirement

Why people cannot make decisions? Because of fear. Fear of making mistakes. What would people say, if the decisions are wrong? Decision makers have the courage of conviction. They are very confident. Those who do not have courage of conviction, they are not confident, hence cannot make decision.

Every manager has to make a decision. In fact, he is required to make more decisions. No one can be a leader unless he is capable of making sound and timely decisions. 'Decisions' and 'QUICK DECISIONS' making capability, make a manager successful.

Be Objective

Decisions without being objective is a futile exercise. Manager must be clear in his views as to what is the purpose of the decision. What he wants to achieve. Is it a problem solving one? If it is so, the manager must understand the problem fully. If the decision is a problem creating one, he must study the anticipated consequence thereof. Decisions must be QUICK, but decisions should not be taken in haste. Therefore, option must be made of the other possibilities. There may be more options to pick up the right decision. Efforts must be made to study the options available and then decide the best of opinions.

Pune is a city of education. It is the only place on earth, where you can have all types of Degrees or Diplomas, right from Film Acting to Military Engineering. I had decided long back that I would take a Diploma or a Degree from Pune University, 'come what may'. With this objective in mind I went to the University with the intention of getting a Diploma or Certificate for any foreign language. I had decided to study German language, when I went there I noticed a 'Board' prominently displayed 'Department of Journalism'.

The objective was to get associated with Pune University for getting a Diploma or Degree, but the decision of doing German language was changed to getting the Diploma in Journalism.

The Director of the Department showed his inability to admit me because this course had already started a month earlier. I pleaded with him and convinced him about my journalistic activities since 1948 and assured him about my bringing laurels to the Department. He admitted me. He was most happy when I stood FIRST in the final examination running into eight papers.

Thus, in decision making the object has to be very clear in the minds of the managers.

Be Decisive at All Times

Any manager who is well organised can be decisive. To take quick decision should be part of his life. He should be habitually decisive. Even if you make mistakes and take a wrong decision, never mind. Making mistakes gives you experience. When experienced, you would be in a better way to make good decisions. It is always better to make a wrong decision than not to take any decision at all. Experience would improve your judgement to make correct decisions.

A fighter pilot, when hit in action, has to take a decision to bail out or not within thirty seconds. His quick reflexes would make him bail out to save his life, which is more expensive than the aircraft. But in order to make this judgement accurate, how much experience, he would have achieved by how many mistakes.

The manager must make out list of options by consulting others, if he himself is uncertain, list out all the options, then consequences, plus and minus points of each option and pick up the best option. The decision should not be delayed. Set some time limit. Set a target for each decision. Every decision has a separate target date. For example, you have set a target date for obtaining a Degree, then post graduation, getting an MBA degree, getting job, settling down and then marriage and so on. For all these decisions, you have to set target dates. Even in offices a manager has to prioritise his jobs and setting a time frame for each action.

Give Weight to Intuitions

There are five prominent senses, which govern our physical structure. There is sixth sense as well, and that is 'common sense'. It has been tried and proved that management by common-sense also works, and works wonderfully well.

Quite often, we go with our instincts. Before making decision, our instincts or the sixth sense cautions us whether the decision is right or wrong. For example, you don't stop your car at the 'Red Signal' and drive down. Your instinct would make you realise that you have made a mistake. Even when you are in a hurry, your instinct would at once make you decide to stop the car at the 'Red Signal' automatically. Long experience has shown that taking decision on intuition have been often right. To quote a true example.

After marriage, I told my wife that our first child would be a girl and her name would be 'Shaifali'. She brushed aside the instinctive proposal as well as the decision. When the baby girl was born she was named 'Shaifali', six months before her birth, which is still continuing.

Again, after three years, I told my wife that we would be getting a boy and she should name him. She again dismissed the inhibition casually; saying hit and run methods are not correct always. My second child is a son and he was named as Saurabh, three months before his birth. Both names of the children are still continuing.

There have been several other decisions, made out of intuitions, which have been very correct and right.

Consult Others When in Doubt

In life, most of the time we get bogged down and cannot take decisions and get confused. In confusion, you either do not take a correct decision or you make an utterly wrong decision, making your life more miserable. In most establishments the managers make decisions and after consulting others especially those who are affected by such decisions.

In the management meetings, when heads of departments meet together to discuss important policy matters, they take decisions by consulting others. You may call this as a management by consensus but the decisions coming out of such consultations are generally good one and easy to implement.

For example, you have taken decisions about the overtime policy, you better consult the representatives of the unions as well as the management to review all the pros and cons of the consequences of the decisions. After such consultations, you arrive at decisions, which are easily implemented because the persons affected by such decision have been consulted.

While consulting others, about the decisions, some questions are exchanged, some experiences are shared, consequences can be analysed and discussed. This process helps in making decisions. During these consultations several innovative ideas are also emerged due to negative assumptions positive attitudes which help make sound decisions.

Decisions not to be Reversed

Before taking a decision all inputs are taken, reviewed, discussed, consulted, where necessary, and there is no further scope for its reconsideration. Instances do occur, when you have to withdraw decisions. That is most unfortunate. Even the Government have to withdraw decision under political considerations or unavoidable compulsions.

Once I had been a Location in-charge of a station and one of my staff members was promoted to next higher grade. In fact, he was to be charge-sheeted for some offence. The promotion order was wrongly issued by our Regional Office. Immediately after the issue of the promotion letter, I was advised on phone to take back the order as it was sent through oversight. When I asked the concerned staff member to return the document, he said he had lost it and would search it and return the following day.

The next day, he gave the excuse that the document was washed along with the other clothes. I told him that another letter could be issued to withdraw the earlier letter. By keeping a letter with him could serve no purpose. The staff returned the letter of promotion.

This is an isolated case. But the reversal of decision is very embarrassing and intolerable.

Implementation of Decisions

Implementation of decision is the real test of management. Some decisions are required to be implemented in toto, while some are to be effected from stage to stage. The decisions which have been taken without the consultation of the affected persons, take time to be explained and implemented. Some decisions are not properly understood, hence these are implemented wrongly. Without the timely and proper follow up the decisions are not effectively implemented.

In the armed forces the decisions are properly explained and communicated before implementation. Even at the last resort the question is always asked, 'Any Doubt?' Any wrongly communicated decision can cause very serious consequences.

Most of the managements decisions are not executed because those are not properly explained and communicated. In our country, the language changes when you cross a river or a State. With so many languages, you can imagine as to how to communicate the decisions for implementation.

What Happens to Bad Decisions

The manager who makes decisions, good or bad, is answerable to some one. The accountability is the check on managers. When losses occur or any serious damage is caused to the company because of the bad decision of the manager, he cannot reverse it. Even the reversal of decision cannot make up the losses.

Due to these situations, some managers try to cover up the bad decision. It is just like a situation when you tell a lie to cover it up you have to lie more. In decision making process, the cover up of wrong decision results in more bad decisions creating a complicating situation.

However, salvage operation can be tried. The persons involved in such situation can consult others who have contributed in the process of bad decisions. Any serious or more complicated decision must be in the knowledge of the boss. It had been our culture in the previous company that any one who made a mistake or took a wrong decision must inform the Location In-charge. A reasonable boss would always help the manager who had taken a bad decision. After all, he had been taking good decision on so many occasions earlier.

I would like to tell a true story on this issue:

I was in the Sales Department and would often guide and advise the young Sales Officers in their day to day assignments. Specially helping them in making their speeches or presentations. They had, therefore, special respect for me.

One day a Sales Officer, who looked very miserable, mentally and physically shaken came to me. He asked me to talk to him in the Conference Hall. I accompanied him, quite concerned. The moment we were together in the Conference Hall he started crying.

I consoled him and asked him to tell me the story. Slowly and steadily he started telling his story:

There was a particular dealer who wanted more loads of a special product than was the fixed quota. Sales Officer refused to oblige him and the dealer insisted upon him again and again. The Sales Officer being a simpleton was induced by the clever dealer who had taken the Sales Officer to Agra. There he fed him well, gave him lots of drinks and took his photographs with a call-girl type woman. When he regained his composure he threatened him to expose him in his company as well as in his social circle. It was a case of sheer 'Black Mail'. I heard his story and made him calm and peaceful.

After the story was completed I advised him not to talk to anyone else, but go to the Regional Manager who was the head of the entire Northern Region, and tell the same story truthfully.

When be told the story in detail to the Regional Manager, he immediately identified the name of his advisor. He complimented the 'advice'. All necessary remedial measures were taken by the Regional Manager so fast and confidentially that no one knew about it.

Thus, the boss must be kept in picture for any wrong or bad decision. Because of his experience and exposure more than you, the solution could be found.

Shifting of Blame be Avoided

Wrong decisions attract wrong reactions. Whenever a manager makes a wrong decision, an attempt is generally made to shift the blame to others. By shifting blames to others, more people get involved in the exercise resulting in more complications. This also sets bad precedents.

Reasons for not Making Correct Decisions

Who makes decisions?

The managers. The people in authority. The people who have been delegated the powers to do so. Those who own the establishment. Those who have to get the job done.

From the above, you see the people who have the powers, authority, experience and knowledge are expected to take decisions. Then why decisions are not taken in time or if taken, wrong or bad decisions. Experience has proved that the decisions are either not taken or taken wrongly due to the following reasons:

Managers Being Weak: The managers who are weak, have no confidence, no experience, are afraid to accept responsibility, timid by nature, incompetent, do not take decisions or take faulty decisions. The actions of such persons put others also in trouble. These managers should not be allowed to hold responsible assignments. But why should such persons be made managers in the first place.

An interesting even comes to my mind when two junior managers were to take a very minor decision, but could not do so:

There were two junior managers who were very close friends. They lived together near Golcha Theatre in Delhi. They studied together. They were married almost the same year and they went for honeymoon to Nainital together and coincidentally they joined the same company. Such was the togetherness.

One day they planned to go to a movie at the Golcha. They arranged four tickets. On the day, they were to go, they sat together, drew out a plan and started discussions for about one hour and even more till one of them went to bathroom. The other one spoke to me in his absence.

Look, how stupid is he? He was insisting that we go for the movie together. Accordingly, we bought the tickets. Now the problem is how to sit together. If we sit side by side our wives would sit separately. If the wives sit together, then we cannot sit together. If we sit alternatively, this fellow does not want to sit near other person in the next seat. I don't mind this arrangement but he does not wish that his wife should sit with some one else, on the next seat. Meanwhile, the other person returned from the bathroom.

They discussed the matter afresh for another forty minutes but could not reach a decision. The discussion turned into a heated argument and they cancelled the programme and returned the tickets.

Now, if such persons are required to take management decisions, you can imagine what would happen. This is how the decisions are either not taken or faulty decisions are made.

No Power To Take Decisions: Some managers, just do not take a decision, since no one gave them any authority to take a decision. Why make him a manager then?

Several instances have been noticed when a manager can place orders to purchase raw materials or other consumable stores from the market, as a matter of routine, but he has no powers to release payments or sign cheques. A stage comes, when his orders are not executed and the logistics management suffers very badly. The managers must be given adequate authority to take decisions. In top companies, delegation of powers are defined in writing the budgets are drawn up, approved. When your authority is known to you, your budget is known to you, it is easier to take a decision, the work continues.

In absence of authority, the decisions are not taken by the so-called 'managers'. For effective management, the down delegation of authority is a must.

Accountability not Clear: The person who is empowered to take a decision must be clear about his accountability. He must know, what would be the consequences, if he crosses his brief. If the accountability is not clear, but vague, he would feel shy to take a decision.

In a saree emporium, the salesman is quite clear as to how much discount he can offer to the customer in respect of particular brand of sarees. If his limits are vague, he is bound to take wrong decisions and the company would suffer losses. If he knows his limit, he would refer the matter to his superior, to offer more discount to click the deal.

In most small enterprises, this situation is either absent or the man who makes decision are not clear about his accountability, so he cannot make a decision. If he does, he would commit a mistake, if not a blunder.

Inadequate Time Limit: Well organised companies have set their goals, systems and schedules to take appropriate actions on time. They have scheduled their activities for filing returns, submission of statements to the respective authorities, granting annual increments and promotions, release of bonus, other incentives on time. The companies, which are not organised properly make a mess of these things resulting in serious damages to its image, morale of the employees and the entire organisation becomes a victim of procrastination.

When the time limits of these functions are not adhered to strictly, the decision-making calibre of the managers suffers a jolt and the functioning of the entire establishment gets bogged down.

If the scheduling of time is unlimited, even then the decision-making exercise suffers. The concerned managers develop an attitude, that there is enough time to carry on and in this presumption the decisions are not taken in time.

Therefore, irrespective of time schedules or lead times given for a particular job, the decision must be taken to meet the situation.

Organisational Culture: It has been discussed earlier, that every organisation has a culture of its own. The culture of the organisation is known by its people who make the organisation known or blown. Sometimes, very efficient professionals become inefficient in the company of slow and disorganised establishment and some time the lazy and unexposed persons become efficient in the well organisation establishments.

It is the culture of the organisation when the managers are given complete freedom to manage their departments and take their own decision. In such culture every manager becomes a 'Management'. Such companies flourish. In the organisation where the delegation of powers do not flow in the hierarchical system the managers shudder to take decision. In this situation, neither the company grows nor the manager. Stagnation takes place at all levels.

Quick, correct and sound decisions, at all levels, make the management vibrant.

Absence of Delegation: A shopkeeper can run his shop single-handedly. A bigger shop, where more salesmen are employed, the duties and responsibilities are shared amongst them. A well established office gets departmentalised, where different activities are divided as per the talents and expertise of the staff. In larger organisations the responsibilities, accountabilities and delegation of authorities flow in a predetermined hierarchical order to conduct their duties and take necessary decisions to run the organisation.

The flow of delegation is regular and consistent. If there is any impediment in the line, the flow of the stream of the organisation stops, then the decisions either get jammed or overflow, flooding the system with confusion and anarchy.

In public companies, in multinational units and in well organised private companies the delegation of powers are well defined in writing. Thus, there is no confusion in taking important decision at critical points.

Imagine the situation where the tender is to be filed at a stipulated time and the authorised person is held up somewhere, and he has not delegated the power to any one just to sign the tender form, how can the company get an order and run his business.

Delegation of powers is the transfusion of blood to vitalise the growth of the body management.

Corporate Policies: When two persons meet politics starts. When more people meet politics is at the peak. Aristotle said that a man is a social animal and by nature and necessities, he is bound to live in a civilised society. Times have changed. Man is a political animal by nature. The necessities of life, made him a leader, political or otherwise. You come across several TV serials where politics in families run the roost.

In management study, the politics in management is a subject by itself. I have not included this chapter deliberately, because the purpose of this book is different.

In the organisation, the managers are required to perform their duties within their assigned roles. The managers are influenced by the pulls and pressures of other departments which are interconnected. This leads them to form their opinionated groups; the interests of which always clashed in the day to day duties.

I have the experience of working in Sales Department, Operations Department, Aviation and Public Relation Department, Stores Department and several others. Working as a Location In charge get you the exposure to Engineering, Accounts, Excise and Customs Departments. I have observed that the Sales Department would not see eye to eye with Operations or there would be clashes between Sales and Accounts, between Operations and Engineering, etc.

These divisions make leaders of the departments as small kings holding their forts and never stop shelling on each other. There cannot be cease-fire amongst them. This prevents managers to take proper decisions in the interest of the organisation. Such decisions, though not always, often are in the interests of the departments. At this point the role of top management is felt necessary. Politics in office is a very interesting subject, where we all are subjected to, either by choice or by compulsion.

Disinterestedness: "To be or not to be, That's the Question" are famous lines of HAMLET written by Shakespeare, hundreds of years ago. The same characteristics appear in this century and shall continue to be present at times to come. The greatness of Shakespeare or for that matter all epics, like 'Ramayana and Mahabharat', is that the characters created therein live in all ages.

So is the manager, who drives his instincts from Hamlet. He is just not interested to take any decision. According to him, making decision is a knocking on the gateway of Dooms Day.

'WHY BOTHER' has become their slogan. This slogan has become very popular in most offices in this country. That's why things are not moving fast as they should be. The successful managers have to take decisions quickly keeping in view of all the pros and cons, in the interest of the organisation. The managers who are decisive are the assets of the organisation.

3.5 Management of Meetings

"Boss is in meeting" is a very common excuse when the Boss is not to meet any person or attend to his telephone call. Meetings are held very frequently in most companies.

A definition of meeting goes like this "Group of people who individually cannot do anything, but collectively in a meeting decide that nothing can be done".

Several managers are of the opinion that the meetings waste the useful time in office; slow down the tempo of enterprising persons, hamper the quick decision making process, consume lot of time on minor issues, overlooking major ones. Meetings are generally dominated by one or two authoritative personalities.

Meetings not Conducted Well

Generally, the meetings are either poorly controlled or inefficiently conducted. Some meetings are conducted suddenly or at wrong times where most people cannot make it possible to attend. The net result emerges either to fix a date for the next meeting and the unwanted debates erupt on the minutes of the last meeting.

Expenses on Meetings

Meetings invite lot of criticism in the organisations, because besides being time consuming, they are very expensive. Imagine, ten to twelve highly paid persons sit together for three to four hours, how much would they cost in terms of their time, paper work, preparing the minutes, typing them, circulating them, reading them plus their transport, accommodation, feeding them and so on.

Scenes at the Meetings: Top companies have kept special funds in their budgets for conducting meetings. They have developed a system to calculate the cost per meeting and per hour for the expenditure. Their purpose is not to discourage or prevent the managers to attend or conduct the meetings. The cost effectiveness is certainly a management responsibility. How the cost effectiveness is not assessed, can be understood from a fact that I had been on some committees of ISI representing an NGO which I left 5 years ago, and I am still getting the minutes of their meetings running into 40-50 pages. I have written to the concerned persons several times that I no longer represent the NGO, but still I am continuously getting the documents of the meetings.

Advantages of Meetings

In most meetings, the members exchange heated arguments and their proceedings are heard several blocks away from the scene. The meetings conducted by many co-operative societies or group housing societies are scenes to be watched. Police vans, ambulances are often called on such meetings.

Sometimes the management meetings also create scenes when departments after departments settle their scores for public display. In principle, the primary responsibility of conducting a good or bad meeting rests on the shoulders of the Presiding Officer.

Despite the negative views about the meetings, well conducted meetings for good reasons have several advantages; some of which are as under.

Knowing People: When persons from different segments of the organisation are called, they interact with each other and know them closely. They also create group identity and introduce each other as individuals and units.

Briefing: An individual or a group gives briefing to the rest of the group about any policy, plan or situation or planning a future strategy to chalk out a disaster plan or any crisis management. Any clarification required thereto can also be debated.

Co-ordination: In a meeting, the participants give an account of their responsibilities or incidents in their own spheres. Meetings help co-ordinate their viewpoints to achieve a consensus. In case, the differences or difficulties are not resolved, these can be referred to some other time after taking the concerted viewpoints. It is not easy to interact with persons who are working at different locations at one go. Meetings can help co-ordinating their efforts at a common place.

Time Saver: Meetings help save time to collect many key persons to gather at one place and take prompt decisions.

Fact Finding Exercise: When members get together at a meeting with different problems, the meetings help to find facts which are common to all. Members contribute their information which becomes relevant to the issue. This helps sort out the issues.

Brainstorming: Meetings are used to provide different ranges of innovations for solving the problems, which are brought out for a detailed discussions. Some times even the lowest cadre brings out brilliant ideas. Such imaginations are analysed and implemented.

In my previous company, we used to have quality circles and in such meetings, we always had the wildest ideas for discussions. We had innovated several useful plans which were benefited to the company, saving several lakhs of Rupees. For example, the staff used to go on the top of the vertical tanks to take dips of the product for measuring the quantity of fuel. By repeated innovations, we brought the quantity of the fuel right on the table of the Shift Managers by devising electrical gadgets at various places. There were several such innovations brought at work stations, the discussion of which would not be relevant here.

Creating an Atmosphere of Commitments: In any modern organisation, the concept of team work has become very vital. Team work is the result of commitment of all members of team. In meetings, all participants commit to the decision taken collectively. With the commitments of the members, the implementation of the decisions become easier.

Evaluations: An element of assessment takes place in a group meeting. While assessing the tasks before the meeting, alternations are also taken into account. In this way, various opinions, arguments and alternations are available for the decision make to take decision.

As a Location In-charge, I had to conduct a meeting with the union leaders, every month. Every time, we would get new problems, new demands, which needed comprehensive discussions and interactions. There are wise and intelligent union leaders who think positive and understand the difficulties of implementing difficult decisions. Such leaders always evaluated the problems very sincerity. The task of the members become easy if the evaluation takes place with a positive approach.

Prompt Decision-making: All participants in the meeting put forward their proposals, views, alternatives, which are evaluated and decisions are taken with the majority support. Such a decision becomes binding on all. In a situation, when the common joint decision is not possible, then the presiding officer plays a prominent role to advise, suggest and explain the subject in logical sequences to convince the members to reach a decision.

Planning and Implementation: The participants of the meeting discuss the different action plans for the implementation of the decisions arrived at. The responsibility of each member is explained to them and in case of difficulties expressed by the members, the same are discussed again if required. This happens when the tasks of members are inter-mixed with others.

Venting of Feelings: The participants express their feelings and personal views in meetings which are generally not redressed in private. The members must give due opportunity to all members to air the feelings without affecting the facts of the issue. This blowing off steam helps in cementing relationship.

Social Get-Togethers: Meetings also help the junior-senior association over a cup of tea/coffee which is normally not possible in heavy schedule of senior executives. Often, very complicated personal issues are resolved in the meetings.

How to Make Meetings Meaningful

In spite of the fact that the meetings are criticised in the companies, the above factors establish that the meetings, if conducted well are very useful. In order to make their work successfully, the followings must be observed :-

The Purpose: First and foremost, the purpose of the meeting must be established & identified. Whether the meeting is avoidable or a MUST. If it is a must, them it should be properly announced explaining the purpose of the exercise.

Who should attend? It must be decided very carefully as to who should attend and why. Those who are not relevant to the purpose of the meetings, should never be invited.

Who would preside? The chairman of the meeting or the person who presides over the meeting plays a very prominent role in the meeting. A person of authority & integrity should preside over the meeting, as he has to function as a guide, a judge, an arbitrator, an umpire, coordinator and a fire fighter. He has to monitor the tempo of the meeting and he has to lead the group as the guard mans the train.

Effective Participation: All members nominated/invited must participate the meeting. Missing of any important person would break the sequence of the agenda.

Proper Agenda: The members must attend the meetings punctually and conclusion of the meeting must end as soon as the agenda is discussed. Each item on agenda must have a time frame for discussion. The chairman must observe the time schedule. Meetings should not run too long. It is ideal if the time schedule of the agenda is specified against each item, and the meeting must terminate with the same punctuality with which it started.

Recording of Meetings: After discussing each item on agenda, the chairman must summarise the discussion and decision, it should be recorded in the minutes. The secretary or any person nominated to do so would prepare the minutes.

The minutes should be brief. This should also include the time, date, the venue, the members who attended and the name of the chairman.

The minutes should also identify the actions to be taken, by whom, and by what date.

The time at which the meeting ended.

The date and time of the next meeting be notified, if decided.

The meetings should not be held in heated debates, arguments and counter arguments resulting in emotional outbursts. The discussion in the meetings should not formulate group formings to avoid counter actions outside the meetings.

Attempts should also be made that the meetings do not end the exercises of rubber stamping by the persons in authority.

Good chairmen conduct the meetings very well and provide good results.

Arrangements of the Meeting

The sources of failure of the meeting depends much on the arrangements. The meetings' venue, time, date and the arrangements for members participation must be carried out immaculately.

The rooms where meeting is to be conducted must be comfortable, airy, assessable, must have right atmosphere with an alternative sitting arrangement with name plates against each member participating. All necessary equipment like OHP, flip, chart, blackboard, paper, pencils, etc. must be available. Necessary arrangements for water for drinking, tea/coffee, light snacks may be kept ready when required. The participants must be advised to confirm their acceptance of the invitation and name of the co-ordinator must be advised to them.

Meetings can certainly be made successful so that these can be advantageous to all.

3.6 Human Resourcing: A Challenging Assignment

The real importance of the human resource of any organisation has in its ability to respond favourably and willingly to performance, objectives and opportunities, and in these efforts to select right persons for right places in order to gain satisfaction from both accomplishing the work and being in the work environment.

This requires that the right people with the right blend of knowledge and skills, be in the right place, at the right time to perform the required work. The organisation is judged by the people hired to work for it. Every company is made or destroyed by the quality, behaviour and attitudes of its people. What actively distinguishes an organisation is its human resource having the ability to use knowledge of all kinds. It is through these professionalised resources that all other resources can be effectively utilised.

The selection of right persons for the organisations is of paramount importance. Every job in an organisation is very important, right from the watchman to the Chief Executive. Therefore, selection of right person **makes** the organisation and wrong persons, selected anytime for any role, mars it. The role of the HRD Department is to select persons of quality. It is the responsible job to identify the qualities of the individual required for the job. It is the people who make and maintain the culture of the organisation. Every organisation has its own culture. So the person, selected must be able to adapt to the culture of the organisation. Generally, the organisations consider the following qualities in the candidates at the time of hiring their services:

Adequate Qualifications: In this age of professionalism, each job in any organisation, has specified basic educational qualification to meet the requirement. These days, specialised education, knowledge of information technology, engineering graduation, medical degrees etc. are necessary for the respective jobs for the optimum performance.

Relevant Experience: When you ask any fresh graduate or candidate, if he has the relevant experience, he would often reply that unless he gets a job, how could he have the experience! So, until he has the job, he cannot be experienced, and conversely, unless he has the experience, he cannot have the jobs. So the question of Hen first or Egg first cannot be answered easily. But the companies have the prerogative to select the experienced person, after all they have to pay for it.

Presentability: The presentation makes the personality of the candidate. It is very important as to how the candidate conducts himself. In my previous companies, I used to be one of the other members of the committees or board it did not matter much but in the present Company, I have shortlisted/selected the persons during the last three years on the basis of the presentation of the persons. The moment the candidate enters the room and walks up to the chair before me, he is fifty percent selected or rejected. The balance fifty percent when he opens his mouth. Presentability is very important, while selecting a person.

Communication Skills: All human beings are required to speak, write or hear. The candidate to be hired for the job must be very communicative. These days, the employers initiate the conversations by saying ""TELL ME ABOUT YOURSELF". In response, the candidate displays his skills of communication. I have come across well mannered, well presented candidates lacking communicative skills. It is often embarrassing when the candidates shyly pleads that he would speak in his regional/national language.

Attitude: From the conversation, it can be easily found whether the candidate is having positive or a negative attitude.

What constitutes a good attitude is different from different person, but a friendly, smiling, willing to help person helps make atmosphere in office more conducive, enjoyable and productive. It is very essential to ascertain whether the candidate would stick to the job or is just for the opportunity to use the organization as a spring board for a big jump else where. Persons, who are stiff looking with negative attitudes are not welcomed by the organizations. Knowledge about his family background must be ascertained. His attitude depends on this.

Hard Working: People are hired who are willing to do any work cheerfully. Often, lack of experience is overlooked in place of hard working candidate. Even experience and skill cannot make up for hard work, initiative or work ethic. One may question, how to know whether the candidate is hard working or otherwise. But by perusing the biodata or tactful conversation, it is very easy to find out the calibre of the candidate. If it is not possible, the HRD person cannot justify his own selection..

Stability: No one appreciates to have a candidate who changes jobs frequently. Such candidates are not stable. The sequence of his previous jobs would indicate that candidate has some attitude problems or he is over ambitious, that he cannot stick to a job for a longer period. It is quite possible that the candidate is over-qualified to get justice in his previous jobs. Unstable candidates can be liabilities thereafter.

Smartness: Quite often, you come across candidates who are very resourceful. Such persons find quick or better solutions for all problems. Smart persons are go-getters. They are so smart that they can get the different or impossible jobs done very easily. Even during interviews, smart candidates would motivate the interviewer to ask questions where in they are expert or confident.

Responsible: Candidates who appear for interview in time, in appropriate dress, carrying relevant documents like well drafted biodata, certificates, proof of achievements indicate that they are responsible and they can hold responsibilities of the jobs profiled for them. Capabilities of candidates, handling higher responsibilities prove that the candidate is very responsible.

Leadership: The details of the biodata and interaction about the previous activities of the candidate can prove his leadership qualities. His attitudes, his willingness to help, his stability and intelligence would prove his leadership qualities. Such persons become motivators, opinion builders in the organisation who become assets of the companies

Updated: Successful candidates are always updated about their knowledge, information around. People who read newspapers, magazines, books, keep their general knowledge updated. Such persons are intelligent and dependable.

Commitment: Commitment of the candidate is quite relevant to his achievement, desire for responsibility and personal motivations. Commitment is also linked with his personal advancement, like his ambitions or liking for money, his attitude towards his family, state, society, college friends. These elements would foretell the potential of the candidate.

Calibre: Calibre of a person tells, how he tackles his problems. Does he take up the challenge himself or he depends upon others? Is he capable of taking fast decisions? What is the strength of his personality? Is he capable of analyzing the activities or consequences thereof? These vital traits are very urgent for evaluating his calibre.

These are some of the important characteristics of good candidates who are needed by your organisations. These would amply indicate the commitment and calibre of the persons you wish to employ. After identifying, the characteristics of the candidate, the next step is how and from where to find the resourcing the humans.

How to Get People?

People are the heart of the organization. Better the people, better the organization. It is very necessary to find the right people for the right job. The followings are the sources from where you can find your people:

From the Organisation itself: Depending upon the size of the company, the persons required can be found from within. If the size of the company is small, the right persons are generally not available. If the company is big and HRD is functioning efficiently, the system of appraisal reports can take, care of this problem. In the very large companies, like Public Undertakings, the HRD can identify the career-path of the employees for the next 10-15 years. The employees are promoted, or transferred to other departments wherever the need arises. Even if the suitable persons are not available either in a small set up or in a large company, the alternative sources, as mentioned here, can be tried to get the candidate for selection, through written tests or interviews.

Business Contacts: Every company or organisation is well connected socially and professionally with allied companies. They are, sometimes, so close to each other that they know the individuals working in the companies by name. These contacts keep becoming bigger and larger with the passage of time. The area of influence spreads far and wide and quite often the executives at the top or any level, recommend talented persons from their relations and friends for employment in the companies. Alternatively the company executives spread the news of their requirements to fill up the vacancies. This attracts the professional candidates to the destination. The candidates are then advised to meet the right persons for preliminary interaction, which may be termed as interview.

Placement Agencies: With the growth of industry, multinationals, and private enterprises, the job requirements have increased, and so do the Placement Agencies. More and more professionally competent Placement Agencies have come to surface. These agencies have well maintained Data Bank of all categories of job profiles.

The companies are in contact with these Placement Agencies and they keep informing them about their requirements.

Conversely, the Placement Agencies are also maintaining a close follow up with their clients and provide them all support as and when required.

On receiving the demands of their clients, the Placement Agencies send the bio-datas of the respective candidates. Some send the biodatas just like post office jobs, but competent agencies short list the candidates from their Data Bank and send two or three candidates only. It becomes simpler for the companies to shortlist the already shortlisted candidates and call them for interview.

Through Advertisements: The most prominent and right method of getting the right persons for the right jobs is carried out through advertisements in the media. The suitable advertisements are written by good copywriters, telling about the organization, the job profile, what type of person is required, i.e. about his qualifications, skills, age, experience, abilities, etc. The salary and perks are also mentioned in the advertisements. It is also classified in the advertisement as how to reply. Either through the prescribed proformas or on plane paper or through letters, telephone or applications.

After the advertisement is published in the newspapers, magazines etc., the applications received are scrutinised and shortlisted. The short listed candidates are advised to appear for interview on a specified date and time. The organisations nominate a person or set a group of persons to form a Board to conduct the interview. Some companies leave the job to HRD personnel to carry out the job independently.

Internet: In this age of IT, the company's requirements are set on the internet giving all the information as given in the advertisements. Similarly the candidates also feed their datas on internet offering their candidatures. The responses culminate in the resultant interviews.

Campus Interview: The method of campus interviews is also very popular these days. The Universities, the Institutes like the Engineering Institutes, Schools of Business Administration write to prominent industries to visit their universities/institutions to interview the candidates and select them as fresh as if could be. Most companies ear mark the candidates much before their courses are complete.

While these are some of the most commonly used methods of sourcing manpower. However, there may be some other methods as well which are not commonly used. All these methods conclude at the stage of interview.

Interviews: To select the required candidates, interviews are conducted by the competent persons to communicate with the prospective candidate, to evaluate them and select the best and the right person for the right job.

An interview of the candidate seeking employment is different from the interviews taken by the media. The journalists, when interview the National Leaders, are not defensive, they are often offensive. Just notice the 'Hard Talk' on BBC, or interviews with famous journalists like Karan Thapar or Vir Sanghvi, you would find how the Leaders & National Figures like Film Stars or Sportsmen, act or react.

The Management Interviews are the conversations of special kind and are conducted in very tense circumstances. Therefore, the situation demands a special method and special skills to have this special conversation.

However, it must be remembered that this exercise should not reflect one-upmanship. It should not appear as a quiz contest or over-show of superiority of the interviewer and the inferiority of the candidate. You are meeting a stranger who is coming to your organisation to seek employment. Therefore, the interview atmosphere must be kept cool and enjoyable. It should look like a talk in the Drawing Room, as natural as courteous and warm. It should be a friendly interaction, with the sole purpose of knowing each other.

Though the interview should be a friendly talk but still the atmosphere looks tense, especially for the candidate who has to compete with other candidates to secure a job. It is the responsibility of the interviewer to ease his tension. He should be made to sit comfortably and the conversation should start as a natural introduction.

Both the interviewer and the interviewee know about the purpose of the exercise. The interviewer seeks information to know about him, his education, his background, his skills, experience etc. The interviewee is eager to get selected. Therefore, the purpose should be to set the questions in such a way to seek more relevant information from the candidate and the candidate should also not involve himself in any unproductive argument or heated discussions.

Since the interviewer seeks more and more information from the candidate, he should make the candidate talk more than he should involve himself. A good interviewer would make the candidate at ease to make him express himself fully.

During my tenure in this company, I have interviewed almost all candidates who have joined our organization during the last 40 months or so. It was a pleasure to talk to the candidates. Earlier, we used to get the vacancies advertised till we appointed two Placement Agencies to provide professionalised persons. These agencies are doing good jobs to cater to our human resourcing requirements.

Whenever the candidates enter my room, I would invariably ask :-

"Any problem reaching our Office?" Mostly, they replied in the negative. As soon as they would be seated, a glass of water or a cup of tea is normally offered. Then the conversation would follow like this.

"Please tell me about yourself" Often, the candidate would start telling the particulars mentioned in the biodata. I would interrupt again, **"Not those details, tell me about yourself, your parents, your family, your tastes, habits, etc."** Again, he would start from somewhere, till such time he gets confidence and start communicating normally. Several candidates reported back to their Placement Agencies that the interviewer took us 45 minutes to one hour, but nothing was asked. I would respond by saying that whatever was required by us, has been known to us.

Some would comment, **"The interview in IAS is not so tough as this one."** My reply used to be **"Yes, the purpose is how much the candidate is updated and informed. Both offer stable jobs with good salaries"**

Many candidates gave us the feed back through their respective agencies that they learnt more through the interview at our company, and had no regrets if not selected. This cycle would continue on and on.

Preparation for Interview

Just as the candidate prepares himself to appear for the interview, the interviewer should also prepare himself to do justice to the noble cause. The cause is noble, you are getting people to work with and you are providing opportunities to the right people to get a job.

Be Clear About the Job Profile: The interviewer, or the Management must be clear about the job profile, for which the candidate has to be picked up. You must identify the qualification, skills, or experience required for the assignment. You must also know about the duty hours of the job, shift timings, if night duties are to be performed. Hardships of the females if they are required to be hired. What would be the salary and perks to be provided? Transport needs! You must be fully conversant with the job description so that the candidate must be kept informed about his expectations.

Identify Strike Questions: Normally the **questions** in the interview emerge from the questions only. In the stereo typed interviews, the questions are kept framed with the interviewers and the candidates are asked the same questions again and again.

Now a days, only two types of questions are asked, viz. close ended questions and open ended questions.

Close ended questions: The close ended questions are very short and the replies are also equally short; like

"What is your father's name?"

"He is Mr. Ram Lal."

Open ended questions: Where as the open ended questions lead the candidate into a longer answers, with detailed explanations like :

"What is your opinion about the Afghanistan scenario?"

"Well, the war may take longer time because the situation is quite fluid, the activities of the terrorists are affecting the entire world" and so on.

However, the questions on specialised subjects like the Balance Sheets, Excise documents, filing of returns, Income Tax formalities, Amendments on Sales Tax, Labour policies, impact on small Companies, Advertising scenario, etc. can be kept ready to get the know-how of the candidates

Whereas the questions emerge from the questions when we ask

"What paper you read daily?"

"What is the main news today?"

"Why India lost the Test Match?

These questions are asked to find out his interests in sports, national events, or his keeping himself updated and so on. When you get involved in these types of informations seeking exercise, the candidate forgets that he is in interview, but the interviewer gets fair information about his communication skills, his presentation, style of speaking, on conversational ticks, his interest and aptitude, his general knowledge and his willingness to learn more. The more the candidate speaks, the more you know about him.

Provide Comfortable Environment: The place where the interview is to be conducted, must be comfortable, devoid of all interruptions. Please ensure that you are not disturbed by the visitors, telephone calls, power shut offs. These disruptions deviate both the interviewer as well as the interviewee from the serious business. It undermines the concentration, particularly of the candidate.

Arrangement must be made to provide drinking water, tea etc. so that the candidate may feel at home.

Avoid Tricks: The purpose of the Management is to pick up the right person for the job in hand. Therefore, no tricks be played on the candidate. Never attempt to confuse the candidate or make fun of him, or underplay him, if he fails to answer a question.

Remember, any person, how-so-ever highly qualified, he may be, and can be confused in an interview. It is very easy. But that is not the purpose of the interviewer.

I have selected persons for the jobs who could not reply several questions saying "I do not know, Sir." Because, they were honest in saying so. They were confident in saying so. It is not possible that everybody knows everything. All managers, all authors, me included, can be confused in any interview. Therefore, such tricks be avoided if you are honest in selecting a sincere person.

Read Bio-Datas Carefully: Before interview takes place, read the biodata sincerely. If already read it, review the same again and underline the salient features which need to be probed further for more information from the candidates. The review of the biodatas would also enable the interviewer to be comfortable in interacting with the candidate. For example, if the candidate is switching his jobs very frequently, it needs to be looked into, to ascertain his stability.

Prepare Notes: It is advisable to prepare notes as to what are the salient features you would like to dwell upon, during the interviews. Which are the questions, which have not been answered in his biodata. You may also feel the need for taking notes, during the interview as well. Like his top class achievements, winning a national award or international recognition or any fantastic experience.

Interviews

The interview is the climax of all your efforts in finding your final chance of the man you need. By, carefully studying the biodatas, you have already narrowed down your choice between two to three candidates. The stage at which the candidate appears for interview has already been processed through filtration by the Placement Agency, through the biodatas and finally through the process of interview. Please ensure that the interview of the candidate must start in time. The interview consists of the following steps.

Welcome: The interviewer must welcome the candidate with a smile or shake hand warmly. He should be seated with all courtesy. He should be involved in the informal talk of enquiring about his difficulty in finding your place, and he should be shown some concern about his journey to your office. Offer him a glass of water or tea. This makes him at ease.

As soon as he gets set in his seat, you may enquire about his family and his personal tastes, ambitions or his achievements. He must feel that he is important.

Job Profile: The interviewer should describe the job profile in details. He should tell the candidate the type of person they are looking for, to handle the assignment. Some relevant questions can be asked if he could meet the job requirement.

While asking questions, note carefully his body language, his mannerism, eye to eye contact; the way he presents his point of view. Observe whether he is relaxed or tense. Whether, he is confident or just beats about the bush. Watch his attitude. Is he of helping hand? Is he arrogant, autocrat, assertive, imaginative,? Does he look pleasant while speaking? Does he stammer? Is he having any speech ticks? Does he repeat the particular words repeatedly? Does he smile frequently or frowns, or lose his temper? Is he submissive or towing the line by saying 'Yes Sir', 'Yes Sir'?

Become Professional: As the momentum picks up, use professional questions. Enlarge your scope. Ask questions to find out his competence and calibre to handle the assignment. You much ask questions in such a way that he gets involved in the debate. You may prompt him to become aggressive by asking uncomfortable questions to judge his maturity and stability. If the candidate is excited, change the topic and talk light topics. I quote an example:

Question: Why do you change your topic so frequently?

Answer: For betterment

Q.:In how much time, you would leave this organisation for betterment?

A.:It depends

Q.:Depends on what?

A: Who offers and how much.

Q.:How can we depend upon you, whether you would stick around or jump again?

A.:It should not concern you, as long as I am around…….

Q.:Why are you perspiring? You are wearing the tie for the fist time?

A.:How can you say that?

Q :Perhaps, you are not comfortable?

A.:I am comfortable. Don't mind my tie please!

B. : When do you get angry?

A. : Normally, I do not get angry. When someone cheats me, I do get.

Q. : Would you like to have a cup of tea?

A. : I would prefer a glass of water.

By this time, the candidate had changed his mood three times. At the end, the candidate must be asked if he has any question for you.

Give Patient Hearing: Listen to the candidate very carefully. While he is talking, you observe minutely. His gesture, his facial experience, movement of his hands. His attitudes, his commitments, his willingness to take the job. His answers would show enthusiasm and seriousness. By this time, you must have understood the strong points and weak points. Your observations should not look biased.

Assessment: Record your observations on the Assessment Sheet, giving your rating on his qualifications, skills, communication, attitudes, presentation, decision making abilities, health, etc.

It must be indicated about his last position, salary, his expectations and your recommendation. While assessing the candidates, you may offer remarks other than the stipulated rating. If anything special like his distance from residence to office, special traits, special concession to be given to the candidate, like his loan commitments of his previous company. Finally, you recommend or approve the appointment.

Checking up References: After you make the recommendations to appoint the candidate, it is advisable to check the references, the candidate has notified on his biodata. It must be verified about his qualifications, why he left the previous organisation, his achievements, his liabilities and all other particulars mentioned in the resume.

Just Before Appointing: Once, you have picked up the last candidate out of the shortlisted persons, it should be reviewed by the HRD people whether or not to have an other round of interview. Professionally speaking, there is always good to have a second or third round of interview or even more for the higher position. The advantage is to have the minutest detail about the candidate covered, which has been missed earlier. In the earlier sessions, the emphasis had been on the candidates professional or personal competencies. In the second or third session of interview, the minor details are taken care of. These minor traits become major issue later on. The minor traits often pertain to very personal habits, attitudinal responses, certain physical deformities which get unnoticed during the interviews. These may also pertain to political, criminal, anti-national and international overtones particularly in the present scenario of international terrorism. These are very minimum risks but once, get escaped, can have far reaching effects.

It has been amply recommended by several professionals that the following topics should not form the basis of the questions in the interviews, e.g.

Applicant's sex
Applicant's debts
Racial affiliation
Foreign country's origin
Marital status
Religion or political affiliation
Physical handicap.
Criminal record

Because of the critical nature of the above questions, certain legal problems can crop up later. These points can be covered more carefully and diplomatically in the second, third or fourth round of interviews. There have been instances where the Management take several months to meet the candidate again and again to make the final decision. But when they make the final decision, they do not regret.

Job After the Appointment: After crossing all these stages, the candidate evaluated, salary and perks discussed, the appointment is given to the candidate, who is supposed to accept the same in writing having read, understood and accepted the contents thereof.

The candidate, after receiving the appointment letter becomes an employee of the organisation. He is referred to as the designated employee, whether he is termed as a trainee or Management trainee or apprentice or the like. He should be imparted the basic training in his department for a specified period, depending from company to company.

In my previous company, the employee who joined the company had to work as a trainee in all the departments, one after the other. After three months of his training, he used to be assessed again for his progress and aptitude. After the training of one year and on the basis of his aptitude & department, he was posted to the department, where he could be more useful.

Any human being having been selected through so many stages, trained consistently, re-assessed periodically his performance & progress, monitored regularly, would carefully and surely become the 'asset of the organisation. It is due to such employees who emerge as the committed, dedicated, dependable stuff, that the organisations are known.

It is believed, and truly believed that the organisations are judged and known by the people they have, particularly at the top.

4

Time Management: Add a Month in a Year

'Time is valuable'. 'Time is money'. 'Time is a great healer'. 'All times are not same'. 'Times change'. 'It is your time now'. 'My time will also come'. 'I have no time'. 'It is difficult to spend time'. All these phrases we have been hearing quite often. In spite of this we don't organise time. In modern management, time management is vital. I placed myself at the right place at the right time. My timing was perfect.

Effective time management is to get better organised. It is only those who are not organised suffer because of time. One should remember that five minutes have 300 seconds. Each second is very valuable. One should not forget that passing of each second we are reducing our life second by second.

All managers are so tied up that they cannot finish the job on schedule. The students are tied up, they cannot cover up the syllabus in time. Housewives are tied up as they cannot finish the work on schedule. It is because they are not organised.

Here are some of the action plans by which you can get organised:

Use of Planner

You may either buy a planner or make a chart yourself on paper or use a date diary. Plan your programmes by writing your line of action on day-to-day and month-to-month basis. Rather, hour to hour basis. In a big organisation systemise the planner into a master plan where you can have action plans for a long period of time even up to five or ten years.

Eisenhower once said, "Plans are nothing, planning is everything". Our Director, Shri Rajesh Mehra, improved upon this by adding, "If planning is implemented effectively then it is good".

In a big organisation where you have got so many activities to perform periodically, like quality control procedures or repair and maintenance schedules or keeping dates with the government authorities for renewal of licences, etc., efficient use of planner is very helpful.

Even for a day-to-day functioning the effective manager must plan his day's function either on a notebook or a date diary or in his computer brain to list out the day's works and priorities and complete the task one by one as per the priorities.

I fix my priorities while taking bath before leaving home for office. I verify the task completed again when I take bath after the day's over. For the long term planning I maintain a date diary. If you have learnt the habit of maintaining and implementing a planner you can be a successful manager.

Identify Goals

Every person must have some goals in life. One cannot become a successful organiser unless he has some specified goals. There are three types of goals:

a. Short-term goals.
b. Medium-term goals.
c. Long-term goals.

Short-Term Goals: Short-term goals are those plans which are organised for a short duration, like a picnic of the family or a go for hiking with friends, jogging early in the morning, a fixed time meditation, going for a movie or a date with a friend. These types of goals are generally not recorded, but kept in memory. Since most of these goals are related with personal habit and actions, these are implemented very effectively, because inter-dependence on others is to the barest minimum, hence decision making is fast.

Medium-Term Goals: Medium-term goals are those goals which are related to a long period of time, e.g. career based like you want to become a General Manager or Vice President or purchase of a car or you want to buy a new house in three years or you want to go on a foreign trip in two years or you want to marry within six months or you want to have a child in the next two years and so on. These goals are also visualised and once the goals are set, the sincere managers start working in that direction. If the visualisation is constant and consistent, all goals are achieved.

Long-Term Goals: Long-term goals are the aspiration for a longer period, e.g. owning a house at Ranikhet; to optimise health for a longer life. Raising a family, providing education to children, saving and investing to enjoy retired life, publishing of a next book and so on. Long-term goals are cherished by every decent living being. To quote personal examples, "When I was a student of 8th standard I set up my goal to do master of arts in English literature. Those days we had just migrated to India from Pakistan and it was next to impossible to pursue studies even after intermediate. During this period we had shifted from Jalandhar to Delhi. Despite severe difficult hurdles I achieved the long-term goals in completing my M.A. in 1961. Since I had been writing regularly, I fixed another goal to do some recognised course in journalism. Although I had joined Indian Oil Corporation, I continued pursuing this goal till I joined the Ranade's Institute in Pune to complete my course in journalism. I set another goal to top the university, which I did in 1971-72 standing first in the university. In January 1987, I set up another goal to go to USA by May-June the same year I had gone to USA. These are some of the examples, they were many more which were achieved after setting up the goals. Every manager must set goals prioritise them and constantly work to achieve those goals. The success is not difficult. While fixing the goals, ensure that these goals match the date diary and the calendar.

Sequence of Activities

In order to achieve goals one must achieve efficiency. While achieving goals certain activities are to be performed. Each activity gives a push over to the other activities for a rapid movement and to keep the march of time and pace, the sequence of activities have to be planned in order so that there is regular flow of activities and not overlapping of each other.

Check Time Wasters

When we have no work, we become the busiest persons. In office our time is wasted in so many ways some of which are as under:

We do work which can be normally delegated to others.

We do things which need not be done at all.

The manager should utilise the optimum use of their secretary or assistant to keep away unwanted visitors and ensure that people keep up their appointments.

Keep some block of uninterrupted time to complete specific jobs.

Minimise conversations and shorten the communication.

Telephone interruptions consume maximum time. Wherever necessary the incoming calls can be diverted to appropriate persons.

Be brief and decisive while on telephone.

Never call a meeting if it is not very necessary.

If you call a meeting, please set the time limit.

Don't deliberate your arguments in the meeting.

Managers do unpleasant tasks and unwanted jobs which must be delegated.

Managers try to do too much at the same time.

Set deadline for each task.

Paper work also distracts the managers most of the time.

Skim the mail.

Please go through the mail which is relevant.

Use telephone instead of writing a note.

Set some portion of time for writing important mail, memos, letters, etc.

Don't allow to accumulate papers on your table.

After taking action all the papers must be kept in respective files.

Keep your desk always clean and don't keep any pending papers on table while leaving for home.

Travelling

Too much time is consumed by travelling. It should be allotted to need base. If convenient some one else can be sent or write to them or use telephone or you can call the other party to your office. If there is no alternative then you have to go; then must go in the most economical way with the fastest mode of transport so that the time can be saved.

The time consumed while travelling may also be used effectively either by reviewing your achievements, reading, progress reports, professional periodicals or attending to important documentation. Time is money it should not be wasted. It should be budgeted and this time budget must be implemented.

Learn to Say 'No'

If you want to say 'No', don't say yes. Several persons have written books on this important subject. Quite often, we are not in a position to do a particular job for a boss or a relation, but we can't say 'no' to him because he may mind or he may retaliate by harming interest. In this process if you don't say no, you are harming yourself more than otherwise. You must learn to say 'no'. This involves courage of conviction, management of your principles and commitment.

The Staff, in day-to-day life, approaches the manager for some concessions, like grant of leave, grant of loan or such allowances which cannot be given because of the pressure of work or certain rules and regulations. Some time it may amount to over-stepping the rules resulting in misappropriation and indiscipline and if you have no courage to say no, you may land in trouble. By not saying 'no', you would be continuously approached for getting your favour. Therefore, it is vital that the manager must say no when its is required. This does not mean that he should say 'NO' always.

Utilisation of Spare Time

People are seen waiting at the bus stand, railway platform, airports, theatres, gardens and other public places. Such waiting time must be utilised at least for reading newspapers, magazines and other valuable books. The most successful people even make the best use of their time by taking books and magazines in bathrooms.

J.M. Barrie a renowned playwright to keep a bevy of steno-secretaries always with him even while in sleep or in the bathroom. You never know when a bright idea may spark his imagination to write beautiful lines in his plays.

Learn to Relax

Time clock does not stop. The man's activities also don't stop, but by nature he is constantly on the move doing some activity at any given time. The body needs rest and relaxation. At least five minutes before going to bed if you close your eyes and review the day's proceedings, it will give you ample time to refresh and relax and plan for the next play. Similarly, as soon as you get up in the morning use the first five minutes in planning your day's programme. As per my personal experience I have produced the best ideas and poems during this time.

My poems "The Witherings; "The Pols Hold A Conference", "Whose street were you are passing" written during this period.

Time Mismanagement

When the time is not managed properly and effectively, it is called time mismanagement. This mismanagement occurs when you have no planning or goal setting. This creates lot of problems, most of which are associated with disorganised or ineffective time management. Some of which are as under:

Constant Rushing: Those who have not planned their time are always in a hurry. This hurry brings them worry. When you have to catch a plane or train, you will have to make sufficient time available to catch the plane or train. They won't wait for you. Those who are always rushing constantly, always miss the train or plane. The top professionalised companies take serious view of the executives who miss their journeys.

Constant rushing always puts extra pressure on your nervous system, thus rushing your adrenaline faster. It can cause heart problem. This will create an impression that you are a disorganised executive. Everything should be done at a proper time and always keep a cushion in between the activities so that if one activity is delayed due to unforeseen problem, preceding activities don't get disturbed. If you plan your time well the constant rushing can be avoided. Constant rushing is very dangerous that it can not only cause accident, it will also make you miss opportunities, which may not come again.

Frequent Lateness: The defective time management makes you reach late everywhere, whether it is office, whether it is catching a bus, train or reaching the examination centre or even to delay your appointments. Successful managers hate late coming of their staff. Those who are frequently late-comers are the most mismanaged individuals.

I had a very good friend by the name of Sudhir Kumar, who was always late for everything. He was selected as the hero of my play, "The Death Of A Salesman", by Arthur Miller. We had rehearsed this play for a period of one year. The prolonged period of rehearsal was the result of Indo-Pakistan war of 1965. Our elaborate rehearsal used to get disturbed because of the late arrival of the hero. All sequences of scenes and dialogues used to get affected by his absence. We analysed the cause for his late arrivals and we found out in a very short time that he used to give appointments to several people at different places at the same time. It was not possible for him to keep up the appointments for any of them with the result that his each appointment got delayed one after another without meeting any of them punctually.

Don't have inter-mixed appointments and organise your time very carefully so that you are not late any time. I hate to be late for any action.

Low Productivity: Mismanagement of time creates low productivity. In order to achieve a high productivity in any activity the time management is a must, e.g. at the time of war when you have to organise a very effective logistics to rush the stuff, like food, guns, tanks, ammunition, etc. The effective time management is required to have the highest productivity to fight effectively. Conversely, the productivity gets lowered if the time schedule is not maintained for maintaining logistics. In such a situation more energy is required and more motivation is needed.

"In the car production in the Japanese technology more than 35,000 parts of a car being manufactured at different places by different companies are brought together for the final assembly where the period of inventory is hardly 6-7 hours, the highest productivity is achieved by observing time management. You can compare with the ordinary workshop in our country where the bad house-keeping always rushing because of lateness the productivity becomes very low leading to frustration."

Frustration: Frustration is the ultimate result of time mismanagement. You don't get things ready-made on time, you miss opportunities, you miss trains, buses without getting the alternatives - all these lead to frustration.

Impatience: In any activity where the results are not forthcoming as expected, one becomes impatient, which leads to chronic vacillation between alternatives. You miss one try for another, try yet another and so on.

Difficulty in Setting Goals: Just as time management helps setting goals and with planning and execution the goals are achieved in time. If no value is given to time it is difficult to set goals. When you don't have goals achieving them is irrelevant.

Procrastination: Procrastination is a stage when an individual becomes lazy, unproductive, demotivated and keep things postponing. All your nerves get numbed, you don't feel like doing anything, you become unproductive and demotivated. Procrastination is very dangerous and it retards and stops the growth of an individual.

"Vilfredo Pareto, the Italian economist noted that 20% of what we do yields an 80% of the results. Conversely, 80% of what we do yields 20% of the results. This is called 80-20 principle.

*E*ffective time management has been used in minimising deadlines, anxiety, procrastination and job fatigue, comes into effect.

This seems like a big investment, considered that the time you spend now will give you more free time in future.

5

Crisis Management

Every management goes into a crisis day after day. The majority of the managers complain that they cannot perform their jobs well, because they are always involved in FIRE FIGHTING. From all around, URGENT works keep flowing in. 'This is 'URGENT'. 'The Director wants it now'. 'THIS MUST BE DESPATCHED TODAY'. "The Chairman wants these statements immediately". "The Ministry wants the information for the Parliament Questions".

These are some of the jobs, which keep the managers away from their routine work. The Targets are fixed, Targets are revised, but they could not be achieved. No doubt URGENCY has its place in every company. The situations demand it.
The global environments demand it. The computer age demands it. The IT systems demand it.

In these URGENT TIMES, the winners are the people who provide best services, best solutions, best comforts, faster than others. Those who cannot provide the necessities of TIME become losers. The losers get surprised, when their competitors get past them fast.

The crisis comes suddenly, unannounced. The crisis is an unannounced and unplanned and unwanted event or a series of events that have undesirable and uncontrollable consequences.

See for instance, the earthquake in Gujarat and an attack of World Trade Centre at New York. Both have caused an enormous death and destruction. The entire economy and political life of Gujarat has been shaken. It has affected the economy of the entire country as well. Thousands of people at World Trade Centre have perished. The loss of property is unimaginable.

Incidentally, I had been to these places, personally. I have visited Bhuj, Kandla, Jamnagar, Ahmedabad and other places in

Gujarat several times. I have also visited New York and the top of World Trade Centre. The collapse of twin towers cannot be imagined. The colossal fall of these buildings on the surrounding buildings and areas caused havoc in USA.

Because of these crises, several industries have been affected. Tourist business has come to a trickle. The airlines industry has come to creaking slow if not a halt. 'Anthrax' has created another world-wide crisis, that the general public is scared to receive or touch his mail.

The crisis in Afghanistan would be longer lasting. It may spread to areas around. The consequences of these crises, have caused serious damage to international peace and tranquillity.

Such devastation's come suddenly without announcements and without appointments. That is why crisis management is so important. These crises bring horrible consequences; and sufferings. The crisis management enables the organisations to dilute the adverse effects of such terrible incidents. The objectives of crisis situations are urgent, immediate and hence the results.

Crisis management deals with the action plans to ensure continuity of operations, providing relief to the victim, and take actions to prepare for the future events.

Some important aspects of crisis management are:

1. Alert compliance.
2. Permanent preparedness.
3. Resource mobilisation.
4. Accurate information management.

Alert Compliance: The crisis management programme provides quick compliance of the need of the hour. It warns and alerts the men in authority in the event of a crisis situations. At State and National levels, the Government agencies are alerted to meet the situations on top priority.

All efforts be continuously made to assess the casualties, loss of properties, the loss of public utility services like Railways, Airways, Road, Hospitals, Fire Brigades, Government agencies, like Army, Police and all those agencies which are mobilised to meet the exigencies.

Crisis management takes effective steps to co-ordinate with all these agencies and institutions. It also complies with the rule of law and provides a platform for anticipating future actions to be taken, if new laws are required to be brought in.

In each organisation, it has become necessary to make some one responsible for setting a crisis management programme. The programme should be implemented effectively. Crisis management should be a part of the planning process. The discussion on this aspect and implementing should be made mandatory.

Preparedness: The preparedness should be the benchmark of the crisis management. Preparedness means taking all measures to prevent, detect, prepare for it, respond to and recover from this crisis. It should also take necessary measures to alleviate the effects of crisis. The preparation for crisis includes all steps to be taken when any organisation is hit by a crisis. This should also include the measures to avert such a crisis, like drawing a contingency plan.

To identify a crisis means to detect it, assess it and declare the crisis situation. To control and recover from the crisis means steps taken to normalise the situation and make the situation safer.

I would like to relate an actual event, which happened in my earlier company:

"In the early eighties, when I was in Nasik, something devastating happened at the Mumbai Airport. I rang up Santacruz from my station at Nasik for some urgent information and I was abruptly told on phone, "THE STATION IN-CHARGE HAS BEEN SUSPENDED. SITUATION IS SERIOUS. CAN'T TALK ON TELEPHONE." This shocked me. I wondered what could happen. I immediately contacted Pune, which was on Air Force HOT LINE. My counterpart at Pune also confirmed the earlier news and added further that three more officers have been suspended including the shift manager. This aroused my curiosity further and I contacted my Regional Office at Mumbai. I was informed about a serious CRISIS at Santacruz. He informed me that officers at Santacruz are being suspended one after the other and it is not possible to conduct the normal refuelling operations. He promised to give me more information later and hung up.

It had become unbearable then, because the real news of the crisis was not coming forth. Suddenly I received a call from my General Manager who curtly talked on phone, "Please confirm by writing that all Quality Control procedures are being followed strictly; and send your deputy to Mumbai today itself", and hung up. My General Manager was very fond of me and he would always enquire about my health, welfare and family and specifically ask if I had written something new. This time, no such thing was asked. I promptly despatched my deputy, who was very reluctant and scared that he too would be suspended as soon as he reached Santacruz. I too was very apprehensive, that if senior and experienced persons were being suspended right and left, my deputy who was very fresh in aviation could have become a casualty.

I was sure that some air accident must have happened at Mumbai and the persons suspended must have overlooked the Quality Control procedures, that's why my General Manager asked me to confirm in writing that QC procedures were being followed. Regarding sending the deputy to Mumbai must have necessitated because of shortage of officers, since more and more were being suspended.

Slowly and steadily the story started coming in. By next morning the story was splashed in the National Press. There were rumours, jokes, and sensations spread far and wide. The most experienced persons were flown in from other places to land at Santacruz to add up the manpower.

"It so happened that a Boeing on international flight was refuelled by a refueller topped up from the newly laid hydrant system. The system required to be flushed first with water, then with fuel before it was commissioned. Another refueller which contained the flushed material containing fuel, water, muck, etc. was parked nearby. It was not for the refuelling purpose. The fuel inside was to be downgraded. In a hurry the change in shift manager ordered his officer to take the refueller at Sahar International Fuelling Station and refuel the flight immediately because it was getting delayed. The officer promptly refuelled the aircraft after inspecting the fuel sample and conducting necessary quality control and documented. After refuelling the refueller was brought back and parked.

The aircraft started and was about to go to the runway when suddenly one engine packed up. The second engine also packed up. Since the flight was getting delayed, the airlines switched over to another aircraft parked nearby and the same was also to be refuelled. The same procedure was followed. The same way shift manager asked his officer to refuel the second aircraft as well. Since the first refueller was used for refuelling of the earlier Boeing and functioned normally, the same refueller was again used. After refuelling the refueller was brought back and parked. The passengers, luggage, etc. was loaded to the second aircraft.

The second aircraft also started and moved to the runway for take off. There was a huge sound of 'phut ... phut ... phut' and engines stopped.

Now the engineers who were working on the first aircraft were engaged in to find out the technical problem as to how and why the engines stopped; then the second aircraft also came to a stop the same way.

Normally when the car or scooter stops, we see whether the current is there, spark plug is giving spark, battery terminals in order, fuel is coming to the engine; or there is enough fuel in the tank. We generally don't check the quality of fuel. Same way the airline engineers were conducting their checks as per the procedure laid out.

Finally the fuel from the tanks of the aircraft was drained out. Lo! there was crisis personified in the bucket full of muck, water and what not from the fuel tank of the aircraft. Similarly, the second aircraft tanks were also drained out, same results. People concerned rushed towards our location and took the samples of the fuel of the refueller. 'Water', muck and what not along with the fuel was found.

As per the international standards the suspended molecules of water up to 30 parts per million are permissible in the aviation fuel. The aqua test is conducted on the fuel samples before refuelling the aircraft. This test is conducted by putting an aqua-test capsule powder in the fuel sample of one litre which can detect suspended parts of molecules of water, which is not visible to the naked eye. This powder would turn pink even if there are 15 parts per million of the suspended water; which is very safe.

The quality control procedures are laid down in the Quality Control Manuals, which are approved by the Director General of Civil Aviation, whose department conducts regular inspections of all aviation fuel station of all oil companies all over the country.

Naturally, therefore, it was a crisis unimaginable. Had any of the two aircrafts taken off, you can imagine the loss of life and property. The image of the company was lowered with the day to day news items.

What happened thereafter is not relevant at this stage. But it started a new crisis management in the company. Quality Control Manuals were re-written, procedures were changed and stricter controls were implemented, officers and staff were trained again and again extensively. Press releases were given to the media to build up the image of the company by telling the TRUTH. The systems were so changed and implemented that such a mistake could never happen again."

All aspects of crisis management were tried successfully in the above true story; from which many lessons were learnt. Crisis management should ensure that the staff handling any hazardous situations must be trained extensively. For this type of crisis organisations need to have the skills, knowledge and methods required for carrying out such trainings. It was not the end here.

The crisis management programme needs to be updated regularly.

In crisis management programme, sharing of information is very important. Managers at all levels must have adequate information of men, materials, machines and their deficiencies. The systems be framed and implemented. The systems should be such that they are self made and implemented so that it is easy to identify, catalogue, prioritise the commitments and profile of designated managers related to crisis management.

It is very necessary to establish and maintain the trust and confidence in the abilities of the work force, especially the managers in organisations. The top managers could easily delegate these duties if the trust and confidence is built up.

The crisis occurs through the untimely decisions of the managers, who are neither planned nor imaginative. Their actions create crisis and other persons are involved to solve these crises. Same managers INVITE crises for nothing.

Here are some of the situations where crises take place:

Situation 1: You have the need to prepare a project report within a stipulated period. You don't take appropriate actions and expect that the project may not come through and the report may not be necessary or called for. The postponed decision becomes an emergency when the top executive demands to have the same project report immediately You have a serious crisis to deal with.

Situation 2: You receive a bulk order from a prominent customer who has built a Grand Hotel. Somehow, either the order does not reach you or you are unable to execute the order in such a short time.

You lose the sales as well as the customer. Crisis stares in your face.

Situation 3: You decide to change the design of a product which is very popular. Your department does not get the right drawing of the design, and the products of old designs continue to be manufactured, resulting in a very heavy inventory of stock, which cannot be marketed easily. You face a crisis.

While you cannot do anything about the crises caused by the unforeseen circumstances, like the aircraft hitting the WTC Twin Towers or the Gujarat earthquake, but you cannot afford to be unprepared to deal with the crises that of aircraft refuelled with off specification fuel. You have to work carefully and work hard within the stipulated procedures whether the quality control measures or procedural regulated systems. Therefore, the most important element of crisis management is the element of contingency plans.

Planning

After all, why we set goals, and involve ourselves in the process of Planning? Just to become a successful company we keep working in a crisis-free environments. But if you continue by-passing the procedures, goals and ignore the Planning you are bound to be busy in FIRE FIGHTING almost every hour of every day and keep enlarging the crisis management group in your organisation. This would not only consume the energy of the managers, but they would lose the ability to recognise a real crisis when it is faced.

Go with Change

Time is changing. It is said that change is the only thing which is not changing. Now the professionals all over the globe agree that even THE CHANGE IS CHANGING. When the change occurs, you cannot do anything about it, you either ignore it or let it happen. You are signing a death warrant for your organisation, and your career by ignoring a change. Remember, fighting change is a losing battle.

I remember, wherever, I have worked, I always worked hard to bring CHANGE; either visually, through systems, through methods and through men. Majority of the person did not agree with it. At Nasik they did not believe that the station could be declared the Best in the Region, if not in India, until it was made true. At Goa, the public there could not visualise the changes within a span of three months. At Santacruz, Sahar any change which was thought of was resisted till implemented. Similarly, wherever else I worked the change was first not appreciated and later, appreciated the most.

Even in the present company I am working as a GM (HRD), several changes have been worked out and implemented. I heard from various quarters that nothing could happen. They all were surprised when actually happened.

Stages of Change

There are several stages of CHANGE which can occur and bring excitement in your working life. Change continues, and shall continue, and you would continue offering responses, some of which are as under:

Immediate Denial: Most people deny whenever change happens. They don't go with it. They don't acknowledge it. According to them it would not work. As per their old habit, they would never let it happen.

Resistance: Man by nature resists change. You change any code of conduct in any office, the people would not accept it and resist it. They would continue following the old habit. Try it. Just change the 'weekly off' in your office and see the resistance. Just change the colour of the uniform. People would oppose.

Exploration: If the change is effected and implemented forcefully, the process of exploring starts. The people generally get ready to give it a try to the new idea. The effected change results in some benefits, and some problems. Both the good and bad points can be examined and you may form a strategy to bring in the change.

Acceptance: When the new change has been effected, given a try and some benefits are visible, the CHANGE is ultimately accepted. The same change which has been denied, resisted becomes the part of your every day schedule.

When the change becomes a regular routine of your schedule you may come across another dose of change. The change is changing always.

What Happens When You Fight Change?

Who fights the change! Every one of us fight the change in onc way or the other, knowingly or unknowingly. We don't accept growing old, even if wrinkles are emerging all over body. The grey hair, wrinkles, losing teeth, unable to walk, breathing heavily, all the signs of physicalchange when getting old. But we don't accept it easily.

Here are other signals when we resist to change:

Using Old Methods: In business, they say, if you adopt yesterday's method today, you would be out of business tomorrow. In this age of computers, you can't afford to continue preparing statements of account manually. Computer literacy and Information Technology shall be the order of day. If you don't play this ball game, you would be left alone, while the other would march ahead of you.

Avoiding Opportunities: Whenever new opportunities come, people avoid them because they are of the view that it would increase the load of your work. You feel you are already over-worked so you can't have an additional one, without knowing that the new opportunities may make your work more efficient and more comfortable. For example using computers instead of typewriters. In absence of computer knowledge makes you resist the change. But when you acquire the knowledge and you accept the computer in place of typewriter, your work becomes more comfortable and more efficient. You can't avoid such opportunities, otherwise, you would be jeopardising your career as well as the future of your organisation.

Retarding Progress: Whenever a new system, a new procedure, a new regulation is brought in the organisation, people take time to adjust and understand it before it is accepted. It is but a natural response of people in any organisation. Newer the things, slower the people. The modern manager cannot be slower if a new and newer methods and assignments are introduced in the systems.

Face the Reality: This is the time for change. Everything is changing. Technology is changing, systems are changing, procedures are changing, markets are changing, habits are changing, man is changing when everything is bound to change, you've to face the reality and cannot resist change.

Who Will Bell the Cat Now: In the past, the traditional management took upon themselves to take all important decisions, whether good or bad. Now, with the extension of business sphere, the modern companies have far reaching units, where the manager controlling the units has to take decision at their levels. So, the companies have empowered their employees to take responsibilities and decisions.

The pressure of time, and global changes demand that the decision should be taken quicker. Therefore, the managers themselves will have to bell their own cats.

It is Inevitable: This situation is ultimate. These days, change seems to be inevitable; so you cannot afford to resist it. The change should not retard your progress. Accept it with grace. Be a role model for others to follow you.

If any of the above factors are noticed by you, make it a personal mission to accept. You must take a lead in bringing change rather than become a slave to other for resistance. Lead a mission announcing boldly, "YES, THIS CAN HAPPEN".

6

Stress Management

The Dictionary meaning of stress is apply more force or pressure on various limbs of body. It also means to create difficult conditions, bringing trouble and danger.

We are all leading a stressful life. We are having the experience of stress at office in addition we carry it out to office from home, as well. Dealing with wife, children, maid servant, neighbours, shopkeepers, visitors and everyone coming in your way strain's your life with a good amount of stress.

You may be a person with cool temperament, with a positive attitude towards life, well educated and experienced in the art of living, some amount of stress is inevitable. Because you are exposed to other persons at home or in office who develop differences with you due to their attitudes and styles of functioning. They certainly create stress for you.

You may not judge yourself about the stress, but the following indicators could identify the amount of stress in your life. As one stress affects the other, it is vital to find out the source of stress in your life for taking remedial measures.

Just check out the symptoms of stress. Once you identify these symptoms, you have to take it seriously to take appropriate measures before it is too late.

Headaches: Several persons come across you in private life and in offices, who have consistent headaches. They are always on pills. They keep checking their eye sight, try for head messages etc. They do not know that it is the serious symptoms of stress. It occurs because they are under constant pressure as they are always thinking about one problem or other. They remain worried most of the time.

Sleep Disorders: Those who are constantly worried, have regularly headaches and cannot sleep peacefully.

Indigestion: Those who are disorganized cannot meet their schedules. They become disorganized in food management and hence develop indigestion. The quantity and quality of food they consume also contributes to this.

Aggression: The people with stress develop pains here and there in head and heart and are bound to be aggressive since they cannot tolerate pain.

Hostility: The disturbed persons who are aggressive are bound to become hostile. Hostility in life and offices can lead to disastrous consequences.

Poor Judgement: The amount of stress which can lead to aggression and hostility affects the nerves and the judgement. Poor judgement adversely affects the decision making faculty.

Nervousness: Stress also puts pressure on the nerves system and results in nervousness. Imagine a manager getting nervous while making a serious decision or handling a crisis management.

Ulcers: Developing ulcers is another symptom of stress. This is very common among people working in office.

Fatigue: While involved in so many mental & physical activities, we get tired and develop fatigue which leads to unhappiness in life leading to procrestination.

Anxiety: In modern times, we are worried about something or the other at all times. We are scared, hurried, we don't meet schedule, don't honour commitment, feel insecurity etc. All these lead to anxiety.

Depression: Most people are depressed from life and its problems. Depression leads to so many disease culminating in suicides and heart failures.

Moodswing: You would meet several persons who are always moody. They change their moods very frequently. They cannot concentrate on anything, unable to remember. Lack of concentration keeps their moods constantly changing.

There are several other symptoms of stress but the above are some of the most common ones. Indication of any of them could be a stress problem. Longer the list of symptoms, the greater is the danger, which could damage your mind and body.

The moment stress symptoms are confirmed, you must take immediate steps to reduce the negative effects on your life.

Steps to Reduce Stress: We must deal with stress seriously because it affects the effectiveness of human. Because of this, managements are also affected. Therefore you will have to reduce the stress yourself. It is well said *"Change the things that you can change and accept the things that you cannot change"*.

Things You Must Change: It is not difficult to do certain things if there is a will to do. You have to learn how to change your life styles, work culture or your environments. People take easier course to run after medicines and don't get consistent habits or treatment with the result the treatment gets disrupted and remains unfinished.

Here are few steps by which you can change certain things.

Be Healthy Always: The most popular saying is "be happy and don't worry". It is simple and can be tried by all of us. Morning walk and regular exercise is yet another step to keep healthy. Eat right and eat tight. Take fresh fruit and vegetables. Avoid smoking, drinking, paan masala and roadside junk food. Remember eating regularly on time makes you healthier. Make Yoga your way of life. It would ward off all your stress.

Enjoy Life: Enjoyment of life means different to different people. Having fun is another way of enjoying life. The system of my life had been to work for eleven months and travel and go places once in a year. Travelling is a real fun. I recall an interesting truth of my life.

The year 1977 was very bad for me. I had just returned from a two months assignment at Ratnagiri, where I was sent to take care of refueling of aircraft serving at "Sagar Samrat" a drilling ship 200 Kms inside sea from Ratnagiri. I was invited by ONGC to visit Sagar Samrat twice. When I returned to Pune, my life had become very miserable, socially, professionally, economically, domestically as if all the bad times had come together.

My friends and relatives advised me to show my horoscope to

a famous astrologer of Pune. I met him and out of the three things he told me, one was "that I was to die within two months". This changed my entire life style. I started counting my days and I enjoyed maximum during those days. I did everything of enjoyment which I never did earlier. My office, friends and all started counting the days. During those days, I was the only civilian who was the member of the Air Force Mess. This became the talk of all mess parties.

I survived all those two months, day-by-day till the last day, when a huge buffalo hit me in my society premises where no animal could trespass, I survived, that is another story but this episode changed my life. All my problems vanished. I started enjoying life afresh".

One must develop the art of having fun in life at home and in office. You should always be remembered as a Funny Guy. Funny persons don't lead a stressful life.

Never Say Yes, if You Want to Say No: You can't please all persons. You may please some people at some time but you can't please all people all the time. And when you don't meet to the expectations of all people even once, you get a problem. You may have your own problems too. How can you add with the problems of others. Please learn to say NO and be relieved. Keep off from notion "what would people say".

Get Relaxed: Look around you and observe how many persons see the birds chirping, enjoy the stars in the skies, formation of clouds, and the colours of a rainbow. Very few. I remember my childhood when we used to see thousands and thousands of birds flying together in one direction in the mornings and then returning in the evening.

In Yoga, there is a "SHAV-ASAN" that is the state of body as if in Death. There is pure relaxation. Relaxation is a very important part of any program of stress management. A sound sleep is yet another form of relaxation. When you relax, your brain gets rest, your nerves get rest and your entire body gets rested and energized. Every minute counts. Relaxing does not mean only lying down or sleeping well. Just be away from your normal run of the mill routine. Therefore, travelling is the best relaxation. You get away from the scene of hectic activity. Laughter is yet another kind of relaxation.

Be Punctual: When I tell my colleagues to be punctual they understand to mean that they must come to office in time. To be punctual means, be organized, manage your schedule, observe your calendar. Can you believe, that throughout my office life, 30 years in the oil company and over three years in the present company, I am never late. I maintain my schedules as far as possible.

Be Systematic: Systems are set for smooth organizing . Maintaining systems make you systematic. It streamlines your discipline. As a successful manager it is essential that you improve the organisation workings in respect of processes and systems. If you regulate your systems you don't waste time and efforts on several unwanted activities. This would save your time and save your fatigue as well as tensions.

Positive Attitude: Be good and have good in anything. Look for good in everything you do and everyone you come across. Be good & hope for the best. If you are cheerful, you would make others also cheerful. Positive attitude makes your life very positive and purposeful.

If You Cannot Change: Every one can't change so fast. If willingness is there, anything can be possible. But if you don't change despite efforts, it may depress you and chances are that you may fall sick. The only alternative is that you change yourself. In doing so, followings are some of the options:

Let it Happen: When you are convinced that the change is inevitable than accept it gracefully. Don't fight. Yield to change. Just compromise with the hope that the change may be good for you as well as for the organization. Once accepted, you must use the change for your benefit.

"For example: The Company changes the systems of marking attendance on a sheet of paper, instead of signing the attendance register, as was earlier done. The reason for the company's directive may be to serialise the reporting timing of the staff or may be all persons are not signing the register, or may be any other reason. If all others are signing on the paper/proforma, you may also sign on paper and let it happen till new system is evolved or the old system is revived."

Show Positive Attitude: If you consider yourself as a part of the organisation, this itself is a positive attitude. And, if you have been with the company for a longer period, you must get the vision of grandeur. Feel important for the organization. Therefore, please adjust your attitude yourself. You should never allow some one else to change your attitude.

No Emotions Please: Any change affected in the company is for everyone, it is not for you alone. Therefore, don't get emotional about and take it personally. Don't get frustrated or angry about the change. Take it easy. Feel cool. Just chill.

Don't Get Victimised: Whenever change occurs, don't be a victim of change. Since you have accepted it, be supportive and stop fighting against the change instead, take advantage of it.

Don't Be Angry: We often get angry over things which are not as per our choice and wishes. We may not be happy about, but we should not express our anger. It is not productive, rather it is counter productive Whenever you are angry, do something productive. Anger consumes your energy.

Don't Worry About the Trivial: We have so many worries at home and at office. Some are small and some are big. We should ignore small matters for which we waste so much time. Keep this energy and time for bigger issues. If you analyse your daily routine, you would find that majority of our time is spent on petty issues. We should devote more time on very big or important issues.

Remember, change has to happen. If it happens, accept it. If you cannot control the uncontrollable, don't take it to heart, don't get angry, don't feel victimised and support it, be a fan of the change. Take the change to your utmost advantage. Why get stressed, if you can avoid it. Avoid it. Be relaxed and happy.

Try These Exercises to Reduce Stress

In every organisation a manager must have spent more than 50% of an average life span, on an average. The balance life must be spent cheerfully. It can be possible if you regularise your habits and daily routine. Yoga is the best method. Being a student of Yoga, I have the experience of its advantages. Here are some of the exercises, which are very useful and effective for any kind of stress. The best part of this is that these exercises can be done at any place.

Shav Asana: Shav Asana is the simplest of all Yogaasanas. You have to lay on the floor like a Shav (i.e. dead body) keeping the entire body relaxed. Feet should be straight and away from each others by at least 9" – 10". Arms be straight side ways, with palms open. Head be slightly tilted to any side. Keep the body motionless and loose. Eyes closed. Inhale and exhale slowly but rythematically. Keep this posture for three minutes. When you get up, you would feel relaxed.

Deep Breathing: Deep breathing is another simple exercise which can be done in any posture. Inhale deeper and hold it and then exhale slowly at least five time. When you feel stressed, the controlled breathing can have a soothing effects. You would feel relaxed after this exercise.

Laughing: Laughter has become a popular therapy in the modern management styles. Full blasted laughter stretches all the nerves of the body simultaneously right from the tip of toe-nail to the end of the hair of the head. Repeat it three times and you would feel the difference. It would regulate your breathing.

Before starting our Training Lectures, we conduct this exercise to defreeze ourselves so that we feel relaxed before training.

Chanting AUM: Chanting AUM three times also relaxes. This exercise is done this way.

"Inhale deep and pronounce AUM with full voice exhale deep

breath slowly for a longer period till you inhale again. By repeating three times with full voice, you would feel the impact from toe to head. Soothing relaxation would be felt by you.

Heavenly Trance: Let me take you to the Heavenly Trance.

Close your eyes...listen to me and follow....In front of you is the Mountain..Lots of snow over there...down below is the valley...miles & miles long...Beautiful trees...green grass....on the left side there are yellow flowers....perhaps daffodils of Wordsworth's time... on the right there are roses and roses....red red roses, black roses, yellow roses...white roses....down below there are more multicoloured flowers....Up there.....several birds are flying......more birds are chirping on the trees.....now it started drizzling....more clouds have appeared....very dark clouds....the colour of the entire valley has changed.....it is getting darker and darker....Rains have started pouring....gentle rain....more rain....more rain.....All the trees, flowers have become wet...Birds are not seen now....rain has stopped....Cool breeze is lulling the plants and flowers...they are dancing in the air....It has become bright....clouds have scattered.....snow on the peaks is glittering and reflecting.......at a distance there is a huge rainbow.....what a beautiful scene....fantastic....open your eyes....rub them and open again. Can you describe the heavenly visit.....you feel relaxed. Absolute stress free.

You can undertake such journeys at any time. No tickets, no rush, no hassles.... Destination is "Relaxation".

Once you overcome the stress, you lead the change. Hold it and maintained the lead.

7

Disaster Management

Disaster means unexpected misfortune. Sudden calamity causing substantial damage. A severe havoc caused by nature or by man, resulting into horrible casualties and huge financial losses. Very recent examples are the terror attacks on World Trade Centre at New York and earthquake in Gujarat.

There are several kinds of disasters which are experienced in forms of:

1. Devastating Floods and Droughts.
2. Fires.
3. Epidemics.
4. Riots.
5. Air Crashes.
6. Rail/Road Accidents.
7. Bomb Blasts.
8. Terrorist Attacks.
9. Earthquakes.
10. Wars.
11. Nuclear Fall-outs.
12. Biological Warfare.
13. Cyclones.
14. Crash of Heavenly Objects.
15. Stampedes.

Notwithstanding the details of all the above mentioned disasters certain consequences are common; like collapse of buildings, damage to properties by fires; human casualties due to epidemics, people killing each other during riots either due to right or wrong causes or due to national or anti-national activities. Imagine the havocs caused by the air-crashes like the twin aircrafts colliding with each other at Dadri, near Delhi. Rail and road accidents are caused day in and day out all over the world.

You are well aware the menace of terrorism being continued throughout the world. Our country is suffering terrorism for the last twelve years or so.

Terrorism does not mean killing people by bullets only. An acid bottle thrown on a girl not wearing veil compels all females to wear veil (burqa) is a terror in itself. Hijacking of aircraft, buses or cars is also an example of terrorism. Spreading biological warfare through Anthrax, whereby people are scared of touching or opening their mail is the recent form of terrorism.

The famous earthquake of Quetta occurred in the early thirties is still fresh in the memories of those who experienced or heard about it. The recent earth-quake in Gujarat has been devastating, causing heavy casualties of men, women, children, particularly, the school going ones, who perished together; and unaccounted loss of cattle and other live stock. The loss of property due to the devastation of buildings is incalculable. All the misery happened on a day when the country was celebrating the Republic Day.

The wars are the man made disasters. We have seen the 1st World War, 2nd World War and now the 3rd one is already on, though it is only beginning. India has the horrible experience of Chinese attack and wars with Pakistan repeatedly. Millions of lives have been lost in these wars.

Humanity cannot forget the holocaust of two Atomic Bombs used on Nagasaki and Hiroshima during the 2nd World War. The sufferings of the nuclear fall-out had been terrible.

The fear of biological and germ warfare is lurking with the ever increasing threat of Anthrax. The havoc caused by the cyclones, particularly, on the Eastern Coasts cause extensive damages almost every year.

The unexpected fall of celestial objects like stars falling on earth cause unexpected disasters. We have not yet overlooked the fear of SKYLAB falling on earth, which came down near Australia. Stampedes at religious places like Kumbh Melas, Mecca and Ajmer also caused severe disasters.

Now, all these disasters were unexpected, sudden,

unannounced, causing severe damages. Wherever occurred, we cannot do anything to prevent such disasters.

When the disasters occur, we start taking steps to salvage the damage. In this exercise, we cause more damage since we are not prepared for such events. Just to refresh your memory, the disaster of Chasnala Colliery, we could not save lives of several labourers who were entrapped in the water filled colliery. Similarly, we could not save lives of school students in the Haryana fire. Even in the Gujarat earthquake, we could not save human lives because we were not prepared for such eventualities. In all accidents whether air-crashes or rail-accidents, the general public reach the site of accidents much earlier than the experts. The public gathered at such sites, do help to some extent, but they are not trained enough to render competent service. Quite often, the public becomes a crowd. And crowd creates confusion. The confusion adds to the disaster.

The management of disaster is generally a mismanagement of disaster because in this management comes into action only when the disasters occur. And the disasters don't happen every day. The preparedness of management is efficient only if it is practised or rehearsed regularly, otherwise it gets rusted and obsolete. Fires take place frequently in most cities. Fire Brigades are summoned frequently. They also conduct fire drills regularly. They keep their equipment in working order at all times. So they are effective.

The disaster managements suffer because of the following deficiencies:

1. Disasters are sudden, unexpected.
2. Lack of awareness how to manage.
3. Non-availability of equipment.
4. Laxity of the administration.
5. Absence of immediate relief.
6. Lack of prompt medical facilities.
7. Inadequate hospitalisation.
8. Non-availability of timely security.

9. Improper communication.
10. Absence of ready transportation.
11. Absence of organised training.
12. Commitment of the Government.
13. Role of the NGOs.
14. Media coverage.
15. Unorganised salvage operation.
16. Ineffective reviews.
17. Unavailability of follow-up measures.
18. Rehabilitation of victims.
19. Disposal of casualties.
20. Inventory of the losses.

Disasters are Sudden, Unexpected: All disasters mentioned above are mostly natural which are unexpected, untimely and sudden for which no management can be made ready to prevent it. Some of the disasters like fires, stampedes, wars, etc. are man-made and preventive measures can take remedial measures to avoid them, e.g. the fires are normally due to the carelessness of men and negligence of operative systems. The subject is being discussed separately for details.

Lack of Awareness: When disasters occur they can be salvaged provided the preventive machinery take prompt action. For instance, weather forecast warns the coastal areas, particularly, about the impending cyclones, the machinery is generally geared up to take necessary measures. In spite of their efforts their messages do not reach the interiors and the poor villagers and other persons are caught unawares. Similarly, when the disaster occurs general public or citizens are not made aware how to manage the disaster. We have invariably seen the crowd gathers around an air-crash or rail accident or even fire. They are not aware how to manage this. Recently an air-crash occurred where the prominent minister was killed along with the journalists and the crowd gathered around the accident, but could not go near the site because of the marshy ground and they could not do anything. Even when the governmental machinery came into action, they did not have the necessary transport to rush casualties to the hospital. Similar thing happened in Gujarat earthquake, the disaster was so severe that people at large and the Government in particular were not aware as to how to manage, because the agencies which normally come to rescue, like ambulances, hospital, police, etc. were also affected.

Non-availability of Equipment: The disaster becomes worst when you do not have the necessary equipment to deal with it. In the Gujarat earth-quake, the affected areas didn't have the bulldozers or the cutting machines to clear the debris. In Chasnala tragedy there were no high power pumps to pump-out the water fast and several lives were perished. In most rail accidents, the non-availability of the cranes, etc. hampered the work. Even at the World Trade Centre and in spite of the necessary equipment available it would take more than a year to clear the debris. Most multi-storeyed sky-scrapers built in the city the proper equipment like ladders or the requisite fire-tenders are not readily available. We have seen most of the time the fire tenders from the neighbouring cities were rushed and by the time they reached the site the damaged was caused.

Laxity of Administration: Due to the lack of preparedness and discipline, the administration is found wanting most of the time to act promptly to give relief. In the cases of stampede whether at Mecca or Kumbh Melas or Ajmer incidents, the administrative measures were not made foolproof with the result the disasters not only occurred but got magnified. We have seen instances where the public gets restive or even hostile when the fire brigade and the police do not reach the sites of disasters in time.

Absence of Immediate Relief: In most rail accidents or even earth-quakes and fires, the necessary relief immediately does not reach the site of accident either because of the communication problems or transport difficulties or due to the vagaries of nature like heavy rain or snow. This also causes disaster over disaster.

Lack of Prompt Medical Facilities: During the disasters

medical facilities are not promptly available because of inadequate facilities and hospitals, sometimes adequate number of ambulances are not available and quite often medicines are not available. Since the disaster is sudden these requirements are not arranged promptly, but the regular awareness and training can take care of the necessary relief measures in readiness to reduce the effect of the disaster.

Inadequate Hospitalisation: Our hospitals, particularly, in the villages and taluka towns are not fully equipped. Most of the hospitals do not have sufficient arrangements to cater emergencies simultaneously, like operations, amputation of limbs or to treat a number of fire stricken victims. In a huge fire where 300-400 people are burnt, at the same time, it is not possible to provide medical assistance in a short time. We have seen the number of casualties treated in tents at Bhuj, Kandla and other areas of Gujarat where there were no arrangements for treatment of broken limbs.

Non-availability of Security: It has been observed that during air and rail disasters, the belongings like ornaments, cash and luggage of the passengers are looted when such disasters occur because the security or police personnel are not easily available to take up the assignment. We have come across instances where the houses of many victims were looted during the Gujarat earthquake and several security personnel were specially deployed on the bank buildings to avoid mass scale looting.

Improper Communication: Disasters generally cut off the communication lines. Earthquakes, cyclones, cloud-burst, floods, fires, etc. dislocate cables and messages of disaster are not promptly relayed preventing the relief to reach at the site.

Absence of Road Transportation: During such instances of massive disasters where the victims are required to be rushed to the hospitals or to the safest place, the road transportation is not at hand with the result that the people who are injured and could be saved, lose their lives because of the non availability of timely assistance which could be made available if that had reached the hospitals or safe places.

Absence of Organised Training: Everybody cannot be trained and is not expected to be trained to meet such eventuality, but a minimum training can be imparted to selected persons, groups, NGOs, the sarpanches so that they can go to rescue sites when required.

Commitment of the Government: The government is committed to not only prevent the man-made disasters, but provide adequate relief to the natural calamities, but the fact is that the government machinery is also made of human beings and if they are not committed it adversely affects the commitments of the government. We have seen the commitments of the Mayor of New York who has been acclaimed as the best manager of the disaster management. So much so that he is being knighted. We also have several committed persons in the governments, in the police departments, in the fire brigades, in the hospitals, but much more has to be done.

Role of NGOs: The NGOs play a useful purpose on such occasions. They are the committed band of people who generally come to the rescue on such occasions, but unfortunately are not adequate to meet all kinds of disasters. If they are trained to meet such kinds of disasters, it is possible to save several lives when the disaster occurs.

Media Coverage: The role of media is very important to tell the truth and nothing but the truth. They should not give a slant to the news and they should project the efforts of the people, of the government, of the agencies, who do some relief work on such occasions. They also should guide, advise, inform the related persons or the general public to get the correct information. Instances have been observed when the media played a prominent role informing the relations of the victims about the information about their kith and kin, collecting funds, blankets, tents, food, etc. and rush to the scene. They also mobilise public opinion to come forward for relief measures. Media should not spread incorrect information, rumours or indirect false information. We have observed on many occasions that Indian media projected a positive attitude on several disasters.

Unorganised Salvage Operation: At the time of disasters the first priority is to save lives and salvage the important property like the jewellery, cash, documents, etc., but the persons who are involved in the salvage are very less in numbers or not adequately trained with the result that more and more people who are not trained, get involved in the salvage operations with the result they make a mess of it. In the Western countries and particularly you would have observed in the WTO operations the affected area was sensitised, demarcated with the temporary barriers and only the authorised persons were allowed to take part in the salvage operations.

Ineffective Reviews: Whenever a disaster takes place the total action, the damage, the consequences, the precautions should be reviewed, so that better methods could be adopted in the disaster of similar kind. The tendencies is that the rescue and relief measures take longer time and the issue of reviews is generally lost in the passage of time.

Absence of Follow-up Action: The disasters and its consequences need to be followed up regularly. Mistakes of one disaster should not be repeated in the next one, but there is no such agency or department on a national level for follow up such measures on a large scale. Now with the series of disasters the Government of India has come up seriously with the issue of disaster management and we hope that it would take necessary measures to follow up the disasters and their remedial measures on a larger scale.

Rehabilitation of Victims: Immediately after the disaster like the floods or earthquakes, the rehabilitation of victims is of a paramount importance. The successful governments make prompt arrangements for rehabilitation of victims. We have seen the prompt rehabilitation of victims at Latoor. Even in Gujarat the rehabilitation was done slowly and steadily.

Disposal of Casualty: This is the most neglected aspect of the natural calamities. The disposal of dead bodies of human beings and the cattle cause a serious problem for spreading epidemics. It has become difficult to remove the dead bodies at the time of cyclones, floods and it is difficult to cremate or bury them because of heavy floods and they cause serious epidemics.

Inventory of Losses: The inventory of losses in respect of property, machinery and the valuables cannot be done because of the rescue and relief measures which need priority. During these operations even those items which can be salvaged cannot be done because of the haste and unorganised relief measures. Inventory of losses mounts up considerably because of this.

In view of the above it is of paramount importance that the management of disasters must be seriously considered by all the units of the government, the industry, the NGOs, who can play a vital role to manage the disasters. Disaster managements are in-built in the organisation. In Defence Forces, Security organisations, various Government Departments, Public Undertakings, the concept of disaster management is very well understood and effective steps are being taken from time to time.

For example, in my previous company, we celebrated National Safety Week during April every year. All units conduct fire drills, lectures, demonstrations, display, posters and live drills and play games, e.g. security and safety.

"One instances comes to my mind is when we invited the local air defence unit at Mumbai to our Aviation Fuel Station at Sahar to participate in the live exercise. The unit gave wonderful display of courage and discipline as how to face the air attack of the enemy aircraft. They explained how the trenches are dug, the equipment camouflaged, the vehicles cleared from the premises, red alert sounded and what to do in the red alert.

At such places, which are earmarked as the enemy targets, the precautionary measures are always taken, by organising permanent teams to act during such red alerts or even the Alarm Bells sounded. Picking up smart, educated and enthusiastic staff members all act immediately when the alarm bells go off. They conduct their duties with utmost urgency and seriousness, these deserve. The identification of the teams and their members are displayed on the painted boards permanently at the most prominent places. Similarly the Disaster Management Teams must have the following teams to work in coordination at least at vital installations, offices:

1. Team Leader.
2. Two Deputy Leaders to act in absence of the leader or during casualty.
3. Fire Fighting Chart, with the identification of Fire Fighting Team.
4. Rescue Team.
5. First Aid Squad.
6. Auxiliary Team.
7. Support Group.
8. Logistic Team.
9. Back-up Party.

Team Leader: For every type of management the Team Leader is a must. The leader selected is appointed must have the leadership qualities. Generally the Chief of the Location Office is self-appointed by virtue of his position because the authority flows from his position. Without 'AUTHORITY' the command is not effectively obeyed. The Team Leader must be very quick, innovative, alive to the situation, a good organiser, adequately conversant with the fire-drills and equipments. He should be an effective manager to co-ordinate with all the groups or teams very closely. The Team Leader must ensure that the following information is displayed very prominently at the most visible site of the office/location or installation.

a. Residential Telephone Nos. of the entire hierarchy.
b. Telephone No. of the nearest Fire Brigade.
c. Telephone No. of the Police Station or the nearest Post Office.
d. Telephone No. of the nearest Hospital or Nursing Homes.

e. Address of the nearest doctors.

f. Telephone Nos. of the Ambulance Services.

g. Telephone No. of the Zonal Warden, if any, in the area.

h. Telephone No. of the Air Raid Alert Unit.

i. Telephone No. of the nearest Taxi Stand or any Transport Office.

j. FIRE CHART, showing the position of Fire Extinguishers, Fire Hydrant, if available, Sand Buckets, Sand Bags, the position of the valves of the water tanks.

k. The Chart showing the Fire Fighting Team, prominently displaying their functions, like telephoning outside agencies, removal of vehicles and equipment outside the premises, taking care of staff and evacuation, if required; keeping safe custody of cash & documents and first-aid team, and any other useful information.

l. Establish information cell/or information office who would monitor the entire information from this cell, to avoid the spread of false information and rumours.

Deputy Leaders: Depending upon the size of the establishment a Deputy Leader or two be nominated or appointed. One Deputy Leader to have all the powers, down delegated of the Leader and other as a stand-bye during casualty or extensive damage caused during the disaster. If the establishment is large, more Deputy Leaders can also be identified. The duties and responsibilities of the Deputy Leaders would be same as those of the Leader. Their function start as soon as the Leader is either not available or he down delegates his authority to the Deputy Leader.

Fire Fighting Chart: In most disasters, FIRE is the first sign of DANGER, Air Crashes, Rail Accidents, Earthquakes, Bomb-Blasts, Wars, always cause fires. Fires when caused, spread immediately. This results in panic.

The Leader of the establishment must ensure that the FIRE FIGHTING CHARTS are made and displayed promptly on a permanent painted tin board. The chart must display the position of the various types of Fire Extinguishers, Hydrants, Sand Buckets, so that these may be handy, when needed.

The Fire Fighting Charts must identify the man-power, like the Chief Fire Master and other team members delegating in the hierarchical order. The chart must indicate the position of the Fire Alarm, Fire Flag, the position of the First-Aid Kit; Stretcher and Gas masks, etc.

The Leader must ensure that the Fire Charts are updated periodically. (**Fire Fighting is Discussed Separately**).

Rescue Team: This team is a dedicated group of persons, picked up from the staff and workers of the establishment, whose job is not to fight the fire but rescue. The team should also be identified on the Fire Chart.

When fire takes place, PANIC spreads faster than the fire. In such a situation, every one runs for his own life. Some people, may be staff, workers, visitors get entrapped in rooms, lifts, lofts, toilets, etc., unnoticed. The Rescue Team should always be alert and notify if any one is found missing or is heard shouting for help. On getting the information, they go all out to save them, either entering the area themselves, or through Fire Brigade, or through ropes, ladders or nets.

During the WTO Disaster, several persons were entrapped in the lifts, staircases and rooms. Some people jumped from the windows. In world famous movie, "The Towering Inferno", you must have seen several rescue efforts by helicopters by fire-men, and several agencies taking part.

The training to Rescue Teams is equally important as to the Fire Fighting Team.

First-aid Squad: This is a specialised group of people who are regularly trained to provide the first-aid to the injured persons in a disaster. The purpose of the FIRST-AID is not to treat the victim, but provide immediate aid in terms of medicine, bandage, artificial resuscitation, prevent bleeding and joining the broken or cut links temporarily and rush the victims to hospital, alive, to get the necessary treatments.

The Leader of the establishment must ensure that some dedicated, committed persons must be regularly trained to perform the tasks in emergencies. The SQUAD must be aware of the names of the important medicines, to give injections, to apply medicines or tie appropriate bandages for the victim to survive, till he reaches the hospital. The team should keep their kit always complete and replenished. A stretcher or a wheel chair, if available, be kept handy. The Gas Mask also to be in the working conditions and easily available.

Auxiliary Team: Depending upon the size of the establishment, an Auxiliary Team is also constituted with the group of staff and workers, who are all rounders. This team, in fact, substitutes all the members of other teams, who are either not available at crucial time or get victimised in the disaster. The Leader of the establishment must have the members of this team handy to utilise their utility.

Support Group: The members of the Support Group strengthen all the soldiers of the disaster fighting teams. They render all support to all the areas of operations, whether it is fire-fighting, rescuing, or removing the casualties, assisting in the removal of debris or even the dead bodies, if such a situation warrants.

Logistic Team: A group of experienced persons forms a Logistic Team whose main function is to provide the stores which are being used or consumed in the management of disaster. These stores pertain to Fire Extinguishers, the Dry Chemical Powder, Foam Tins, CO2 Cartridges; medicines, food supplies, tea, coffee, milk, etc. It is not only in major disasters, but in minor accidents and fires, the importance of Logistic Team is always felt. They have not only to handle the stock in hand but to regulate the supplies from other sources.

Back-up Party: Back-up party is constituted by senior persons or the men in authority who keep a keen eye on the over all situation. They keep reviewing the progress of the Disaster Management and change or modify the strategy from day to day requirements.

Like in the Gujarat earthquake, the strategy and reviewing was constantly done on the day to day progress which was modified even from area to area depending up the situation.

These teams and the members of the team can remain active and effective only if the periodic and regular training is provided. Unfortunately, the smaller establishments do not take exercises seriously. But the bigger and well organised companies spend good amount of money and time to keep their personnel active and alive to the situations at all times. Whatever be the size of establishment, the Disaster Management has to keep the above teams in all preparedness to get optimum results.

All major companies especially Oil Companies or those handling hazardous products are required to conduct Fire Drills once every month. During the month of April, Oil Companies conduct Safety Week. During the Safety Week, Disaster Management exercises are also conducted. During one such exercises the following game was played in order to make the officers and staff aware of the need for such preparedness and to conduct rehearsals for live management of disasters.

The following is the striking example:

We picked up 120 persons from our installation and made three groups of 40 persons each. Each group was identified by a name, A, B, & C. The smartest of the group was made the leader. The task of each group was kept as a SECRET in such a way the other group didn't know.

There were three Marshals to conduct the game and one Chief Co-ordinator:

Task of Group A

The leader of Group 'A' conducted a meeting of his people in a secret place which was not known to the other groups. Since the other groups were also conducting the meetings at the same time, the members of one group could not interact with the members of the other groups.

The leader of the 'A' group received a sealed cover which was opened in the presence of other 39 members and the task of the group was read out by the leader. The text of task was as under:

The Task: 'This is very Secret and this should not be leaked out at any circumstance. Violations would be seriously punished.

'This group has been assigned to plant a dummy bomb in the premises of this installation at any place, any time, without getting it noticed by any one, within the next 72 hours from 5 p.m. onwards. The person planting bomb, if caught would be expelled. The leader of the group would nominate any one from the group without notifying to others. All the remaining persons would help in doing so.'

In another secret document, it was notified to the leader, how to deploy other members and ensure that the dummy bomb is planted within next 72 hours. As soon as the bomb was planted he had to notify to the Chief Co-ordinator.

Task of Group B

The leader of the Group 'B' read out his secret message to the members of his group. The text of the task read like this:

This is Top Secret. Any one leaking the secret would be punished.

From 5 p.m. onwards, a mischievous group of persons is going to plant a bomb within 72 hours inside the premises of the location. We have to keep all the persons of this group alert during the next 72 hours in three shifts to prevent the plant and catch any one do so. Any suspicious person should be handed over to the 'Marshal'; one Marshal with an Arm Band was prominently spotted in each shift.

The leader deployed persons in smaller group at each strategic position.'

Task of Group C

The leader of the Group 'C' also read out his secret message to the members of his group. The task of this group read like this:

This is Top Secret. Any one leaking the information would be punished.

There is an information that a group of mischievous persons is about to plant a dummy bomb within 72 hours in the premises of the installation. We shall have to be vigilant. As soon as the attack takes place we would have to trace and defuse the bomb. We would inform you, the moment action is required. Be alert. Any one is found suspicious, should be notified to the 'Marshal'.

The game started with lot of activity, tension and silence. Every one looked suspicious of each other. No one knew as to whose group belongs the next person standing with you.

After 52 hours the Chief Co-ordinator got the information that the dummy bomb was planted successfully. The 'B' team was eliminated as they could not prevent the plant. The Chief Co-ordinator alerted the 'C' group to defuse the bomb in the next 20 hours. The role of the Marshals was to ensure that no one played foul and the game continued with the same seriousness.

After hectic searches and taking various leads from various persons in the same group, the bomb was detected hidden in the water tank of the bathroom flush.

The person who detected the bomb was deployed near the bathroom to keep a watch on any one entering, for consistently 12 hours. After each suspected visitor, he would search the bathroom thoroughly and finally detected the bomb.

The game became so interesting and gripping that maximum persons participated in the game and the 'C' group was given handsome prizes. The team which planted the bomb also was awarded.

I don't have the copy of the script of the game, which was written very carefully and the role of each was clarified in all tasks. We were lauded for the success of this exercise.

Even the representatives of the Army who were invited to become Judges also appreciated and complimented the Exercise."

From the above exercise, you would notice that the serious game, when played seriously can be a source of interesting exercise, which teaches more than a series of lectures. Such exercises must be conducted regularly when there is a danger of Terrorists throughout the world.

Fire Fighting

Fire is a very common form of disaster which occurs almost everywhere, any time. More fires are caused by the negligence of people or improper house-keeping. Fires are also caused by short-circuits, which are due to faulty wiring, poor maintenance of equipments.

Fires cause scare and panic, which is more dangerous than fires. Fires when noticed, should be immediately extinguished.

Triangle of Fire

There are three elements of fire commonly known as the triangle of fire, viz:

a. Combustible material.
b. Air (oxygen).
c. Temperature.

If any of the three elements is removed, the fire is killed.

Combustible Material: Any material which can put on fire is the combustible material, like paper, dry grass, cloth, cotton, oils, petroleum products, cardboards, plastic material, etc. In case of fire if the combustible material is removed from the scene of fire, the fire is extinguished. In huge fire, it is not possible. For example, if there is a fire in the paper godown or a plastic factory or a kerosene tank, it is not possible to remove the combustible material immediately.

Under such circumstance, the immediate remedy is to localise the scene of fire and prevent it from spreading

Temperature: Fire spreads heat. Rather heat spreads fire. To cool down the temperature the water is used in most fires. The water should be sprayed not only on the scene of the fire but its surrounding areas also to prevent it from spreading.

Oxygen (Air): It is the oxygen, supplied by air which helps causing the fire and spreading it further. In all the three elements of fire, it is the easiest to remove this element. When fire takes place, the air is cut off from the scene of fire by putting a blanket of layer, either by sand, foam or dry chemical powder. All these items foam, sand or dry chemical powder when sprayed on the fire it forms a layer to cut off the oxygen to prevent spreading of fire.

Fire Safety

Most managements are not directly involved in the fire fighting exercises. But it is the responsibility of the managements or establishments to make sufficient arrangement to prevent fire or to fight fire when it takes place.

Fire safety precautions must be made efficiently in all offices, big or small, factories, stores, godowns.

During such disasters the primary responsibility of the management is to take care of the following:

a. Safety of human life.
b. Safety of property, buildings, etc.
c. Safety of cash and important documents.
d. Safety of machinery.
e. Safety of neighbourhood.
f. Safety of environments.

All these things mentioned are very important in the modern civilisation; and are very expensive. The managements must involve their managers to take special care of the following:

a. A very good housekeeping.
b. Adequate fire extinguishers.
c. Sand Buckets.
d. Fire Fighting Team.
e. Regular exercises.
f. Fire Fighting Chart.

All the above factors have already been discussed in this volume at respective places except the fire extinguishers. The following fire extinguishers must be positioned at strategic points and well maintained. A brief discussion on important fire extinguishers is necessary here:

Fire Extinguishers

The need of the Fire Extinguishers that will be required in a fire situation depends upon the nature of the material involved in the fire. There are different types of fire extinguishers in different sizes, portable, semi-portable, any of which could be installed in the office, factory or other premises, depending upon the requirements.

Dry Chemical Powder Fire Extinguisher: These are the most commonly equipments contain finely prepared powder (sodium bicarbonate) that is so fine that it flows like a liquid. The powder is pushed out with the pressure of CO2 gas cylinder which is fixed inside the cylinder. This fire extinguisher is highly effective for oil fires, flammable gases, cloth, paper, etc.

Foam Type Extinguisher: In these types of fire extinguishers, the foam produced from it forms a blanket over the fires involving flammable and volatile liquids. The other advantage is that any burning material that falls on it goes through it and the cover closes again preventing fires to reignite. However, these should not be used where they can come into contact with a live electrical apparatus not only because of the danger of shock, but the foam can also cause short-circuit.

Carbon Dioxide Extinguisher: CO2 type fire extinguishers have become very handy and useful for office fires since they leave no powder or residue in the electrical gadgets like air-conditioners, computers. These are very effective because the sudden rush of gas when operated will be enough to blow out the fires in these gadgets.

Halon Type Extinguisher: This type of extinguisher is very powerful and rapid fire killers for intensely flammable liquids and pressurised flammable gases. It also leaves no residual after use.

Water: Hydrant systems or like fixed fire fighting

installations using water are used for major purposes; for extinguishing, for controlling spread of fire by reducing temperature, for exposure protections, and for fire protection.

Water absorbs not only heat but also many toxic gases released during a fire and has tendency to clear away smoke.

Sand Buckets: Sand buckets must be kept with moistureless/dry sand at strategic locations to be used wherever fire is noticed. The use of sand helps only in the spread of a layer on fire and which cuts off oxygen.

All these equipments must be maintained regularly, must be painted in red so that these are easily identified from a distance and can be picked up instantly in emergencies.

The disaster management has to be alert, committed and dedicated, well trained and ever ready to come into action with electrifying speed. You may not prevent the disaster, you can certainly prevent the damage from taking dangerous proportions.

8

Enjoy Your Job: Thrills at Work Stations

Every man is involved in some kind of activity to earn his livelihood. Those who are doing their work for a long time their job becomes monotonous. Lives of such people become dull. They don't have any further interest to grow. They reach a stage of procrastination much before time.

There are majority of people who are doing good jobs, getting good salaries, good perks, getting elevated periodically and they are bubbling with life. Even if they are continuing in the same job for a longer period they start losing interest. As per Peter's principle every top executive becomes inefficient at some point of time. It is, therefore, very necessary to keep your job lively. Whatever job you are doing, whether you have the aptitude or not, it should be enjoyable. The job must give you a pleasure. No job is good job if there is no thrill.

I have come across several defence personnel, particularly, the fighter pilots, who enjoy flying dangerously. The fighter pilots want to repeat their sortics in war because they enjoy dog-fights. They enjoy rolling of aircrafts, they like action. But all are not fighter pilots.

The sportsmen in the respective games enjoy their games, specially, when they play against stronger teams. We have heard senior players announcing that they are enjoying their game, whether it is boxing, wrestling, sword fighting, swimming, cricket, hockey, food-ball, golf, any game for that matter, the sportsmen get the ultimate thrill from them. Even the chess players, card-players also enjoy their games. Good students enjoy their studies. Children get enthusiasm from their games. Smaller kids enjoy picking up things, throwing them up and picking up others.

In Rabindranath Tagore's Gitanjali he described children

playing on sea-shore picking up pebbles throwing them, picking them again and throwing them again. They enjoy this life.

Life without bubbling enthusiasm is no life. In fact, it is worst than death. Lucky are those people who die in action.

The life of a manager is very responsible. It is a rush rush job for most of them. He is always involved in FIRE-FIGHTING. He looks ever busy, tense, often frustrated, most of time over-worked. He is sandwiched between management and the work-force, but he is the pivot around which the entire activity, of the organisation revolves. The manager of this century is a changed person. He is the torch-bearer of the organisation. His life can be wonderful if he is in a position to make his job interesting. How to make the job interesting, we give below some of the tried and tested methods whereby you can enjoy your job:

Know Yourself: It has been experienced that people forget themselves as to what they are, what they want to become and what are their goals. When you ask people as to tell their mission or goal in life, majority of the people can't tell. One should know his existence. Every one of us is talented, one way or the other. Human being is the most beautiful creature. If you view it negatively it is the most ferocious animal. One of the basic needs of man is self-esteem. One must preserve his self-esteem. If the manager conducts himself well, he knows his inner qualities, his capabilities, he can lead others by comparison. Be proud of yourself. Enjoy yourself and your existence.

"I Had the Blues Because I Had No Shoes, Until Upon the Street I Met a Man Who Had No Feet"

Always remember the above two lines and you would realise that you are much better than thousands and millions of people. Enjoy this thought. Cherish these feelings, you would get a thrill.

Be a Self-Starter: We have learnt our discipline, our ethics, our nationalism from our leaders, teachers and the institutions like NCC, Scouting and the armed forces. They prepare you to have a purpose in life. Whenever you watch the Republic Day parade, jawans and officers marching pace by pace, you get thrilled, you become jubilant, you feel proud of the achievement of the nation. When the nation achieves some milestone like sending man in space, a nuclear explosion, victory in sports or on the front, you automatically get proud of the achievement. No one comes to you and to tell you to be proud of. These are all natural.

When you are on duty, you are aware about the call of the duty, your job assignment, your responsibilities, your obligations, your purpose in life, your purpose in office, these should thrill you. These should make you motivated. No one should come and tell you of these obligations. You motivate yourself. You become a self-starter. I have the proud privilege to have the feeling of achievement that none of my students have ever failed. I did no magic, but I encouraged them to become self-starters. Create interest in their subjects and the subject will give them thrill and they would cycle back to study the subject again and again in order to have the thrill. This thrill makes him self-starter. The people who have made their lives successful they were self-starters. It is suggested that you read the lives of succcssful people regularly and you will get thrilling feelings.

Pleasant Communication: We have discussed this subject in this book separately, but the purpose of touching this topic again is to emphasise that this is the best weapon any person is having. How to use it to your advantage, is the problem. It does not become a problem if you understand the depth of communication. How wonderful this weapon is that you can create wonderful relations with wonderful people just through the art of communication. In my life I have produced remarkable results through letters, through other means of communication. Quite often it used to be a thrilling game.

So, in other words, if you speak well, soft, using good language, a measured tone and pitch with a soothing voice, you can give thrills to others as well, rather than getting yourself thrilled. A good conversation can not only make you popular in your circle, but people would like to come to you again and again. Your communication should be so soothing and effective that the other persons should cherish to talk to you. If a person is a good communicator he wins all battles whether it is an interview, a debate, a party or even a matrimonial alliance. Blessed are those people who are good communicators.

Innovate New Styles: Bring something new in your work style. Innovate new things in your organisation. Any new thing in life gives freshness.

My wife keeps on innovating the position of furniture of our sitting room regularly. This gives a new look to the room. It looks pleasing.

For example, we planted over four hundred trees at Ozar location. Firstly, the planting of trees itself was a time-consuming exercise, which kept all of us busy taking interest in the planting of trees in a straight line, in various geometrical figures. Thereafter, another idea came to our minds. We started naming the trees, like Akbar, Birbal, Gandhi, Bhagat Singh, Indira, Ashoka, Kanishka, Chanakya, Saleem, Nalva, Keats, Shelley, Byron, Shakespeare, Sant Tukaram, Shivaji, Rana Pratap, Edison, Eliot, Hitler, Churchill, Stalin, Sikandar, Dhyanchand, Mankad and all the rest up to four hundred or so.

As we named more and more important persons from history, literature, sports, science, we became more and more interested in the exercise. Our staff did not feel the compulsion of going home after the duty hours.

The staff who normally used to be absent frequently, were not only regular, but would keep the station spick and span. There was all round progress, of quality control, house-keeping and over all their own turn out.

A new kind of enthusiasm developed amongst all the staff. The word spread in the HAL and Air Force units. More and more officers and staff from these units started visiting our location and appreciated our new styles and innovative ideas. This encouraged the staff further. Majority of the staff, who were alcoholic, started enjoying their work and kept away from drinking habits and became more happy. Their family members were more cheerful than before. Similar innovative ideas were implemented at Santacruz, Sahar and Goa. Jobs became a pleasure when you are involved in it.

At Jaquar also, several new ideas were brought and implemented. It created a new wave of cheerfulness. This is not one time effort. It is a continuous process. Make your job fun giving ritual. People who visit you must be compelled to visit you again, by displaying something new.

Face Challenges Cheerfully: Don't make your life stale. Doing the same job continuously make your work monotonous and dull affair. Always look out for challenging jobs. The jobs which others are not comfortable to do. A marketing executive always accepts challenges. He probes barren markets, push up sale, launches new products. Keeps his customers well stocked at all times and keeps a constant touch with them. He is always liked by his customers, dealers and all outer publics. He clears bad debts, clears outstandings and keeps his chief executive or the management happy.

Doing challenging jobs is a thrill, a great opportunity enjoyed by brave men. The rotational assignments in most companies give opportunities to employees to undertake challenging jobs. To visit the field of activities in adverse conditions, like heavy rains, scorching summers, showers, riots is certainly a challenging job. Good managers always make their work enjoyable by taking up new and new challenging assignments. Trying impossible jobs and doing successfully would give you wonderful feelings.

Getting Difficult Jobs Done Successfully: As a matter of fact there is no difficult job at your desk. A job which you are doing for such a long time cannot be termed as difficult. Occasionally, you are required to complete an assignment before the dead line is set by your boss. In order to complete this additional assignment within a limited period, you are also required to get in touch with other departments, new in-charges, handle difficult persons. To add to this problem, you don't get the material required. You don't get the right person to make the sale document. You don't get the despatch clerk, the transport, sometimes the driver is not available. Telephone lines are dead. Power is shut off. Under these difficult conditions, if you deliver the goods and complete the assignment in time imagine your sense of achievement. Next time, such a situation won't frighten you.

I have come across some young men who do not improve their educational qualification, because they think, it is not possible. They say that don't get time to do so. But, when there is a will there is a way. Nothing is impossible. You can do everything provided you have a determined mind. To brave all this, you need an attitude. A positive attitude. When you succeed in doing so called 'difficult' jobs. You would feel a sense of achievement. You cannot only make your job interesting, but the whole life meaningful.

Just try it. Make a list of difficult jobs at your desk. Prioritise the list depending on the most difficult on the top of the list and the rest, one after the other. After making a list of difficult jobs, start completing the jobs as per the list, one after the other in your normal working style. The job would certainly look enjoyable and interesting.

Start Taking Decisions: Your job appears to you as difficult because you don't take decisions. You feel scared to do so. Or, you take longer time to take decision. One scare leads to another and a stage comes when the entire job makes you afraid of making mistakes. If you develop the courage of conviction and take decisions yourself, it would look enjoyable.

For example, your pending work is piling up. You are not taking decisions to clear your papers and dispose of the files. The tension and pressure would keep mounting leading to frustrations and depression.

Take prompt decisions on any one document or matter that comes to your desk. The completion of task after the other would keep you ready to receive more task. This would not only give job satisfaction but pleasure.

9

Finer, Final Fill-ups for Managers

Every manager tries his best at work. In spite of his sincere efforts, some of his tasks are left undone. As you do good work more and more, you feel more could be done. Man is never satisfied. Which are those finer points? Which make the task a successful one?

From my experience, observations and study the following tips have carefully been assembled. These must be implemented for the success of the Managers, in the process of management.

Pre-Post Period - Transition to Manager

Before becoming a manager, you must be holding a position lesser than that of a manager. You may be a skilled worker, a clerical staff, a supervisor before getting a position of a manager. The influence of the pre-post period takes time to get adjusted to the new status.

I remember, there was a character in my previous company who was promoted from clerical position to an officer. Even for going to the officers' bathroom, he would wait for some time before entering the bathroom, until some one noticed him using the officers' bathroom. He was so conscious of his newly attained status. Before becoming an officer he was doing his own job in his own way, only responsible for the jobs of his juniors.

As a manager, you are accountable for the entire team. You become responsible for the results of the entire team; their skills, their developments, their motivation, their mistakes, their achievements. This change of position needs a careful transition.

I have come across several best technical persons, some engineers included, who could not become successful managers, because they failed to make the transition from junior to the manager.

Give Your Time to Employees

As a manager, you are the leader of the team. The members of team consider you as their guide, philosopher and a seer. You are a source of inspiration for them. You are their Light House. They look up to you for support. Management is the people's job. Manager has to look after his people. He has to give time to his team mates. This brings the team workers closer to their leader; the manager.

All Round Communication: The people in the organisation must have information, as to what is happening in the organisation. Knowledge of information is power. It adds to the vitality of the organisation. Lack of communication enflames rumours. Manager must be communicative. He must share the joy and grief of his employees.

If a manager talks to his employees one to one, especially about the personal life of his, he endears himself to the employees. He must participate and often take active part in social get togethers and personal events.

Delegate Down the Line: Manager may be the most indispensable person for the organisation. He may be an expert of everything. He may be capable of doing all things by himself, it is not possible to run the affairs of this organisation single handedly, for all the times. The pressure of responsibilities may burst the seams. The bubble will get burst.

Delegation is the only option to get your responsibilities shared. It gives you opportunity to share the talents of others. The other experts in the team also get opportunity to contribute. It helps the company to grow.

Set Targets for Employees: We all have a mission in life without any goal, we go nowhere. To achieve something in life, we set clear targets in life; and we aim at the targets to get results. Management must set targets for managers and the managers must set targets for his employees. If the employees are advised about their goals, they get clear message to achieve their targets. The momentum of works gears up.

Softening the Attitudes: Good managers always succeed. They take it for granted that whatever they do, they would succeed. This often hardens their attitude. When this happens, they always want things done, as per their whims and fancies.

The process of development of the organisation passes through several stages. The journey through these stages needs adjustments to accept the changes of various stages. This requires softening of the attitudes. If the managers do not change their attitudes, the organisation suffers.

Accept Change: Change is happening minute by minute, day by day, month by month. No one can stop this process. Everything is changing. Time is changing, man is changing, attitudes, life style, values and total life is changing. Earlier, we had a notion; that change is constant, everything else changes. Now, we are convinced that even 'change' is changing. Managers must accept the change in everything. They should lead others to accept the change. Use it to your advantage and for the good of the organisation.

Recognise Achievements And Encourage Talents: Every one is a talented person within his own limits. Some talents are known, some are hidden. The work is being carried out by people because of their talents. The talents of the employees must be recognised. All achievements of the employees must be acknowledged. Even a 'THANK YOU' to a peon for bringing a glass of water is a REWARD for him.

There are many writers, teachers, singers, artists and good managers, innovated organisers. They must be recognised.

Lucky are those, who work in good organisations, because they and their talents are recognised. **This book is an example by itself**. I published my first 'book' while in Railways. I wrote much more and published while working in Indian Oil. The company supported me when, 'Death Of A Salesman', was translated and staged for the first time in the country. There are several others' achievements which were recognised by other organisation, where I was associated .

You must have come across many sportsman who are sponsored by various successful companies. Managements must recognise achievements. Those who do not, kill the talents and demoralise the employees.

Stop Fire Fighting - Prevent Fires: All those organisations, which are not well organised are always involved in solving minor problems. When all managers are involved in the fire fightings, lot of time is wasted.

If the systems are set, procedures are formed and implemented, the fire fighting is not carried out. Prevent fires by organising systems.

The professional companies do not get involved in fire fightings. The systems take care of them. There are no fires in the well managed units.

Casual Approach is Dangerous: 'Sab chalta hai' is a common phrase used very frequently. Things are taken for granted when systems are not followed, the procedures are overlooked, fire-fighting taking care of lapses, the attitudes become habits and efforts become casual. This approach is dangerous for the organisation. The companies collapse because of the employees and more so, of the managers.

Make Job Enjoyable: Managers must make their jobs enjoyable and lead others to make their jobs enjoyable. (This has been elaborated separately).

Search for Excellence: Quantity is a way of life. The life of every one must be qualitative. Values & ethics chisel life. Set goals in search of excellence. Excel others in all activities.

Remain Organised All the Time: Ideally, a manager is an organised person. An organised person is always successful. This should not be an exception, but rule. Whether at home or in office, he should remain organised at all times and at all levels.

Be Human and Remain on Earth: The label of a 'MANAGER' and its status should not blow his head, or trumpet. He should have empathy, consideration, love for fellow colleagues, respect for customers, regard for all publics internal

& external, of the organisation He should not build castles in the air, live in space but be an earthy person. He should be approachable. The Manager should be a 'people's man'. The Management should also be for the people.

Lead by Example: The Manager must fight the bull by the horns. He must lead his team by his own example. His own actions motivate his team-mates. By leading his team, he should remain a member of the team.

Live an Ethical Life: It is said that 'Values & Ethics' are not easily seen these days. But all is not over as yet. There are several Managers, several men in many organisation who have values. Perhaps, such Organisations are functioning because of these people only. It is a fact of life.

Manager must have ethics and values in his life. The employees look to his manager for these things.

Be an Organiser: Manager is an Organiser of the Organisation. He must co-ordinate all resources, talents, help of all the employees in the Organisation to achieve results and success. Without being Organiser, the Managers do not exist. Manager is an Organiser, always.

Celebrate Success: We always celebrate the successful events. All good things in life must be celebrated. Often, we do miracles in life. Sometimes we achieve certain unbelievable success. At that moment, we reward ourselves, either by planning a trip abroad or buying a car or anything. It is a celebration par excellence.

Managers must celebrate the achievements of their employees, whether it is about completing their sales targets and the filing of the Balance Sheets of the company in time or earning record profits. Celebration motivates.

Reserve Sense of Humour for All Occasion: How many times have you seen your boss, smiling or laughing? The Managers who do not laugh, lead a dead Organisation; Laughter is a natural instinct of man. Manager must have the capacity and capability to enjoy laughter. Manager's role is to manage people.

People must know people. They way to know people is to understand them by living together, working together and coming closer to each other. Sense of humour is a cement of togetherness. Laughter is an essence of life. Manager must be lively.

Enjoy the Remaining Life: Most managers, must have lived half or more than half of their lives. In reaching this stage, they must have crossed several hurdles in life, must have met several defeats and experienced failures. The balance life must be enjoyed.

By 'enjoyment' means one should get a thrill at every moment. All the 'senses' must be entertained. All basic needs must be fulfilled. All goals must be achieved.

The Mission of life must be complete. The word 'ENJOY' has different meaning to different people. Here, the word 'ENJOY' is a message to the Managers. And I am confident the Managers do understand the meaning.

The above tips are the tips of the 'Ice-Berg', which are visible only one third. Two third of the Ice-Berg of Management is still not covered. The unconquered land of the Ice-Berg has to be covered by the Managers. Goal is great. Target may be torturous, journey is long. The task is not yet finished.

'YOU; The Manager has to complete the Mission. **Over to you.**

10

Glossary

Here are some of the best worded quotes; one of which is displayed daily on the Notice Board of Jaquar, to inspire its people.

1. Successful people don't do great things, they only do small things in a great way.
2. Man is still the most extraordinary computer of all.
3. For one who has no objective, nothing is relevant.
4. Grief shared is half grief; joy shared is double joy.
5. Drink nothing without seeing it, sign nothing without reading it.
6. When a mouse laughs at a cat, there is a hole nearby.
7. To a friend's house, the road is never long.
8. Some books are to be tasted, others to be swallowed, and some few to be chewed and digested.
9. Kindness is a language the deaf can hear and the blind can see. Kind words never hurt the tongue.
10. The buyer has need of a hundred eyes, the seller of but one.
11. It is surely a good thing to know how to command as well as how to obey.
12. A good neighbour doubles the value of a house.
13. Hospitality must be extended even towards an enemy who comes to your house; the tree does not withdraw its shade from the woodcutter.
14. I had no shoes, and I murmured, till I met a man who had no feet.
15. Leaders must be seen to be up front, up to date, up to their goal and up early in the morning.
16. If you would know the value of money, go and try to borrow some.
17. Language is the dress of thought.

18. Ability without dependability, responsibility and flexibility is a liability.

19. Healthy pride is a feeling of the pleasure of accomplishment with humility. Ego gives a swollen head while pride gives a swollen heart.

20. A sense of humour makes a person likeable and attractive. Laughter is a natural tranquilliser for people all over the world.

21. He who has a good friend has no need for a mirror.

22. If you want to make something believable, whisper it.

23. Force rules the world - not opinion; but it is opinion that makes use of force.

24. Never answer a letter while you are angry.

25. Rudeness is the weak man's imitation of strength.

26. Our costliest expenditure is time.

27. If there is one thing that builds any kind of relationship, at home, at work or society, it is integrity.

28. Plans are nothing, planning is everything.

29. If your children are bad they should not inherit any property; if they are good they need none.

30. Silence and modesty are very valuable qualities in the art of conversation.

31. Talking and eloquence are not the same, to speak and to speak well, are two things. A fool may talk, but a wise man speaks.

32. The **five Ds** for quality of work - **D**edication, **D**evotion, **D**iscipline, **D**iscrimination and **D**etermination.

33. A man who has committed a mistake and does not correct it, is committing another mistake.

34. People who drink to drown their sorrow should be told that sorrow knows how to swim.

35. You can never plan the future by the past.

36. A straight path never leads anywhere except to the objective.

37. Vision is the art of seeing things invisible.

38. A broken friendship may be mended, but it always sounds

cracked.

39.Great minds discuss ideas, normal minds discuss events, small minds discuss people.

40.The wise learn many things from their foes.

41. Better dabble with work than not work at all.

42.Treat people with respect on your way up, because you will be meeting them on your way down.

43.An ounce of loyalty is worth more than a pound of cleverness.

44.A liar is not believed when he speaks the truth.

45.You must learn to obey before you command.

46.He who does not understand your silence will probably not understand your words.

47.Think much, speak little, and write less.

48.Life is meaningless, but we give meaning to it through sensible activities.

49.May your right hand always be stretched out in friendship, but never in want.

50.Necessity turns lion into a fox.

51.A cat that is locked up may turn into a lion.

52.A man is as old as he feels, and a woman as old as she looks.

53.Grey is a sign of age, not wisdom.

54.Much travelling teaches how to see.

55.Silence is emotional turmoil and a soothing balm. It is healing all ailments.

56.Never laugh at others' falls; the road ahead is slippery.

57.The mills of the God grind slowly, but they grind exceedingly fine.

58.Never trouble trouble, till trouble troubles you.

59.Daggers and spears are not as sharp as tongues.

60.Laughter can be heard farther than weeping.

61.It is beautiful to be famous. It is glorious to be rich. It is heavenly to be loved.

62.The world is full of willing people, some willing to work, and the rest willing to let than.

63. Success is not measured by how high we go up in life, but by how many times we bounce back when we fall down. It is this bounce back ability that determines success.

64. Don't be afraid of a loss, then you will get a profit.

65. To read without reflecting is similar to eating a lot without digesting what is eaten.

66. Blessings never come in pairs, misfortunes never come alone.

67. To have friends is good, but not to have to use them is better.

68. It's only the people with push that have pull.

69. Don't buy the house, buy the neighbour.

70. A man of virtue, judgement and prudence speaks not until there is silence.

71. Silence is more eloquent than words.

72. Less words, more action.

73. It is disgraceful to stumble twice against the same stone.

74. Any fool may make money, but it takes a wise man to keep it.

75. He who has not tasted bitter doesn't know what is sweet.

76. Proverbs are the daughters of daily experience.

77. A nail may save a horse shoe, a horse show a horse, a horse rider, and a rider, a country.

78. Every time you forgive a man, you weaken him and strengthening yourself.

79. A listener needs more intelligence than a speaker.

80. You give money with your hand, but go after it with your feet.

81. He who does not climb will not fall.

82. For him who is lucky even the cock lays eggs.

83. No one has so big a house that he does not need a good neighbour.

84. Man is received according to his clothes, but sent according to his mind.

85.Good things are sought after, bad things are found.

86.Do you love life? Then do not squander time for that's the stuff life is made of.

87. What you are, speaks so loudly that nothing you say can be heard.

88.The liar tumbles much sooner than the lame man.

89.Put a frog on a chair of gold, and it will jump back into the swamp.

90.If you lend, you either lose the money or gain an enemy.

91.The wound from a knife heals, the wound from a tongue never.

92.Good order is the foundation of all good things.

93.It is always easier to talk about change than to make it.

94.Without the past, the pursued future has no meaning.

95.Errors, like straws, upon the surface flow / He who would search for pearls, must dive below.

96.Think well, feel good.

97.He who fondles you more than usual has either deceived you or wishes to do so.

98.The heaviest burden on road is an empty purse.

99.The whole of science is nothing more than a refinement of every day thinking.

100. Man's mind is his basic means of survival - his only means of gaining knowledge.

101. The wife of a careless man is almost a widow.

102. You can never plan the future by the past.

103. Even the lion has to defend himself against flies.

104. Tears are a language; only he who weeps understands them.

105. New opinions are always suspected, and usually opposed, without any other reason but because they are not already common.

106. Never stand begging for what you have the power to take.

107. A piece of bread eaten in harmony, is enough to feed a hundred persons.

108. The better you think you are doing, the greater should be your cause for concern.

109. Don't be too sweet, you won't be eaten; don't be too sour, you won't be spat out.

110. Books and friends should be few and good.

111. There is no pillow as soft as a clear conscience.

112. Fortune is accumulated by drops and is poured out by pails.

113. A good word travels far, a bad one farther.

114. Trust not a new friend, or an old enemy.

115. Flattery is like cologne, smell it, but don't swallow it.

116. He who clothes himself in another's garments is soon undressed.

117. When you go to buy, use your eyes, not your ears.

118. Riches take away more pleasure than they give.

119. If a man deceives me once, shame on him; if he deceives me twice shame on me.

120. Man learns little from success, but much from failure.

121. Good judgement comes from experience, experience comes from bad judgement.

122. However securely you climb, never say you cannot fall.

123. When the blind man carries the lamc, both go forward.

124. Where the words are excessive, the quality is deficient.

125. It is good to give advice, but better to give me remedy.

126. With money in your pocket, you are wise and you are handsome, and you sing well.

127. To an ant, a few drops of rain is a flood.

128. He who has come through the fire will not fade in the sun.

129. The bitter taste of poor quality remains long after the sweet taste of low price is forgotten.

130. Only one digs the well, but many come to drink out of it.

131. When there is more than enough, more than enough is wasted.

132. Better face a danger once than be always in fear.

133. Admonish your friends in private, praise them in public.

134. Love lives for a short while, but hate lives for long.

135. On the day of victory no fatigue is felt.

136. By asking, one learns.

137. Waste not, want not.

138. Daggers and spears are not as sharp as tongues.

139. Never trouble trouble, till trouble troubles you.

140. A man without a smiling face must not open a shop.

141. When I did well, I heard it never, when I did ill, I heard it ever.

142. Anger is a wind which blows out the lamp of the mind.

143. Life is like a mirror. We get the best result when we smile at it.

144. Anyone can make a mistake, a fool insists on repeating it.

145. The diamond cannot be polished without friction, nor the man without trial.

146. Lies buzz like flies, but truth has the brilliance of the sun.

147. Time spent in laughing is time spent with God.

148. A man of character will make himself worthy of any position he is given.

149. Pay attention to your enemies, for they are the first to discover your mistakes.

150. A closed mouth catcheth no flies.

151. A wise man does first what a fool does last.

152. The pitcher that goes too often to the well is broken at last.

153. There are no menial jobs, only menial attitudes.

154. A candle by consuming itself, gives light to others.

155. A listener needs more intelligence than a speaker.

156. Fallen blossoms leave their perfumes behind.

157. Riches take away more pleasures than they give.

158. Choose what you say rather than say what you choose. That is the difference between wisdom and foolishness.

159. The courteous learns his courtesy from the discourteous.

160. Be a friend to thyself and others will befriend you.

161. Even the prayers of an ant reach heaven.

162. It is not enough to do the **right thing**, it must be done at the **right time** and at the **right place**.

163. Brute force can't achieve what a gentle smile can.

164. Talent knows what to do; tact knows when and how to do it.

165. The greatest ability is dependability.

166. After love, help is the most beautiful verb in the world.

167. The crown of all facilities is common sense.

168. An optimist is a guy that never had much experience.

169. Hard work pays off in the future. Laziness pays off now.

170. It is the neglect of timely repair that makes rebuilding necessary

171. To be vanquished and yet not surrender, that is victory.

172. Good name in man or woman is the immediate jewel of the soul.

173. Success always occurs in private, and failure in full view.

174. The law believes that language must be precise, leaving nothing to imagination.

175. No one is listening until you make a mistake.

176. Cash in hand is always worth two promises in the air.

177. The worst company anyone can keep for long is oneself.

178. Our sweetest songs are those that tell us saddest thoughts.

179. Values should be **caught**, not **taught** in the millennium.

180. He who listens learns.

181. Growing old is mandatory, growing up is optional.

182. Truth is one but the learned describe it in different ways.

183. Everybody is ignorant, only on different subjects.

184. There is no happiness in life greater than a clear conscience.

185. Ideas are more powerful than guns.

186. The greatest sin is to think yourself weak.

187. Crime never takes a holiday.

188. Positive thoughts are wings of success.

189. Let noble thoughts come to us from all side.

190. Burn impurities instead of calories.

191. Turn vision into action.

192. Egos are strong and unbending.

193. Knowledge blossoms in silence.

194. Discretion is better part of valour.

195. Contentment is the biggest virtue.

196. Who is the enemy hard to be won? Yudhishtra replies, "ANGER".

197. Silence is gold, noise destructive to peace and happiness.

198. Successful people don't do different things they do things differently.

199. Tough time never lasts, but tough people do.

200. We cannot motivate people, but we can inspire people to motivate themselves.

201. A national that reads is a nation that leads.

202. Dignity comes to light during difficult times.

203. Break the walls that divide and build bridges that unite.

204. Your grace and diplomacy take you through difficult personal and professional situations smoothly.

205. The remedy for weakness is not brooding over weakness, but thinking of strength.

206. Strength does not come from physical capacity. It comes from an indomitable will.

207. It is beautiful to be famous. It is glorious to be rich. It is heavenly to be loved.

208. You are where your thoughts are. Replace the negative thoughts by positive ones.

209. Work is worship, worship is not work.

210. Great buildings stand on strong foundations. So does success.

211. The harder you work, the luckier you become.

212. It is impossible to find God outside ourselves. We are the greatest temple.

213. What a great man does, is followed by others. People go by the example he sets.

214. In times of adversity, it is infinitely advantageous to be near a wise man.

215. To be free from despair is real happiness.

216. The good are never rendered arrogant by wealth.

217. Give love, give help, give service, give any little thing you can, but keep out barter.

218. Skilfulness in action is called Yoga.

219. A loving relationship flowers into commitment.

220. Work develops ability, fortifies self-confidence and enhances the sense of self-esteem.

221. Work saves us from three great evils - boredom, vice and need.

222. Learn to pull together and not pull apart.

223. Strength does not come from physical capacity. It comes from an indomitable will.

224. Visioning is a means of determining our own future.

225. Life is about reaping what you have sowed.

226. Faith is the nectar of life. It engenders power, zeal and self-confidence.

227. A wise man hears one word and understands two.

228. Keep your words soft and tender because tomorrow you may have to eat them.

229. If fortune turns against you, even jelly breaks your teeth.

230. The wise man pauses, while the fool crosses the stream.

231. Acquire a good reputation and go to sleep.

232. Wise people learn from other peoples mistake.

233. He conquers twice who conquers himself in victory.

234. The five **D**s for quality of work - Dedication, Devotion, Discipline, Discrimination and Determination.

235. The angry man defeats himself in battle as well as in life.

236. The desire and anger lead to error, so gain mastery over yourself.

237. I want to know how God created this world.

238. Most men would rather say a smart thing than do a good one.

239. Opportunity never knocks twice at any man's door.

240. Never laugh at others' falls; the road ahead is slippery.

241. Hope is the physician of every misery.

242. Change what you can and accept what you cannot change.

243. Words are like weapon, use them with caution and care.

244. If you don't drive your business you will be driven out of business.

245. Suffering ennobles you. It makes you a better person.

246. The family that eats together stays together.

247. Modesty pays, arrogance costs. Be modest and be winner.

248. Borrow their virtue and reject their error.

249. Brevity is the real key to success. Why not economise on words.

250. Happy is that country which in time of peace thinks of war.

251. The worst prison would be a closed heart.

252. Don't eat fast - haste makes waste.

253. Unless you love yourself, you love no one.

254. One kind word can warm three winter months.

255. Good judgement comes from experience - and experience comes from poor judgement.

256. Cultivate health instead of treating disease.

257. Never put too much trust in friends, learn how to use enemies

258. He who hesitates is lost.

259. Never give advice unless asked.

260. Riches take away more pleasures than they give.

261. Books and friends should be few and good.

262. Tell your friend a lie, and if he keeps it secret tell him the truth.

263. Let us never negotiate out of fear, but let us never fear to negotiate.

264. Where secrecy or mystery begins, vice or roguery is not

far off.

265. Beware of a silent dog and still water.

266. Superstition is the religion of feeble mind.

267. Keep cool; anger is not an argument.

268. If a tree is firm, why should it fear the storm?

269. The greatest thing in the world is to know how to be self-sufficient.

270. To tear is easy, and to sew is difficult.

271. Where words are excessive, the quality is deficient.

272. Small faith will take you to heaven but great faith will bring heaven to you.

273. Love truth, but pardon error.

274. To have a grievance is to have a purpose in life.

275. Learning is a treasure which accompanies the owner.

276. Let us make our work a source of joy to ourselves and to others.

277. To be trusted is a greater compliment than to be loved.

278. To bow the body is easy; to bow the will is hard.

279. Better a thousand enemies outside the house than one inside.

280. What use is a jewel if it is not polished.

281. Don't drop out of school ... a little knowledge is a dangerous thing.

282. Envy eats nothing but its own heart.

283. If you run after two hares you will catch neither.

284. Punishment does not right a wrong, but it prevents hundred others.

285. Don't be afraid of a loss, then you will get a profit.

286. A listener needs more intelligence than a speaker.

287. Keep a green tree in your heart and perhaps a singing bird will come.

288. Confidence, like the soul, never returns to us whence it has once departed.

289. Where wisdom is called for, force is of little use.

290. The greatest of evils and the worst of crimes is poverty.

291. Vice and virtues are products like sulphuric acid and sugar.

292. Study the past, if you would divine the future.

293. If poverty is the mother of crime, stupidity is its father.

294. People don't grow old. When they stop growing, they become old.

295. There is no evil in the atom, only in the men's souls.

296. Patience is bitter, but its fruit is sweet.

297. Behold, the kingdom of God is within you.

298. What is action? What is inaction? - As to this even the wise are bewildered.

299. Footprints on the sand of time are not made by sitting down.

300. Heaven is blessed with perfect rest, but the blessing of earth is toil.

301. Friends are made by many acts - and lost by only one.

302. The foundation of truth is self-restraint and dedicated work.

303. Giving and forgiving must be done intelligently, to prevent exploitation.

304. Opportunities are usually disguised as hard-work, so most people don't recognise them.

305. Fame is the food that dead men eat.

306. Hard-work has a future pay off, laziness pays off now.

307. Execution of law is more important than the making of them.

308. Work is much more fun that fun.

309. Inflation is a sin; every govt denounces it and every govt practices it.

310. If a free society cannot help the many who are poor, it cannot save the few who are rich.

311. God! defend me from my friends, from my enemies I can defend myself.

312. Nothing is so exhausting as indecision, and nothing is so futile.

313. Knowledge, like religion, must be experienced in order to be known.

314. Public opinion is always in advance of the law.

315. If one sticks too rigidly to one's principles one would hardly see anybody.

316. In nature there are neither reward nor punishment - there are consequences.

317. They, who know the great in man, know the supreme being himself.

318. Within Hastinapur, we are five and the Kauravas 100. But to an outsider, we are 105.

319. Your faith is what you believe, not what you know.

320. Duty is what one expects from others, it is not what one does oneself.

321. An ass can swim in seven ways, but when he sees water, he forgets them all.

322. The problem with you, Watson, you see, but not observe.

323. Forgiveness is perfect when the sin is not remembered.

324. No one can make you inferior without your consent.

325. If the beginning is good, the end must be perfect.

326. Scatter with one hand; collect with both.

327. Where there is no vision, people perish.

328. Praise the wise man behind the back, but a woman to her face.

329. Justice without force is powerless; force without justice is tyrannical.

330. We make our fortunes and call it fate.

331. A man consists of the faith that is in him. Whatever his faith is, he is.

332. Admonish your friends in private, praise them in public.

333. Learning preserves the errors of the past, as well as its wisdom.

334. Laws are like cobwebs, which may catch small flies, but let wasps and hornets break through.

335. Always respect the hand that works rather than the mouth

that preach.

336. The lottery is a tax on people who are bad at math.

337. A fine is a tax for doing wrong. A tax is a fine for doing well.

338. He who is too busy doing good, finds no time to be good.

339. God gives each person a hook with which to pluck his fruit.

340. To have money is to be virtuous, honest, beautiful and witty. And to be without is to be ugly, boring, stupid and useless.

341. The patient must combat the disease along with the physician.

342. He who has thousand friends has not a friend to spare, and he who has one enemy shall meet him everywhere.

343. When I see through men I find in them divine incarnation.

344. There is a limit to a violent action, and it can fall. Non-violence knows no limit and it never fails.

345. Some comrades apparently find it hard to understand that democracy is just a slogan.

346. A banker is a man who lends you an umbrella when the weather is fair, and takes it away from you when it rains.

347. All laws are important, but some are more important than others.

348. He that falls by himself never cries.

349. The more you speak of yourself, the more you are likely to lie.

350. How is it that little children are so intelligent and men so stupid? It must be education that does it.

351. Why fear death? It is the most beautiful adventure in life.

352. A rain of tears is necessary for the harvest of learning.

353. When I did well, I heard it never: When I did ill, I heard it ever.

354. There are those who despise pride with a greater pride.

Select Bibliography

Select Bibliography

1. *Principle of Management* by Terry and Franklin, 8th Edition, 1994.

2. *Effective Management Skills: Managing People* by John Scott and Arthur Rockester, British Institute of Management, 1984.

3. *The How to Manage Handbook,* Excel Books, 1995.

4. *Strategies for Success: Winning Formulas for Successful Living,* John Dornan, 1997.

5. *Skills for Success: A Guide to the Top for Men and Women*, Adele Scheele.

6. *Brainstorming for Managers:* Promod Batra, Susan Brady, Maitra, Vijay Batra, 1996.

7. *Training is Everything*, Denis Waitley, 1996.

8. *The Manager's Case Book*, Elwyn Thomas and Mike Woods, 1994.

9. *Notes to Myself: My Struggle to Become a Person*, Hugh Prather, 1990.

10. *I'm O.K., You're O.K.*, Thomas A. Harris, M.D., 1993.

11. *Write It Down, Make It Happen*, Henriette Anne Klauser.

12. *Beware: The Naked Man Who Offers You His Shirt*, Harvey Mackay.

13. *The Tao of Management*, Bob Mersing (An Age Old Study For Modern Managers).

14. *How to Enjoy Your Life and Your Job:* Dale Carnegie.

15. *How to Win Friends and Influence People*, Dale Carnegie.

16. *Successful Time Management in a Week* by Declan Treacy.

17. *Managing For Dummies*, Bob Nelson & Peter Economy.

18. *The Relaxation and Stress Reductions Work-Books* by Martha Davis, Ph.D Elizabeth Robbins, MSW, Eshelman Mathew McKay, Ph.D.

19. *You Can Win* by Shiv Khera.

Index

Index